"*Heaven & Nature Sing: 365 Daily Devotions for Outdoor and Nature Lovers* is a welcome addition to the growing body of literature encouraging God's people to return to Him in praise and adoration through both the special revelation of His Word, and the general revelation of His creation.

"Grounded in scripture, this daily devotional book inspires the reader to daily pause in reflection on the Lord's goodness, and with special consideration of how God's creation calls us to walk with Him. Written by a number of Christian thinkers (including several friends of mine!), each daily devotion calls us to remain rooted in Him, and to open our eyes to how the Lord continues to teach us through the smallest flower to the grandest vista.

"It's a pleasure to endorse this wonderful devotional book, and encourage you to get several of them—for you and for friends who will be encouraged each day."

Joel Vermillion
Director, Wilderness Ministry Institute
www.wildernessministry.org

"Many times as I hiked in Montana, Colorado or the Winds with my brothers, we stopped and looked at the sky, mountains, trees, waterfalls or bears and marveled at the beauty and majesty of God's creation. We kept wondering and talking to each other, that there is a spiritual lesson here and we should write a devotion about it.

"Well, Sharon and her friends have just done that. The first several days of reading already brought me back to the woods and helped me remember so many wonderful memories.

"*Heaven and Nature Sing* draws us closer to God through the lens of the outdoors and teaches us many biblical truths. As I am reading these pages, I feel that my backpack for the next trip just got a little heavier, as I sure want to bring this book with me and read it when I watch the sunrise or sunset, or by the campfire."

Ed Wu
Founder & CEO, Premier Education Partners
www.premier-edu.com

"One does not have to read very far into this book to discover that the authors have a living relationship with the Lord Jesus and love to speak of His wonderful creation.

"Each author approaches their topic with a unique perspective born out of their experience living out the text. This results in a diversity of writing styles and teaching that will be helpful to many people. The affect that appreciating God's creation has had on their lives is very apparent. As each one shares, they hope that the Lord will give you His life through their words.

"I encourage every reader to take one short devotional per day and meditate on the Scripture, allowing the Lord to speak His life into your heart. As you do this, you will come to a greater appreciation for the Word of God, and for the God of the Word who created such a wonderful world for us all to enjoy."

Dr. Del Broersma
Retired Entomologist, Purdue University
Pastor, Upper Room Christian Fellowship

"As booksellers of nearly 30 years, my wife and I have longed for more books that do what *Heaven and Nature Sing* sets out to do—offer daily devotional readings for those who love the great outdoors, who want Bible-based, Christian insight right alongside stories of the goodness of creation, the joy of wilderness adventuring, offering insight about deepening faith from those who backpack and kayak and rock climb or stroll through the pastures near their homes.

"With a bit of creation-care virtue, natural history and popular science *Heaven and Nature Sing* is a rare resource, good to give to fans of the outdoors, or even the armchair variety, whose faith will come alive as they enjoy these meditations by those who have found God in creation."

Byron Borger
Co-owner, Hearts & Minds Bookstore
www.heartsandmindsbooks.com

HEAVEN
and
NATURE
Sing

HEAVEN
and
NATURE
Sing

365 DAILY DEVOTIONALS
FOR OUTDOOR & NATURE LOVERS

EDITED BY
Sharon Brodin

BRODIN
press

WORTHY ARE YOU, our Lord and God, the Holy One, to receive the *glory*, the *honor* and the *power*—for You created ALL THINGS, and because of Your desire they existed and were *created!*

Revelation 4:11

All Scriptures references are the World English Bible translation, unless otherwise stated. Public domain.

Published by Brodin Press LLC, Minneapolis MN
www.brodinpress.com/devotional

Book and cover design by Sharon Brodin, Brodin Press LLC
Proofreading and Editing: Jamie Mayes and Kathleen Schalla

ISBN 978-1-7365349-2-2
ISBN 978-1-7365349-4-6 (Hardback)
ISBN 978-1-7365349-3-9 (eBook)

Contents

Introduction

The idea for this devotional came out of the blue one morning when I was in prayer. I don't remember what I was praying about. All I know is this idea suddenly dropped in my mind to write a 365-day devotional focusing on God's creation of the natural world and the many ways our love and involvement with it applies to our life with God.

As I started to pray through this idea, I knew I was to invite many others across the outdoor space—those working in both for-profit and non-profit organizations—to contribute their wisdom and experience, too.

This book is the result of that morning's time with the Father.

I've loved nature and being in the outdoors all my life. I was raised by parents who loved nature and the outdoors. The older I get, the more I value this amazing world and the loving, amazing Creator who put it here.

If you're reading this then you, too, value it and value Him. Or maybe you simply love nature and are searching for God. Maybe you already know how much the Bible speaks of the natural world and its connection with both us and our God. Or maybe this is new to you. In all cases, welcome!

Each devotional starts with a scripture from the Bible. Then a one-page devotional, written by me or one of the contributors, the name you see at the bottom of the page. At the end of each devotional it says: *Dig deeper*. These are related scriptures that invite you deeper into God's word that day.

At the back of the book is a section that includes each author or artist and a short bio. You can find out more about them on the website: *brodinpress.com/devotional*.

Be blessed as you journey through God's word as it relates to nature and the outdoors throughout this coming year!

Sharon Brodin
Brodin Press LLC
January 2022

January

S. BRODIN

January 1

"For you shall go out with joy, and be led forth with peace. The mountains and the hills shall break forth before you into singing..." Isaiah 55:12

What a way to begin a New Year!

To *"go out with joy"*—the Hebrew word is *simchah*—it means exceeding gladness.

True joy is *not* the result of our circumstances or achievements. If it were, every person of wealth, success and power would be a joyful person. True joy comes from the source of joy—the Lord Himself.

Joy is both a choice and the result or fruit of the work of the Holy Spirit. We choose it and we grow in it. When its source is the Lord, it's a fountain on the inside that keeps producing clear, pure living water—independent of circumstances and achievements.

And to *"be led forth with peace..."* This is the wonderful Hebrew word *shalom*. Its meaning is so much more than the mere absence of conflict. It speaks of wholeness, soundness, welfare, completeness, abundance, favor and peace.

This is the peace Jesus spoke of when He said, *"Peace I leave with you, My peace I give unto you..."* (John 14:27)

"The mountains and the hills shall break forth (or burst) *before you into singing..."* The Hebrew word is *rinnah*. It's more like a joyful shout or cry than melodious singing. It's power-packed... it's full of passion and emotion...it's loud!

Have you ever felt that when you're in the mountains? A breaking forth of joy, the stunning beauty and majesty? That's creation acknowledging its Creator.

How do we position ourselves before God to be led forth with that kind of blessing?

Humbly...surrendered...fixing our eyes on Jesus...seeking first His Kingdom and righteousness...giving Him our attention, worship and praise...believing and obeying His word.

Move into this New Year with joy! Be led forth by His shalom!

Dig deeper: Isaiah 55

January 2

"Now may the God of hope fill you with all joy and peace in believing, that you may abound in hope, in the power of the Holy Spirit."
Romans 15:13

I've had one rock climbing experience in my life, more than 30 years ago. My most vivid memory of that episode was the fear I felt right before starting to rappel back down.

My friends said, "Lean back! More!" With my feet at the edge of the cliff and my full body weight leaning back to that 90 degree angle—it was so hard for me! Even though I wasn't that high. Even though my friend held the belay rope firmly.

It's not that I didn't trust my friend or the rope. But my fear of the unknown momentarily took control over my trust.

I eventually *did* lean back far enough and *did* make it back down safely (it was even fun!). For one thing, I knew I didn't have a choice—I had to get back down there eventually! And I had great hope that my friends knew what they were doing, and could coach me on what I needed to do.

People face the new and unknown differently. We're heading into a New Year. How do you feel about that? Does it fill you with expectation and excitement? Or does it fill you with dread and anxiety? Maybe it's both, or somewhere in between.

As believers in our Heavenly Father, in His Son Jesus and in our Helper and Comforter, the Holy Spirit—we have very good reason to have hope. He's the *God of hope*! As His children we're offered that hope freely, along with *all joy and peace* as we trust in His goodness, His love, His faithfulness, His wisdom and His judgments.

We don't go into this New Year alone, but *in the power of the Holy Spirit*. That's how we can abound in hope! He's got our belay rope securely in His hands even when we can't see the way ourselves.

One more time: *"Now may the God of hope fill you with all joy and peace in believing, that you may abound in hope, in the power of the Holy Spirit."*

Dig deeper: *Ephesians 1*

January 3

"Yours, Yahweh, is the greatness, the power, the glory, the victory, and the majesty! For all that is in the heavens and in the earth is Yours. Yours is the kingdom, Yahweh, and You are exalted as head above all. " 1 Chronicles 29:11

The creation theme is sprinkled liberally throughout the whole Bible. It isn't confined to the first couple chapters of Genesis.

Why is that important? If we call ourselves *believers*, then what we believe is extremely important. Before we can worship God, we need to believe that He is, and did what He says He did.

Yes, we believe God the Father sent Jesus the Son to earth as a man and as God. Yes, we believe Jesus came to break the power of darkness and restore us to relationship with the Father. Yes, we believe He did that through His death on the cross and His resurrection three days later.

Do we also believe *all that is in the heavens and in the earth* is His because He created them? It's in the same Bible over and over and over again. Or do we believe scientific naturalism that claims the heavens and the earth came about by random chance over billions of years?

These two ideas don't complement each other. They're mutually exclusive. That means one or the other is true—they can't both be true.

Unlike what many would have us believe, we don't have to ignore science and stick our heads in the sand to believe God made it all! In fact, many modern scientists are ignoring all kinds of evidence because they need to believe there's no God involved. Look for some of the many books and publications out there written by high-level scientists who are creationists and you'll see what I mean.

Believing that God is the author of life, of the universe, is central to our faith. And when we can plant our flag there, we can worship God with conviction and hope. *Yours, God, is the greatness, the power, the glory, the victory and the majesty!*

Dig deeper: *Psalm 104*

January 4

"Therefore let them also who suffer according to the will of God in doing good entrust their souls to Him, as to a faithful Creator."
1 Peter 4:19

The Bible calls God by so many different names. Isn't it interesting that in this particular verse Peter chooses *Creator*? You'd think he'd talk about God being Father, or Shepherd (a caretaker) to those who suffer.

And while God is those things, too, here it's His identity as Creator he emphasizes.

The Greek word translated Creator is *ktistés*. Sometimes it's used for the founder of a city. It refers to creating out of nothing.

This God who created everything we see—the earth, seas, mountains, plant world, animal world, galaxies—out of nothing brought order into it and keeps it going. This takes a kind of wisdom and power that's so out of reach for us humans!

We think we know so much until we really dive deep into the hows and whys of the created world. The more we learn, the more we're amazed. And the more we realize how small and limited we really are. And it's this God, this Creator, who we can entrust our souls to.

Suffering comes in all shapes and sizes. It takes many forms. In this letter, Peter is talking to Christians who are being persecuted for their faith. In all the ways we *suffer according to the will of God* (yes, it's backed up in the Bible that suffering is part of His plan at times) we are encouraged and can even rejoice, because we are *"partakers of Christ's sufferings"* (verse 13 of chapter 4).

When we recognize God as Creator...when we see from the perspective of how He keeps the entire universe in hand, we can easily entrust our soul to Him. Because He's not only Creator, He's a good Father, He's our Good Shepherd. Nothing can separate us from His love (Romans 8:31-39).

Are you suffering today? Entrust your soul, your suffering, your pain to your faithful Creator.

Dig deeper: *The book of 1 Peter*

January 5

"I planted. Apollos watered. But God gave the increase." 1 Corinthians 3:6

The great miracle of the plant world is the mystery of the seed. A seed falls to the ground (is planted) and receives the sunlight and nutrients necessary for growth (watered). But the growth process isn't from those things, but from within itself.

Inside the seed is its genetic blueprint. The instructions it needs for growth, for photosynthesis, for fruit-bearing.

It happens around us every day. We see it in forests, deserts, jungles, prairies and under both fresh and salt water. We see it cultivated in fields, on farms and in home gardens. People make their living by this process called agriculture. Our lives depend on it for food sources, medicines, cosmetics and a host of other products. While we can control our part in it—the planting, the watering, the fertilizing—we have absolutely no control over the genetic process itself. It's built into each seed by God's design, through His wisdom.

That's Paul's point in this section of 1 Corinthians 3. People in the Corinthian church were taking sides according to their favorite preacher (hmmm...does this happen in our day, too?). Some sided with Paul, some with Apollos, some with Peter.

Paul says to them—No! It's not about us: *"Who then is Apollos, and who is Paul, but servants through whom you believed?...So then neither he who plants is anything, nor he who waters, but God who gives the increase."* (verses 5 and 7)

We can teach, preach, minister, witness, disciple. But it's God's work in someone's heart—that spiritual genetic blueprint—that causes growth and maturity in that person's life.

That's both humbling and encouraging. Humbling because we recognize we only have a part. Encouraging because we have a part! Paul says, *"...each will receive his own reward according to his own labor. For we are God's fellow workers..."*

We work with the Holy Spirit by planting and watering spiritual seeds in peoples' lives...and God handles the miracle of increase.

Dig deeper: *1 Corinthians 3*

January 6

"Don't love the world or the things that are in the world. If anyone loves the world, the Father's love isn't in him. For all that is in the world, the lust of the flesh, the lust of the eyes, and the pride of life, isn't the Father's, but is the world's." 1 John 2:15-16

Even though Jesus says in John 3:16 that God loves the world, in this verse the message is: don't love the world. The world John is referring to in this passage is the world system that's under the control of the prince of this world, Satan. It's the arena of the kingdom of darkness—the pull of negativity, discouragement and evil desires.

When Jesus washed the disciples' feet, He demonstrated the need we all have to be cleansed of the influence of the world we live in. Jesus and the disciples, like everyone else in Israel, spent a great deal of time with dirty feet. They walked everywhere in sandals and the dusty trails and roads were part of everyday life. When we live in this world we're impacted by its dusty negativity and we have a critical need to be washed.

There's a species of legume called *beggar's lice* that illustrates this dusty world reality. The tiny seeds have a Velcro-like sticky coating that's tenacious. After walking through a patch of beggar's lice, you'll have pants covered in them and an hour's worth of time removing them. God designed this bean plant to have the ability to aggressively spread its seed...good for the plant but irritating for the hiker!

The world system that attempts to constantly assert influence over our lives is like beggar's lice. It sneaks up and attaches itself to you. That's why it's so important to have fellowship with Jesus and one another, to allow the Spirit of God to wash us from the influence of the world, to pull off the sticky seeds.

This cleansing comes from God's word and our willingness to humble ourselves and receive the washing of the word through fellowship, scripture reading and the reality of His cleansing presence.

Dig deeper: *John 7:14-16; Romans 12:2; James 4:4*

Brian Rupe

January 7

"...not that we are sufficient of ourselves...but our sufficiency is from God, who also made us sufficient as servants of a new covenant..." 2 Corinthians 3:5-6

There is tension everywhere in life. There is beauty and there is pain. There is joy and there is aching. Even water feels the tension, like a droplet hanging off a broad leaf after a rain—gravity pulling it groundward while molecular forces strain to hold on and hold together.

God made this world good, and we would be remiss in dismissing all His good gifts by feeling overwhelmed by the brokenness we also experience. The Lord whispers to us of His power and love in the beauty of a sunrise, in the sunlight reflecting off calm waters, in fellowship and laughter. But in the clouds, in the storms, in diseases and death, God isn't whispering. He calls to us to seek Him, to know where we truly belong and are fully accepted.

While we bring nothing to the table because we have absolutely nothing to offer, we are enough because our Father has made us enough. A tension and mystery that we must know is that we can never be good enough to affect any eternal good, but God, in His grace and power, makes us adequate to do His work. His work!

Not only can we have confidence through Christ toward God, we are given a job in the kingdom. God doesn't stop at saving you and me—He wants to use us to bless, exhort and encourage others. To bring life! His grace is sufficient for this work, which should both keep us humbled before Him and also empowered in this world. Either one of these pulls would be dangerous without the other. One would lead to crippling despair and the other to puffed-up arrogance.

May we learn to listen to God's whispers and pay attention to God's calls. Then we will know where our value is found and have appropriate confidence in what God has done for us and what He wants to do in and through us.

Dig deeper: *Isaiah 54:10; 2 Corinthians 9:8; Hebrews 13:20-21*

Beth Poliquin

January 8

"Look! Praise Yahweh, all you servants of Yahweh, who stand by night in Yahweh's house! Lift up your hands in the sanctuary. Praise Yahweh! May Yahweh bless you from Zion, even He who made heaven and earth." Psalm 134

Are you a night owl? This psalm is for you! We each have a different inner clock. Some of us are best in the morning, others are at our prime during the night hours. Do you use your best mental energy time in Yahweh's house?

It doesn't have to be in a church building like this psalm talks about—the sanctuary. In our times the Holy Spirit lives in us, and we can meet with Him anywhere. But give Him your best time. If you're a morning person, it'll be in the morning. If you're a night owl, spend dedicated time with Him during the night.

It might be a specific place where you can get alone and focus on Him—a room in your home, maybe. Other times maybe you'll meet with other people to bless Him—a home group meeting, a prayer room, a church building.

You may ask: How often should I meet with God like this, to bless Him? Well...how often do you want to be blessed by Him?! Once a month? Every week or two? Every day?

I love how this psalm talks first about us, the servants of God, coming to Him and blessing Him, praising Him, honoring Him—*"He who made heaven and earth."* It's an amazing privilege to be able to do that. To worship and bless this amazing, powerful, creative God who made us and everything we see in the natural world.

And it's even more amazing that when we do that, this powerful, creative God blesses *us*. And the blessing of God isn't just words—it carries spiritual authority, wisdom and power. How often do you want that kind of blessing?

"May Yahweh bless you from Zion, He who made heaven and earth." Personally, I want that blessing every day!

Dig deeper: *Numbers 6:22-27; Psalm 63; Luke 6:12-23*

January 9

"Seek Him who made the Pleiades and Orion, and turns the shadow of death into the morning, and makes the day dark with night; who calls for the waters of the sea, and pours them out on the surface of the earth, Yahweh is His name..." Amos 5:8

The nations around Israel in those days worshiped various things in nature—the sun, the moon, the stars, calves, the sea, the mountains. They had gods for everything.

Amos wasn't a well-known prophet in his day—he was a shepherd and farmer. But God gave him a message to speak to the people of his country, Israel. They were deep into idol worship...worshiping the things in nature rather than the God who created nature.

Here's another verse that reminds us who this God is:

"For, behold, He who forms the mountains, and creates the wind, and declares to man what is His thought; who makes the morning darkness, and treads on the high places of the earth: Yahweh, the God of Armies, is His name." (Amos 4:13)

Yahweh, the Lord God, isn't the mountains or winds or seas or high places. He's the one who formed them. He's the one who created the physical laws by which they exist. But the people resented this God who interfered with the way they wanted to live. So they didn't seek Him, they chose to worship His creation instead. That caused all kinds of havoc in their society—you can read about it in the rest of Amos.

Our society today is pretty similar! For hundreds of years "enlightened" people have been doing their best to do away with a God who has authority over them. So they've constructed a worldview without Him, trying everything they can to make Him unnecessary for the origins of our world and the running of the universe.

And all the while the Lord is waiting for us to seek Him.

"Those who know Your name will put their trust in You, for You, Yahweh, have not forsaken those who seek You." (Psalm 9:10)

Dig deeper: *The book of Amos*

January 10

"If I speak with the languages of men and of angels, but don't have love, I have become sounding brass, or a clanging cymbal. If I have the gift of prophecy, and know all mysteries and all knowledge; and if I have all faith, so as to remove mountains, but don't have love, I am nothing. If I give away all my goods to feed the poor, and if I give my body to be burned, but don't have love, it profits me nothing."
1 Corinthians 13:1-3

These verses say a lot, but here's the big part: If you don't have love, you gain nothing.

This is so true in worship, my friends! We should do everything for the glory of God. This in and of itself is an act of worship! Like doing the dishes, changing diapers, ministering to a friend, or singing a song. All are acts of worship because of how we position our hearts. Music is the same.

We place such an emphasis on music being the way we worship God. But as I've been diving deeper and deeper into this topic, I've learned a huge lesson: anything that takes our focus away from worshiping God is idolatry.

When we focus on how well it was presented, or why are we singing this song, or this music is bad and we should be only singing a certain style of music. Family, that is idolatry.

We are focused on the wrong things and our hearts are certainly NOT in a loving place to connect with God! We are becoming like that clanging cymbal and going through the motions of the music rather than worshiping our amazing God and Father! How much we miss in those precious moments.

So when you walk into service on whatever day your body of believers meets, have a heart check in the car before you even walk in the door. Say, "Lord, I want to meet with You here. I want to engage with You here. I want my eyes to be on You, and only You! Let my offering be sweet smelling to You!"

Dig deeper: *1 Corinthians 13*

Laura Watson

January 11

"Come to me, all you who labor and are heavily burdened, and I will give you rest." Matthew 11:28

Trees can withstand many injuries. Wildfire, wind, losing limbs and invading species. Similarly, our bodies can be pushed to the limit as we explore the reaches of God's creation. When we weather the storms of life, our souls and spirits can become injured or wearied. God created us to have an extraordinary ability to heal, both physically and otherwise.

Trees and humans heal differently, and this gives us a parable that can teach in part how God wants us to look at healing. Trees don't heal, they seal. When a tree is injured, it isolates the injury by putting callus or walls of scar tissue around the wound. That keeps the damage from spreading and killing the tree, and allows the tree to continue to grow and flourish. For the rest of that tree's life, it'll carry that wound deep within its structure.

Human brains compartmentalize trauma, separating the experience from the rest of our memories so we can continue to function and survive until the hard season is over.

For people, this is a short-term strategy. We're not meant to remain with closed-off areas of our hearts and minds as the tree does. If we do, those places will eventually start leaking mindsets and reactions that aren't healthy or sustainable, and may allow toxic mindsets and habits to form. We're not meant to spend our lives putting up walls, trying to continue on, when there are places of brokenness within us the Lord wants to touch.

Have you "sealed" anything that God might want to heal? What's the Holy Spirit saying to you today about how those closed areas are affecting you and others around you?

If you feel prompted, ask the Holy Spirit to begin this journey with you today.

Dig Deeper: *Psalm 107:13-16; Lamentations 3:21-23; John 8:32*

Emilie O'Connor

12

January 12

"He heals the broken in heart and binds up their wounds." Psalm 147:3

Yesterday we examined how we're not meant to have parts of ourselves closed off due to past hurt. God wants to restore us. We contrasted this with how trees survive by creating scar tissue that remains part of them for the rest of their lives. So, what does it look like to be different? What does it look like to walk boldly into the unknown territory of healing with the Lord as our companion?

When past hurt and pain tempt us to isolate and compartmentalize, this is where we look at the tree and do the opposite. Christ asks us to open our places of hurt and pain and enter into the process of healing. God comes as *Jehovah Rapha*, the Healer.

Sometimes God shows us where He was in those memories and it redefines the memory. Other times the Holy Spirit brings truth to break off lies and strongholds. We open up to the Holy Spirit and to safe people around us to walk forward into healing, transformed from the inside out.

The goal of healing isn't to cover, but to reveal. And in the process to walk forward into a transformed life with courage. In this way we don't hide from the pains of our past. We're not ruled by our past.

2 Corinthians 5:17 says we're new creations in Christ. The power and blood of Jesus transform us from the inside out. The Bible uses the Greek word *sozo* to describe our salvation. It means we're healed, saved and delivered. Jesus said on the cross "It is finished." Trees aren't capable of replacing or repairing damaged tissue. But Christ can repair the places where we've been hurt and make our hearts whole again.

Where can the *sozo* power of Christ bring new meaning to the power of restoration in your life today? Are there any next steps you feel led to take?

Dig Deeper: *Isaiah 53:5; Jeremiah 17:14; 1 Peter 2:24*

(Research from US Forest Service and northernwoodlands.org)

Emilie O'Connor

January 13

"Yahweh's Spirit will rest on Him: the spirit of wisdom and understanding, the spirit of counsel and might, the spirit of knowledge and of the fear of Yahweh." Isaiah 11:2

Have you ever built a successful campfire? One that doesn't just start a flame going, but one that keeps burning, and gets nice and hot?

There are three essential ingredients: fuel, a spark or flame, and air. When we're camping, the most common fuel around us is dead wood (or split wood, if we're at a campground). Gather some fire starter, then kindling, then bigger pieces to keep it going. Once that's ready, get your spark or flame started and you're off to the races.

Unless you don't give your fuel any air. If you stack the kindling and then the bigger pieces too tightly, air can't get through and your fire dies out. The fire needs space and air to do its work.

God designed our brains to work that way, too. He's given us amazing amounts of creativity, solid ideas, the ability to solve complex problems. But if our mind is too crammed full of stuff, if we don't give it any breathing room, the fire dies out.

The same is true for our spirit. We need to open up, give it space, give the Holy Spirit breathing room to work in our spirit.

Do you know what both the Hebrew and Greek words for the Holy Spirit are? The same words they use for wind and breath! *Ruach* in Hebrew, *pneuma* in Greek. It's the Spirit of God that causes the fire to keep going.

Let's ask ourselves: Am I giving my mind, my brain room today? Am I making space for thoughts, ideas, creativity and problem solving? Or is it so jam packed with social media, TV, music, news and other distractions that the logs can't burn?

Am I giving my spirit room today? Does the Holy Spirit have room in me to blow and breathe as He wants to? Does He have room to burn?

Dig deeper: *Romans 8:14; 1 Corinthians 12:1-11; 2 Corinthians 3:17-18*

January 14

"He who has the Son has the life. He who doesn't have God's Son doesn't have the life." 1 John 5:12

"I'd rather have life begging for structure than structure begging for life" is something a friend and church leader has said for years. In other words: If our church or our spiritual life is so structured that the life is squeezed out, it's dead!

Structure is essential, there's no doubt about it. God designed our body with an inner skeleton that provides structure for all kinds of things: for muscle tissue, tendons and ligaments to attach to...it gives us the ability to sit, stand and move.

That skeleton, while essential, is hidden. It provides the framework for the rest of the body to do what it's all designed to do. It's there to support life. As another friend recently pointed out in his sermon: If you see bone, something's wrong! That body is either wounded or dead...or on display in a museum somewhere.

Just like in our physical body, structure is necessary in our spiritual life, too. Structure is gathering weekly at a church or home group. Daily Bible reading. Going through a devotional like this one. Set times for prayer and intercession. Learning spiritual truths through podcasts, sermons, books and videos.

But like how our body's skeleton is there to *support* life, not *be* the life, so these spiritual structures are there to support the life of the Son in us. If we have all the structures in place yet aren't connecting with Jesus or growing in our walk with Him, we've missed the whole point.

On the other hand, a vibrant spiritual life without underlying structure to give it stability is temporary at best. Like the way a body without a skeleton would flop all over the place and eventually get exactly nowhere.

So...we don't do the structure things to check them off our list or chalk them up as ways to make God happy. We do them so the structure will support the life of Jesus in us.

Dig deeper: *John 6:63; Romans 8:14; Galatians 5:25*

15

January 15

"In the beginning God created the heavens and the earth." Genesis 1:1

This is the way our Bible begins.

What do you do with that if you grew up believing the heavens and the earth exist because of random natural forces over billions of years?

They can't both be true—these two belief systems are mutually exclusive. Neither of these can be proven by standard scientific method because neither is observable (it happened before people were around to witness it) or repeatable.

Either everything is the result of random chance...or it's the result of intentional design.

And if it's intentional design—if the author of Genesis is correct that God is the one who created everything around us, including ourselves—then that means God is real. And, as Christian philosopher Francis Schaeffer wrote, He's not just real—He's the God who is *there*.

The rest of the Bible goes on to tell us how that same God involved Himself in peoples' lives—first individuals, later a nation and then the nations. In fact, that God eventually became a man in order to re-connect people to Himself.

The creation story isn't a throw-away fable for Christians. We can't just ignore the first couple chapters of Genesis and call it good. God as Creator is a repeated theme throughout the entire Bible (you'll find that out the more you go through this book).

So what do we do with this God who has the power and wisdom to create galaxies...planets...interdependent ecosystems...a human who starts as one cell then turns into trillions of cells with dozens of interrelated systems many times more complex than any computer?

This God is the one who created *you*, and who wants you to know Him. Who wants you to *"walk in the cool of the day"* with Him—today—as He walked with Adam and Eve in the garden, in the beginning.

Dig Deeper: *Genesis 1*

January 16

"...but those who wait for Yahweh will renew their strength. They will mount up with wings like eagles. They will run, and not be weary. They will walk, and not faint." Isaiah 40:31

As a Christian paraglider pilot I've combined my passion for Christ and His creation with my passion for paragliding.

Many years ago I volunteered with a friend who worked for Indiana's Department of Natural Resources reintroducing bald eagles into the wild. I was privileged to hold 2-foot-tall "baby" baldies while my friend weighed them, measured their talons, and recorded their growth. It was always miraculous watching them attempt their first flights.

Many years later as I took my first flights on a paraglider, I had the thrill of experiencing what those fledgling eagles experienced as they took off from the hacking tower. After spending the morning running up and down the hill, practicing, and ground handling the paraglider, I was exhausted.

Finally, it was time to try to fly. As I ran to launch, I felt the wind fill my wing and my feet left the ground. I glided for what was supposed to be a short hop, but instead I felt the warm rising air of a thermal. Instead of going down, I began to go up...and up!

Suddenly the vistas before me opened and I could see the sea twenty miles away. I was lifted "up with wings like eagles." My weariness fell away from me and my "strength was renewed."

Isaiah 40:31 took on a whole new meaning as God brought together these passions of mine in one epic moment.

That was twenty years ago. Through creation, paragliding and my love of everything that flies, I've experienced how God is my sustainer, my provider, and the lifter and restorer of my soul.

When I feel oppressed or stressed or anxious, I go out into God's creation and contemplate His beauty and worship Him through hiking and flying.

Dig Deeper: *Psalm 3:3; Psalm 54:4; Philippians 4:13*

Brian Doub

January 17

"If we confess our sins, He is faithful and righteous to forgive us the sins, and to cleanse us from all unrighteousness." 1 John 1:9

I had sinned. I felt sick and couldn't eat. It was as if *"my bones wasted away through my groaning all day long"* (Psalm 32:3). So, even though the day was overcast, I packed my paraglider and went for a walk in England's Lake District National Park.

Maybe I would go flying, but in my mind, my paraglider had become my burden of sin – 22 kilos (50+ pounds). I would climb the highest mountain, pray and repent under my burden. It didn't matter if I could fly or not. I needed to physically express my repentance.

As I climbed I had to cross a bog. It reminded me of Christian crossing the Slough of Despond in John Bunyan's *Pilgrim's Progress*. I was despondent and bogged down in my guilt and sin. Sinking ankle deep, my boots became covered in mud. I confessed my sin, begging for mercy and that He would wash me white as snow.

I came upon a large boulder where I stopped to rest. There beneath the boulder a small spring of water trickled out, clear and clean with a sound of glass chimes in a gentle wind. Was this a promise from God? *"He is faithful and righteous to forgive us the sins, and to cleanse us from all unrighteousness."*

I accepted it.

As I reached the top, I let my burden slip from my shoulders. I dropped my paraglider and rejoiced in tears upon my knees. I was forgiven. My burden was laid to rest at the cross of Christ. He is faithful to forgive my sins and cleanse me.

The clouds parted. The sun came out and a refreshing breeze began to blow. I laid out my glider, pulled it up and launched into the air. I immediately began to rise higher and higher as if upon the wings of an eagle.

Dig Deeper: *Psalm 32:1-6; Acts 3:19; 2 Corinthians 7:9-10*

Brian Doub

January 18

"Those who are wise will shine as the brightness of the expanse. Those who turn many to righteousness will shine as the stars forever and ever." Daniel 12:3

The best place to see the stars at night is wherever the sky is intensely dark. That means away from the lights of cities, away from even streetlights in a neighborhood.

The wilderness is a great place to go if you love to star gaze. Without artificial lights around us, the night sky there makes it easy for the stars to pop out. Especially in areas and during seasons when the air is clear and dry, stars appear by the millions. Constellations are easy to find. It's awe-inspiring. Have you been able to experience that?

The darkness, rather than crowding out the light, gives place for these stars and their light to really shine.

This verse from the last chapter of Daniel is in a section talking about the Last Days, which many Bible scholars think we're in now. It's one of many parts of the Bible that talk about these last days and how hard it'll be—and in many parts of the world, now is—for followers of Jesus.

The Bible often describes sin and evil as darkness, and those who live their lives rejecting God and His ways as walking in darkness. It tells us this darkness will increase the closer we get to the end. That's the setting for this verse in Daniel.

Even as the darkness in our world intensifies, *"Those who are wise will shine as the brightness of the expanse. Those who turn many to righteousness will shine as the stars forever and ever."*

Too many people live their lives for stardom—worldly fame with people. Most will compromise godly wisdom and righteousness for it. It's the people who remain faithful to God and His ways that will truly shine like bright stars in dark skies.

The darker the times get, the brighter these stars will shine in God's eyes. And in the end, His eyes are the only ones that matter.

Dig deeper: *Isaiah 42:6; Matthew 5:13-16; Ephesians 5:8-9*

January 19

"The mystery which has been hidden for ages and generations. But now it has been revealed to His saints, to whom God was pleased to make known what are the riches of the glory of this mystery among the Gentiles, which is Christ in you, the hope of glory." Colossians 1:26-27

Paul explains how there was a mystery, a story that had not been completed and that no one really understood.

Watching or reading a good mystery is fun because you're constantly trying to figure out how it will conclude. Who committed the murder? Who'll receive the inheritance? How will the hero escape the present danger?

No matter how much conflict there is, in a good story we know it'll have a good ending.

There are countless mysteries in creation. One favorite is the mystery of how water travels from the tree roots deep in the ground to the very top of the tree. Though scientists will teach about several forces that may assist in this process, all of their explanations fall short. It's still a mystery! Standing in front of a tree and imagining the amount of force it takes to push or pull water to the top of the tree, it seems amazing that we don't know how it works. But for now it's a mystery.

One of the mysteries of the Christian faith is Christ in you, the hope of glory. What a mystery that Christ has chosen to live inside of those who put their faith in Him—that His very presence is carried in our hearts. Paul tells us that's a rich and glorious mystery.

Christ in us, the hope of glory speaks to the power of God that's in us. It speaks to the authority we have to gain the victory. It speaks to our ability to be fruitful, and to be salt and light in the world. We're a mystery that's been revealed—so let your light shine in the darkness!

Dig deeper: 1 Corinthians 2:7; Ephesians 1:9; Colossians 4:3

Brian Rupe

January 20

"For the invisible things of Him, since the creation of the world, are clearly seen, being perceived through the things that are made..." Romans 1:20

We can know what God is like by looking at His workmanship. I think that's why I love being in the outdoors so much. I don't even have to go to a wilderness area to see it. I can walk in my own neighborhood and be reminded of God's character and goodness through what's around me.

In the next few days we'll dig into some of God's character attributes we can plainly see through nature, His creation.

The first is *Creativity.*

We see God's creativity in the astounding variety in the natural world. How is it possible He could think up such a vast array of living things? Let's take a look at some numbers:

- There are about 6,400 species of mammals in the world
- There are 18,000 species of birds in the world
- There are 32,500 species of fish in the world's waters
- There are 60,000+ species of trees
- There are almost 400,000 different types of plants
- To rule them all, there are 900,000 different species of insects in the world. At any one time there are some 10 quintillion individual insects living somewhere on earth— no wonder it seems like bugs are everywhere!

How much fun it must've been for our God to speak all these species into existence. His is the most creative mind in the universe! And as His children *"we have Christ's mind,"* too (1 Corinthians 2:16).

That means we're not only *born* with creativity, we can ask God for *His* creativity in our day-to-day living: in our work, our relationships, school, problems we face. How do you need your Heavenly Father's creativity today?

Dig deeper: *Psalm 104:24-25; Psalm 8:3-9; Job 12:7-10*

January 21

"For the invisible things of Him, since the creation of the world, are clearly seen, being perceived through the things that are made..." Romans 1:20

Yesterday we started looking at how God has displayed His character—*the invisible things of Him*—in what He's made.

The second part of His character we'll focus on is *Strength*.

There are lots of things that might come to your mind when you think of *strength* in the natural world. Here are a few examples I think of:

- One African elephant can carry up to 19,000 pounds.
- I got to drive a team of Belgians for a short distance once— the power in those two 1-ton horses blew me away.
- Yellowstone's Lower Falls dumps 63,500 gallons of water per *second* into the canyon 308 feet below.
- Horseshoe Falls, the Canadian side of Niagara Falls, dumps 682,000 gallons of water per second. The force from all this water creates crazy winds in the gorge. I experienced them near the foot of the falls in one of those tourist boats.
- Mountains give us a sense of immovable strength. Solid rock going up and up for thousands of feet.
- And yet the power underneath the mountains can pulverize them in a matter of minutes. This happened when Mount St. Helens erupted back in the 1980s.
- The gravitational pull of the moon is so strong it creates tides in the earth's oceans 238,000 miles away.
- The gravitational pull of the sun is so strong it keeps eight planets, one demoted planet and innumerable asteroids in orbit from as far away as 4.5 billion miles.

And now think of the God who created all of this, and the strength that's in Him. *"Yahweh's name is a strong tower. The righteous run to Him, and are safe."* (Proverbs 18:10)

Dig deeper: *1 Chronicles 16:11; Psalm 73:26; Ephesians 6:10*

January 22

"For the invisible things of Him, since the creation of the world, are clearly seen, being perceived through the things that are made..." Romans 1:20

Let's keep looking at what we can know about God by looking at the natural world around us. The Bible says these things are clearly seen. One of the things that's clearly seen is *His love of Beauty.*

How do we know God loves beauty? Because we're surrounded by it! Even as I write this, the sun is rising, casting bright oranges, reds and yellows on the clouds. It's like the song says: *"I see You in the sunrise every morning. It's like a picture that You've painted for me..."* ("Nobody Loves Me Like You" by Chris Tomlin)

One of my personal favorite expressions of God's love of beauty is in birds' feathers. The colors! Some birds are graced with extraordinary, bright, expressive colors, like many of the parrots and the peacock. Others seem drab and dull until you get a glimpse of them in the right sunlight. Then we can see the brilliant iridescence. Why would God do that?

I love going to the mountains in late spring when the alpine wildflowers are blooming. They're exquisite! So many tiny plants produce so many bright petals that thrive in this harsh environment. And God's put these flowers on mountain tops where very few people ever see them. Why would He do that?

It's only been in the last few decades that people have been able to see the beauty of stars, supernovas and galaxies lightyears away from earth. God splashed beauty even in the far reaches of space. Why?

I believe it's because He loves beauty for beauty's sake. It doesn't have to accomplish anything. It's just there because it's wonderful. God delights in it.

And He created us in His image to love and delight in it, too. That's amazing! What a gift to be able to recognize and appreciate beauty. Thank you, Father!

Dig deeper: *Philippians 4:8; Matthew 6:28-29; Psalm 139:14*

January 23

"For the invisible things of Him, since the creation of the world, are clearly seen, being perceived through the things that are made..."
Romans 1:20

We've seen a bit of what God is like by some of what we see in nature. His creativity, strength and love of beauty. Today we'll look at another way we can clearly see God in what He's made: His *Attention to Detail*.

No matter what system or kingdom we look at in nature, it's jam-packed with detail. In fact, the way scientists classify the various species of whatever they study is by their details. The beak shape of a bird...the web pattern of a spider...the bark of a tree...all are details that make them different from each other.

The details of our own body are absolutely astounding. We have all these different systems that work together—our heart and blood system, our digestive system, our brain and nervous system, our skeletal system, our skin and hair. They each have their own function, but work together in perfect harmony to make a whole body.

Even more astounding is what we can't see—the cell level. Each of our 37 trillion cells contains DNA, the human genome—our genetic map that's hidden inside the nucleus of each cell. This genome "consists of two sets of 3 billion individual letters each... [These letters] directly encode the roughly 100,000 different human proteins and the uncounted number of functional RNA molecules found within our cells. Each of these proteins and RNA molecules are essentially miniature machines, each with hundreds of component parts..." (*Genetic Entropy and the Mystery of the Human Genome*, by Dr. JC Sanford—a fascinating read, by the way)

That's detail!

The same God who created that mind-blowing detail in our body knows and cares about the details of our life. It doesn't always seem that way, living in this sin-filled world as we do. But Jesus assures us *"the very hairs of your head are all counted"* (Luke 12:7). He knows.

Dig deeper: *Matthew 6:27-33*

January 24

"For the invisible things of Him, since the creation of the world, are clearly seen, being perceived through the things that are made..." Romans 1:20

Like an artist, God has signed His name to His works in a way. We can know what He's like by observing and learning about the natural world around us.

Part of His character that's evident through nature is *Tenacity*. Tenacity means not letting go, not giving up. A determination in the face of hurdles and set-backs.

One of the best examples in nature of tenacity are the trees—big ones—that grow out of solid rock. We see them on cliff sides, on mountainsides, in steep ravines.

How in the world do they find the nutrients they need out of the tiny amounts of soil there? And yet their roots find places to cling to, and they grow despite the impossibility of it. Their roots wrap around rocks and cling to crevices, hanging on for dear life. It's inspiring!

Tenacity reminds me of one of our yellow labs, too. Brandy loved to fetch tennis balls and wouldn't stop until she was exhausted. I'd fake a throw to get her running off, then hide it somewhere in the yard. That dog would run around, sniffing, and not give up until she found it. Then she'd bring it back to me for another round.

God's like that, too, did you know that? Psalm 139:7-10 says, *"Where could I go from Your Spirit? Or where could I flee from Your presence? If I ascend up into heaven, You are there. If I make my bed in Sheol, behold, You are there! If I take the wings of the dawn, and settle in the uttermost parts of the sea, even there Your hand will lead me, and Your right hand will hold me."*

What comfort to know our Father tenaciously pursues us—like Jesus' story of the shepherd who leaves the 99 sheep behind to go after the one.

Dig deeper: *Matthew 18:12-14; Romans 8:35-39*

January 25

"For the invisible things of Him, since the creation of the world, are clearly seen, being perceived through the things that are made..."
Romans 1:20

Part of God's character that we clearly see in nature is that He is a God of *Order*. A wonderful example of order is space and the heavenly bodies that fill it.

I love looking up at the stars when we're in the wilderness. There are no city lights to dull their brightness. There are millions of them, seemingly spread out randomly across the sky. But they're not random! God has placed them in precise order. How do I know that?

When I look into the sky on a clear night I look for constellations that are familiar to me. As soon as I spot the Big Dipper, I know where north is. From the Big Dipper I can find the Little Dipper and then the North Star, Polaris.

In the late summer through the winter here in Minnesota, when I look into the southeast sky at around 10:00 at night I can see Orion the Hunter. I find it oddly comforting to see him up there! I can get my bearings. He reminds me of my big God.

Centuries before radar and GPS, people navigated by the stars. Why? Because they're in a specific, dependable order.

God's order is stamped all over the physical world. And He's placed order within us. It comes out in some of us more than others! But as children of the Father, we all have access to His order for our lives.

It comes with being filled with the Holy Spirit. One of the fruits He develops in us is *self-control*, or self-management—order (Galatians 5:23). Even if it doesn't come naturally to you, you can depend on Him to grow it in you as you allow Him to.

And you know what's interesting? According to 1 Corinthians 14:33, the opposite of disorder is peace. When we live in God's order, our lives are settled in His peace. What good news!

Dig deeper: *Job 38:31-33; Colossians 1:16-17; Deuteronomy 7:9*

January 26

"For the invisible things of Him, since the creation of the world, are clearly seen, being perceived through the things that are made..." Romans 1:20

The final character attribute of God we'll talk about from Romans 1 is *Redemption*. God is the God of Redemption. It's been His plan all along. Way back in the Garden, as He confronted Adam and Eve about their rebellion, He spoke of a Redeemer who would crush the head of the serpent. (Genesis 3:15)

One of the most vivid examples of redemption in nature is the aftermath of a forest fire. Fire is so destructive. And yet new life is born into the forest within weeks...days, even.

Some varieties of trees can only seed when the heat of a fire unseals the heavy resin that envelopes their cones! One of those is the lodgepole pine that grows all over the mountains of the American West. Another is the Jack pine found in the boreal forest of Canada and the northern US. The eucalyptus and banksia trees of Australia fit into this category, too.

I'll never forget going to the Boundary Waters within a month of one of its biggest wildfires a few years ago. There was already lush, green grass and blooming flowers in the ashes. And that ashy, fertile soil produced some of the best wild blueberries that area had seen in years.

God is an expert at redeeming hardship, disaster and even death. As His children, we can expect and trust Him to redeem any area of our life we give over to Him.

"I have blotted out, as a thick cloud, your transgressions, and, as a cloud, your sins. Return to Me, for I have redeemed you." (Isaiah 44:22)

"He has sent redemption to His people. He has ordained His covenant forever. His name is holy and awesome!" (Psalm 111:9)

"But as for me, I know that my Redeemer lives. In the end, He will stand upon the earth." (Job 19:25)

Dig deeper: *Ephesians 1:7; 1 Peter 1:18-19; Revelation 5:9*

January 27

"Set your mind on the things that are above, not on the things that are on the earth." Colossians 3:2

At church one day I had a vision. Or more to the point, I had a vision impairment that opened my eyes.

It was a small church with warm, bright wood trim and ceiling panels that focused the eyes toward the front. The space had a podium and the usual accessories, and was backed by a white wall. The only adornment was a large wooden cross.

It was a bright sunny day so the front wall was quite well lit. The preacher was off to one side, so I could somewhat vacantly gaze at the cross while he spoke. Which I did. No particular thoughts. Just listening to the words of Jesus.

The sermon ended and we bowed to pray. As I closed my eyes, all I could see was the after image of a bright neon-like cross in my closed-eye vision. I opened my eyes and it persisted...for a long time. It was so prominent I was still seeing it when I exited the building after a few minutes of "Minnesota goodbyes" on my way out. I could still see it out in the bright sunlight.

How long do I need to gaze at the Savior and listen to His words until I see Him no matter how bright and hot the troubles of life get?

Am I able to be honest enough to admit that it's more than I am doing right now? Am I willing to choose the discipline of putting aside other things for the best thing? When I really get right down to it, do I really believe He *is* the best thing?

Dig deeper: *Colossians 3:1-4; Ephesians 5:13-16*

Matt White

January 28

"Behold, to Yahweh your God belongs heaven, the heaven of heavens, and the earth, with all that is therein." Deuteronomy 10:14

"To Yahweh your God belongs..."

Why, as followers of Jesus, do we have a mandate to care for God's creation? Because it belongs to Him—He made it. And then gave us *stewardship* over it. Genesis 1:26 says, *"God said, "Let's make man in our image, after our likeness. Let them have dominion over the fish of the sea, and over the birds of the sky, and over the livestock, and over all the earth, and over every creeping thing that creeps on the earth."*

Stewardship isn't a word we use much anymore in our culture. In the days of aristocratic lords and noblemen, a steward was the person employed by the estate owner to manage the estate. The steward managed everything that belonged to the owner: the mansion or castle or manor house...the lands belonging to the estate...often the tenants who farmed the land on the estate and their homes.

The steward had a lot of responsibility and a lot of authority. You can imagine how valuable a trusted, competent steward was to the master of the estate.

Just so, our Heavenly Father, the Master of heaven and earth, gave people dominion over the earth. Not *ownership* of it, because the earth and the heavens belong to God. But *stewardship* over it.

As stewards, we care for what He's made. That can look different for different people. Some love trees, some love gardening, some love farming or ranching, some love animals. Some love to photograph nature, some love to paint it. Some love to help set aside natural areas for parks, others like to help clean up waterways and trails. Some want to breed healthy animals, some want to rescue abandoned and mistreated animals.

What has God put on *your* heart to do to help care for His creation?

Dig Deeper: *Genesis 1:26-31; Job 12:10; Psalm 65:9-13*

January 29

"Blessed is the man who doesn't walk in the counsel of the wicked, nor stand on the path of sinners, nor sit in the seat of scoffers; but his delight is in Yahweh's law. On His law he meditates day and night." Psalm 1:1-2

Several years ago a pastor from Uganda challenged the members of our church in Minnesota to "saturate in the Word" by reading 10 chapters of the Bible a day. Their church had done that for years, and their people were rich in God's word and in prayer.

Many of us took on that challenge, and I can testify how it changed our view of the Bible.

Americans are more likely to "snack on the Word." We're more likely to go for the 5-minute devotional or 2-minute prayer. Something we can get in quickly between everything else we're doing. Something that doesn't inconvenience us too much.

Saturating in God's word—meditating on it day and night—is like getting the flyover view of the Bible.

The arctic tern makes the longest migration of any bird on earth. Twice a year these amazing birds fly between the Arctic and the Antarctic. That's incredible! Let's pretend they pay attention to the continents they fly over. What different terrains, regions and features they see!

They truly get a big picture look at the world. They see the vastness, the way it all connects together. It's a much different view of the world than, say, a penguin would get, that has to walk it step-by-step.

That's how a "flyover view" of the Bible works. Reading long chunks of it every day—saturating in it—gives us the big picture flyover of God's work in human history. It brings out the story of Jesus differently. Instead of seeing Him suddenly appear in Matthew's Gospel, we see Him from the very beginning in Genesis, and throughout the whole Bible.

Would a flyover view of God's word change your life, too? I don't know...you'll have to try it! What's stopping you?

***Dig deeper:** Psalm 119*

January 30

"You, Lord, in the beginning, laid the foundation of the earth. The heavens are the works of Your hands. They will perish, but You continue. They all will grow old like a garment does. You will roll them up like a mantle, and they will be changed; but You are the same. Your years won't fail." Hebrews 1:10-12

The writer of Hebrews is quoting Psalm 102 here, verses 25-27. It was written centuries before Jesus came on the scene. Centuries before Jesus' disciple, John, wrote of Him: *"All things were made through Him."* (John 1:3) And before the same John had those wild visions he wrote down as the book of Revelation, which include this: that the current heaven and earth will one day pass away (Revelation 21:1).

All the created things on earth and in the heavens are part of God's long-range divine plan. They had a beginning and they'll have an end. The writer of Hebrews is pointing all these events, past and future, to Jesus.

This man, Jesus, lived in a specific time in history in a specific place in the world and did specific things that specific people witnessed and wrote about. This man, Jesus, wasn't just a man, though! He was God who *"became flesh, and lived among us."* (John 1:14)

Jesus, who *"laid the foundation of the earth"* will one day *"roll them up like a mantle."* Many people worry about our planet's doom, that climate change or environmental disaster will destroy it. Or maybe an asteroid.

But the Bible teaches the Creator of heaven and earth Himself will one day cause the current heavens and earth to perish.

Even though the man, Jesus, lived in a specific time on earth, the God, Jesus, always was and always will be. He was there in the beginning with God (John 1:2) and will be there at the end (which is really a new beginning, Revelation 21-22) when He's called the Lamb.

He is the same. His years won't fail. He has a plan that won't fail. And we're part of it!

Dig deeper: *Hebrews 1*

January 31

"God thunders marvelously with His voice. He does great things, which we can't comprehend. For He says to the snow, 'Fall on the earth,' likewise to the shower of rain and to the showers of His mighty rain." Job 37:5-6

We spent three days holed up in what was a beautiful rustic suite along Lake Superior. The plan was for my associate and I to update our business website and spend time snowshoeing, Nordic skiing, and enjoying the natural setting of our room facing the largest freshwater lake in the world.

Yup, we were going to work hard and play hard in the beautiful north.

Then there was the website. It just didn't seem to want to cooperate. New templates fighting us, tweaks, glitches, errors, mobile versus desktop issues. It just seemed to be one thing after another.

Frustrations and more time-consuming issues meant we only got out of the suite to get some quick exercise to refresh our brains. Then it was back to the task at hand. Our planned fun outdoor adventures were thwarted by the clock and the issue of lacking in website expertise.

It was now Monday morning. Having worked since Friday night, I woke up a tad bit disappointed in our lack of weekend adventures. I brewed a pot of coffee, feeling a bit sulky.

Then God spoke.

My eyes glanced out the window to see graceful drifting snowflakes gently swirling and falling to the ground. A fresh blanket of snow covered everything. The setting was pure white bliss. The voice of my loving God rang out to me: *"Be still and know that I am God."* (Psalm 46:10)

I lingered by the window with peace and contentment in the moment and in the weekend. My weekend was just as it was supposed to be and God was in every part of it.

Dig deeper: *Psalm 32:8; Isaiah 46:4; Matthew 6:33*

Tracy Blesi

February

February 1

"There is no fear in love; but perfect love casts out fear, because fear has punishment. He who fears is not made perfect in love."
1 John 4:18

There are so many ways this verse can apply to us, but let's focus on just one today: *"There is no fear in love"* as it refers to our relationships with others.

I was recently on a four-day kayak camping trip with six other women. Trips like this, when you're with the same people day and night in a situation you can't get out of, can be pretty intense!

Even without realizing it, thoughts like these can come into our mind: "What if they don't like me? What if I say the wrong thing? What if I can't keep up? What if I'm not as good as they are?" You get the picture.

After I got home I read the verse above as part of my daily Bible reading. It dawned on me—for the first time, even though I've read this verse countless times over my life— why there's no fear in the kind of love this verse is talking about.

This love—*agape*, in the Greek—God's kind of love, the kind talked about in 1 Corinthians 13—isn't focused on me at all. It's focused on the other person. The other people. If I'm busy loving other people with God's kind of love, I don't have a lot of time to be thinking about myself or what others think of me.

And if I'm secure in God's love for me—with His perfect *agape* love no matter what I do or don't do—then I don't need to be so focused on what others think of me.

Ask the Holy Spirit today to show you the love of the Father more and more. Say, "Father, help me know Your love for me." And then ask Him to help you love the other people in your life the way He does.

The more love is perfected in you, the more it pushes out fear. There isn't room for both of them in your heart and mind!

Dig deeper: *1 John 4*

February 2

"So he went and did according to Yahweh's word; for he went and lived by the brook Cherith that is before the Jordan. The ravens brought him bread and meat in the morning, and bread and meat in the evening; and he drank from the brook." 1 Kings 17:5-6

The "he" in this story is Elijah, a prophet of Israel. In this instance, the Lord sent Elijah to this wilderness place immediately after he'd delivered a prophetic word about a 3-year drought to Israel's evil king, Ahab. The Lord provided for his needs and protected him from Ahab's anger and revenge.

Have there been times in your life when the Lord "sends you" to the wilderness for protection, or a period of rest or healing? For us who love the wilderness, what an awesome time! He uses nature to minister to us in so many ways.

But there's another story about Elijah high-tailing it to the wilderness—this time out of fear instead of God's direction. In fact, it's a couple of chapters later in 1 Kings.

He had just bested 400 prophets of Baal and called fire down from heaven to burn up an offering. Right after this amazing high-point in Elijah's ministry, Ahab's queen, Jezebel (who was even more evil than Ahab), blew up and threatened him with death.

Elijah fled for his life, again into the wilderness (1 Kings 19). The Lord still provided for his needs through an angel. But then He said to him, *"Elijah, what are you doing here?"* (1 Kings 19:9) God had not sent him this time. He had other things in mind for Elijah.

Have there been times in your life when you've escaped to the wilderness out of fear? Or to avoid uncomfortable, even hostile relationships? To put off something you knew the Lord told you to do and you opted for a distraction instead?

It won't help! It only lets in discouragement, as it did for Elijah. As followers of Jesus, let's listen for *His* direction for us.

Dig deeper: *Numbers 9:23; Isaiah 30:21; John 10:27-29*

February 3

"All the congregation of the children of Israel traveled from the wilderness of Sin, starting according to Yahweh's commandment, and encamped in Rephidim; but there was no water for the people to drink." Exodus 17:1

The Hebrew word *Rephidim* means: *in the desert*. This place was desolate. The text says they camped there according to God's command. So sometimes it's God who brings us into the desert to camp for awhile.

But sometimes we set up camp in desert places ourselves. Have you ever set up camp in Regret? Or Unforgiveness? Or Offense? There are many desert places we can settle into that don't have life. There's no water there.

When God commands a desert campsite, His provision is hidden somewhere. We can be sure of it. But when we bring ourselves to the desert and set up camp, we're on our own. He's patiently waiting. His grace is available. But we have to make the choice to break camp and follow Him.

What does it look like to set up camp in regret, or unforgiveness or offense or other desert places? It looks like constantly rehashing either my own mistakes or how others have hurt me. It looks like focusing on the problem. It looks like complaining, or out-of-control fear and anxiety.

But what does it look like to break camp and follow Jesus instead? It looks like green pastures and still waters. (Psalm 23) It looks like freedom and life. It looks like the fruit of the Spirit—joy, peace, goodness and the rest. (Galatians 5:22)

Even when life isn't going the way we think it should, it's still our choice where we set up camp. Sometimes life is green and wonderful. Sometimes it's harsh and awful. But in our inner life, we still choose where we set up camp.

Will it be in the desert away from the water of life...Jesus Himself? Or with Him and His living water? (John 7:38)

Dig deeper: *Deuteronomy 30:15-20; Joshua 24:15; Galatians 5:25*

February 4

"In fire by night...and in the cloud by day..." Deuteronomy 1:33

Do you ever feel like you're living in a fog? Sometimes it's difficult to know what in the world is going on!?! It can be pretty scary to get caught on a trail or back road in a thick fog.

God led the children of Israel with fire at night and a cloud by day. The cloud by day makes me wonder if He was hiding the view ahead—expecting obedience without complete vision for the next step.

During one Minnesota winter we experienced an unusual amount of fog. Along with the fog, we were treated to a spectacular display of hoar frost and rime ice. The rime ice happens with the right combination of atmospheric pressure, moisture and temperature. The freezing fog collects as ice crystals, and creates sparkling ice on every surface. Hoar frost is when the normal dew mist skips the liquid phase and forms tiny ice crystals on grass and trees.

The fog penetrates every area of our atmosphere. God is present everywhere. Just as God used a cloud to lead the children of Israel and His presence was in the cloud, so the Lord wants us to know He's always present with us and always working in us. The rime ice, produced through freezing fog, is a message of God's presence and guidance in our lives.

Sometimes we feel the cloud is like a deep fog of despair. We're not sure what God's doing or where He's taking us. But we can be confident He's always leading us towards a good destination, teaching us how to listen to His voice, to trust and obey.

After the rime ice forms through a dark foggy night, suddenly the sun comes out and the result is a spectacular display of sparkling ice crystals. Indeed, God has never stopped working. His grace and power never gives up forming in us His ultimate glorious intentions.

Dig deeper: *Psalm 27; Acts 3:19; Hebrews 10:19-22*

Brian Rupe

February 5

"Shepherd the flock of God which is among you, exercising the oversight, not under compulsion, but voluntarily, not for dishonest gain, but willingly; not as lording it over those entrusted to you, but making yourselves examples to the flock." 1 Peter 5:2-3

Peter, the apostle who wrote this letter, wasn't a shepherd, he was a fisherman by trade. But in his day shepherds were common and could be seen with their flocks on hillsides around Israel.

In these verses he's talking to pastors, leaders, even fathers of families. Today it could be business owners, ministry leaders, house church leaders. *"Shepherd the flock of God..."* Care for, tend, take care of those under your care, under your leadership. Just as a shepherd takes care of his sheep, so you take care of those you have influence with.

Psalm 23 tells us more about what shepherds do: *"Yahweh is my shepherd: I shall lack nothing. He makes me lie down in green pastures. He leads me beside still waters. He restores my soul. He guides me in the paths of righteousness for his name's sake. Even though I walk through the valley of the shadow of death, I will fear no evil, for you are with me. Your rod and your staff, they comfort me."* (verses 1-4)

Who wrote Psalm 23? David, Israel's shepherd king. He knew shepherding well. He cared for his father's sheep for many years. He knew what it was to protect his sheep from enemies, to lead them to pasture and water, to tend their injuries. That's where David was trained by the Lord for his ultimate purpose, to be *"shepherd of My people Israel"* (2 Samuel 5:2).

So Jesus' assignment for leaders in His kingdom is to *"shepherd the flock of God which is among you...making yourselves examples to the flock."*

You can do this whether you're officially a "leader" or not. Who does God have in your life that He wants you to minister to? They are your current "flock"! Whether it's super casual or from an "official" position, shepherd God's people well!

Dig deeper: *Psalm 100:3; Isaiah 53:6; John 10:11-15*

February 6

"I press on toward the goal for the prize of the high calling of God in Christ Jesus." Philippians 3:14

Anyone who's ever hiked, backpacked, paddled, skied, biked, climbed—especially with the challenge of covering a long or challenging distance—knows what it means to *press on toward the goal.*

Whether the goal is the end of the trail, the next portage or the summit of a mountain, it's amazing how much time, effort and money we're willing to devote to press toward and reach it.

And not just once! Many of us will do this time and time again. We'll invest vast amounts of resources, mental energy and time to get that prize. For many of us the prize is as simple as the personal fulfillment and satisfaction that comes from "conquering" our own limitations and our environment. Sometimes it's as simple as being surrounded by the beauty of the natural world.

As followers of Jesus, are we putting that same value, those same resources into pressing toward the goal of the calling of God on our lives? Do we value the prize of that high calling to the point that we're willing to *"forget the things which are behind, and stretch forward to the things which are before..."* (verse 13)

It's a reality check to stop once in awhile, to slow down enough to ask ourselves: What am I pressing towards today? This week? This year? Am I distracted by my own "high calling" or am I in tune with my Father's high calling for me?

No matter what goals we're pressing towards in this physical world—a through-hike, a kayak or canoe trip, a cliff face, a back-country campsite—the most important goal we'll ever pursue is this *"high calling of God in Christ Jesus."*

In fact, let's use our times of pressing in the natural world to press in our walk with God. They go hand-in-hand so well.

Dig deeper: *Hebrews 12:1-2; 1 Corinthians 9:24-27*

February 7

"I press on toward the goal for the prize of the high calling of God in Christ Jesus." Philippians 3:14

When was the last time you had to really *press on* to reach a goal? For us who are followers of Jesus, we *press on daily* toward the goal, the prize of God's high calling for each one of us.

Sometimes the pressing gets hard. Exhausting. Discouraging. We want to give up. Quit. Look for an easier life that doesn't require so much from us.

But then we remember the prize—our friendship with the Creator of the universe. Our place in His kingdom, our role in His family, and eventually an eternity with Him.

That remembering helps us with the *pressing on*.

One of the very best ways to teach us what it means to press on is to participate in a wilderness trip of some kind that involves lots of time, uncontrollable conditions and no way out of it!

When you're in the wilderness, no matter how exhausted, fed up or discouraged you get, you can't just quit. You can't call Uber to come get you. You usually can't call anybody, because you probably don't have cell coverage.

There's no easy way out when you're miles into the wilderness, whether it's in a canoe, on a backpacking trail, on skis. The only way out is to keep going. To finish. To press on.

We'll find that even when we think we can't go any further, we can when we have to. When we have no other choice but to press on, we'll find reserves of strength (both physical and mental) we didn't know were inside us. We discover these reserves only when we're in these kinds of situations.

The same is true for our spiritual journey. When we come up against barriers to our goal—which we will—that's when we pull on the reserves inside us. That's when we learn to pull on the strength of the Holy Spirit's life in us.

We learn to *press on* by pressing on!

Dig deeper: *Romans 5:3-4; James 1:12; Galatians 6:9*

February 8

"As therefore you received Christ Jesus, the Lord, walk in Him."
Colossians 2:6

There is nature to be found in ordinary places that aren't usually associated with words such as *wild* or *backcountry*. Nature reclaims spaces that man has developed and claimed as urban or industrial.

City blocks that are overgrown with what looks like weeds can actually be diverse ecosystems that allow vanishing species of wild grasses and insects to flourish. Wildflowers peek through the cracks in cement and sing praises to the King of Kings with their very being.

Living in a city has taught me to look for nature not only when I leave the city, but also in small parks and tucked-away lots. In yards and community gardens. This perspective has taught me about how God wants to walk with us daily. So much of our walk with God and others is found in the journey. In the in-between moments.

Just like I can't wait to only see beauty when I'm in nature's purest habitats, I can't wait to talk to or relate to God only when I'm in the perfect faith environment, such as church or a worship service.

I've come to treasure the small moments of nature I see in the city, just as I treasure the small moments with God throughout the day. And so often, God uses those small moments to surprise me with beautiful things. I'm reminded of how He knows me, loves me and cares for me.

Those small moments and conversations with God turn into the longer journey that shapes our lives.

What is God using to show you His presence in your life today? Where can you see beauty in unexpected places around you today?

Dig Deeper: *Psalm 113; Matthew 13:31-32; Colossians 2:5-7*

Emilie O'Connor

41

February 9

"...Exercise yourself toward godliness." 1 Timothy 4:7

The Greek word in this scripture that's translated exercise is *gumnazó*. It means to train by physical exercise, with your full effort, working out intensely. It's how the Greek athletes of the day trained—with intention, discipline and regularity.

Anyone who's trained for a long-distance race of any kind knows what that's like. The training slides to the top of your to-do list. You eat according to your training schedule. You sleep according to your training schedule. You train your body for more distance and speed.

Lots of us have paid the price of taking on a long hike, bike ride, paddle, backpacking trip—whatever—without being in shape. What's the result? Days of unnecessary soreness at best, maybe injury, maybe failure of your goal.

As a woman in my 50s now, one of my top motivators for regular exercise is so I can keep doing the outdoor activities I love well into my "mature" years. I want to be able to enjoy them and not hurt myself in the process!

Is our spiritual training as high on our to-do list as our physical training? Paul goes on to say, *"For bodily exercise has some value, but godliness has value in all things, having the promise of the life which is now, and of that which is to come."* (verse 8)

Yes, physical exercise is hugely important. It's one of the ways we steward this one body God's given us. Our destiny for the kingdom is partially dependent on our health. But, our spiritual health is even more important!

It's that strong spirit in us, the fruit of the Holy Spirit, our faith walk with God that we need when we face life's greatest obstacles. If we're not prepared to face them by having exercised ourselves toward godliness—Jesus in us—we risk getting taken out by them. Some even walk away from their faith because of them.

What's on your to-do list today? How will you exercise yourself toward godliness?

***Dig deeper:** Romans 12; 2 Peter 1:1-11*

February 10

"...Exercise yourself toward godliness. For bodily exercise has some value, but godliness has value in all things, having the promise of the life which is now, and of that which is to come." 1 Timothy 4:7-8

I don't want to give myself to the wrong things! To train, discipline, strive, learn—and then to realize it was all after temporal, worthless things in the light of eternity. Or even to realize it was good, but not the best—not the things on God's heart for me.

How tragic to run the race only to discover I was on the wrong course.

In the world of sports that would disqualify me. On a long hike in the wilderness it could lead me to a swamp instead of the mountaintop. On a canoe trip it could mean taking the wrong portage to end up miles off-course.

In the realm of God's kingdom and eternity the consequences are much more serious.

We've all heard "God has a plan for your life." And He does! Each of us has a God-given destiny. *"In your book they were all written, the days that were ordained for me, when as yet there were none of them."* (Psalm 139:16)

But unless we exercise ourselves toward godliness, toward following Jesus, toward life in the Spirit, it'd be easy to miss it. It's easy to focus on exercising ourselves toward things that don't really matter. They might have some value...but what has *eternal* value? What has the promise of both life here on earth and eternal life?

One of the biggest benefits of training our physical body for a physical adventure—whether it's a marathon, a backpacking trip, a canoe trip, a mountain bike excursion—is the way we can apply our experience to exercising toward godliness. We can learn the same things: perseverance, work ethic, discipline, self-management.

So don't stop doing the things you love. Get outside and hike, bike, ski, paraglide, paddle, pack, camp. Do it. But keep God's life in you at the forefront.

Dig deeper: *1 Corinthians 9:24-27; 2 Timothy 4:7; Hebrews 12:1*

February 11

"The secret things belong to Yahweh our God; but the things that are revealed belong to us and to our children forever, that we may do all the words of this law." Deuteronomy 29:29

I was meditating on this scripture one day and found some insight on *unlockingthebible.org* that really blessed me...

There are secrets that belong to the Lord including "the future of our children, the reason for our suffering, the manner of our death, the salvation of our loved ones, the events of tomorrow, the outcome of our ministry and the progress of our Christian life."

Isn't it ironic that even though we can't control our own future, it's often so hard for us to surrender our future to our loving Father? And not just the "big" future, but the unknown of today and tomorrow.

I was on a canoe trip in the Boundary Waters with three other women not too long ago. We innocently believed this would be an easy trip.

We launched on a glorious sunny July morning. All went flawlessly until early afternoon. Then the rain started—which under normal circumstances would be no big deal. But our trip was about to go horribly wrong.

No, no one got hurt. Nothing like that. But we encountered a series of the worst portages we'd ever been on. There isn't room to go into details here, but trust me, by the end of the third one, we were exhausted physically and emotionally. And with just an hour of daylight left, we hit a dead-end.

Sometimes life is like that. Everything is going along smoothly and suddenly we're faced with challenge stacked on top of challenge. There's nowhere to go.

It's at those times we cling to those things that are revealed to us—God's character. His love. His faithfulness. Will we still trust Him even when we don't know all His secrets?

Dig deeper: *Deuteronomy 29*

February 12

"I will plant it in the mountain of the height of Israel; and it will produce boughs, and bear fruit, and be a good cedar. Birds of every kind will dwell in the shade of its branches." Ezekiel 17:23

The Book of Ezekiel is mostly a collection of prophecies given to Ezekiel by God while he and his fellow Israelites were held as refugees in a foreign land, Babylon. As in verse 23 here, these prophecies often use allegory to get their point across.

In all of Ezekiel 17 the allegory is trees and vines—how God is able to plant and uproot. To give life to something that's dried up and take life from something that's flourishing.

Let's look at the whole passage:

"The Lord Yahweh says: 'I will also take some of the lofty top of the cedar, and will plant it. I will crop off from the topmost of its young twigs a tender one, and I will plant it on a high and lofty mountain. I will plant it in the mountain of the height of Israel; and it will produce boughs, and bear fruit, and be a good cedar. Birds of every kind will dwell in the shade of its branches. All the trees of the field will know that I, Yahweh, have brought down the high tree, have exalted the low tree, have dried up the green tree, and have made the dry tree flourish." (verses 22-24)

God (*Yahweh* is the Hebrew word for God) is saying here that He'll do the planting of the kings and kingdoms. He'll bring down powerful people and exalt lowly people. What's prospering, He'll dry up. What's dry, He'll make flourish. All according to His plan.

This can bring life to our prayers! When we pray about a situation we know is evil, we can pray that God would bring down the high tree, dry up the green tree. When we pray about something that seems hopeless, we can pray that He would exalt the lowly tree and make the dry tree flourish.

And then keep praying this way, trusting in God's ability to make it happen!

Dig deeper: *Ezekiel 17*

February 13

"Therefore behold, I will allure her, and bring her into the wilderness, and speak tenderly to her. I will give her vineyards from there, and the Valley of Achor for a door of hope..." Hosea 2:14-15

In these verses, God is speaking through Hosea about how He would handle the nations of Israel and Judah that He had compared to an unfaithful wife. *Achor* in Hebrew means disturbance or trouble. God would restore them there in the wilderness, and turn their *Valley of Trouble* into a door of hope.

In those days the wilderness wasn't somewhere people went for a good time! It's not like us, who want to escape the city to get into the wilderness for some hiking, kayaking or backcountry camping.

It wasn't a rejuvenating experience for them, it was a harsh and desolate place. If you've ever been to the wilderness areas of Israel, most of it's in the southern part of the country. It's vast areas of desert—sandy, rocky hills with very little vegetation or water. The Dead Sea is in that desert.

And yet it was God's mercy that He would bring His people there. They were too caught up in their own lives—idol worship, selfishness, sin, conflict with the nations around them. He knew once they got into the wilderness He could get their attention.

Sometimes that's what it takes for Him to get our attention, too. Here's the thing, though. If you're a child of God, a follower of Jesus, the purpose of a wilderness season isn't punishment. He's not bringing you there, or allowing something, because He's mad at you.

He could be taking you away from the noise in your life to get your attention.

Don't resist His alluring you into the wilderness. Let Him give you vineyards (abundance) there, and watch Him turn your Valley of Trouble into a Door of Hope.

Dig deeper: *Read the book of Hosea to understand the lengths God goes to for His people*

February 14

"The wind blows where it wants to, and you hear its sound, but don't know where it comes from and where it is going. So is everyone who is born of the Spirit." John 3:8

The Greek word in this scripture for *wind* is *pneuma*, which can mean wind, breath or spirit. In the same verse, John 3:8, the Greek word for the Spirit is *Pneumatos*, also using the root word *pneuma*.

19th Century minister, Albert Barnes, notes in his commentary for this verse, "As the 'wind' sometimes sweeps with a tempest and prostrates all before it, and sometimes breathes upon us in a mild evening zephyr, so it is with the operations of the Spirit. The sinner sometimes trembles and is prostrate before the truth, and sometimes is sweetly and gently drawn to the cross of Jesus."

While people have harnessed wind and taken advantage of its power, we've never been able to tame it. We can see its effects but we can't stop it or start it.

So it is with the Holy Spirit. We can see His effects on people, a changed life. But we can't tame Him. We can't control Him. We can't predict Him, stop Him or start Him.

But there's one thing we can do with the Spirit we can't do with wind—have a relationship with Him! The Spirit is a Person, a part of the Trinity like God the Father and God the Son.

We can love Him, talk to Him, partner with Him, listen to Him. We can also grieve Him, disbelieve Him, disobey Him.

And just as wind is a mystery—it's stops and starts and affects our paths—so is the Spirit a mystery in many ways. On this side of eternity we can't comprehend the full mystery of His purposes and ways. And that's OK.

We can still welcome His work in our lives, trust Him and be available to Him.

***Dig deeper:** John 3*

February 15

"...whatever things are lovely...if there is any virtue and if there is any praise, think about these things." Philippians 4:8

Beauty is an amazing gift from an amazing God. If it serves no other purpose than to bring us joy...a smile...an *aaah!* feeling inside...then it's worth it.

Whether it's a sunset over the ocean, wildflowers blooming in the spring, layers of mountains in the distance—the beauty in nature feeds our soul and spirit. We don't know why, other than that God designed us to respond to it in that way.

One morning in a very intense week, a scheduled work call was canceled by the other party at the last minute. I jumped at the chance to get outside for a walk.

It was cold that day—about 5 degrees (Fahrenheit). But the few new inches of powdery snow, deep blue sky and sunshine called my name, and out I went.

It was the best therapy I could've chosen! That hour in the fresh air surrounded by so much visual and sensory beauty did wonders. I came home relaxed and ready to get back to work.

It also gave me some free mental space to thank the Lord for all this beauty, and to pray about some of the issues and relationships I'd been struggling with.

I used to think beauty was more fluff than substance. I felt I had to justify spending money and time enjoying it. I don't believe that anymore! God loves beauty, or He wouldn't have put so much of it in the creation He made.

Beauty isn't the same for all of us. For example, lots of my Minnesota friends hate winter and can't wait for spring each year. There's no beauty in it for them. And that's fine. What we appreciate as beauty is personal.

What kind of beauty moves you? How can you feed your soul and spirit with more of it? When you do, you'll experience more fulfillment and joy mentally, emotionally and spiritually. And that means more health physically, too.

Dig deeper: *Psalm 19:1; Psalm 111:2; Philippians 4:4-9*

February 16

"...Whatever things are true, whatever things are honorable, whatever things are just, whatever things are pure, whatever things are lovely, whatever things are of good report: if there is any virtue and if there is any praise, think about these things." Philippians 4:8

Neuroscientists have been discovering things about how the human brain treats our thoughts. Repetitive thoughts form pathways in our brain—literal, physical pathways.

It's like how hiking trails are formed. When you walk through the woods, bush-whacking your way the first time, you won't make much of a dent. But if you walk that same route through the woods many times a day for many days, before long you'll have a pretty nice trail.

Here's a Tale of Two Trails: One was a portage in the Boundary Waters. It was the most horrible trail I've ever been on. We had to navigate mud, rocks, swamp water up to our knees, muck, overgrown vegetation and tree branches. And then it just ended. Beavers had flooded the rest of it. Bad neuron pathway!

The other is one I still consider the most scenic trail I've ever been on. It's high in the Snowy Range Mountains of southeastern Wyoming, 10-11,000 feet. Every step of the way we could see mountains, wild flowers, windswept trees, snow left from the winter and wide vistas of gorgeousness. It wasn't easy, but so worth it for its continuous spectacular views for all five miles. Amazing neuron pathway!

If I have the choice, which trail will I take again?

Now, let's go back to our thoughts. Thinking thoughts over and over will cause our neurons to make pathways in our brain, whether they're through swamp water or on the mountaintop. Our neurons don't know the difference.

But we have *choice* in our thought life. The Bible makes it clear: we're to bring *"every thought into captivity to the obedience of Christ"* (2 Corinthians 10:5). Let's choose to think on the true, honorable and lovely things! Let's stay out of the swamp water.

Dig deeper: *Romans 12:2; 2 Corinthians 10:3-5; Philippians 4:4-9*

February 17

"For everything there is a season, and a time for every purpose under heaven." Ecclesiastes 3:1

In life there are times, circumstances, or seasons that feel overwhelming. There are those moments when, in the middle of it all, you find yourself at a loss and are maybe asking yourself, "Where are you God?"

We can all relate to feeling like everything is out of control and life as we know it has changed.

The many challenges and lessons I have learned from leading wilderness expeditions for years has trained and prepared me to embrace and even find comfort in the unknown and unknowable.

I find that during times when life feels overwhelming and chaotic, creating space for a Solo Retreat with God is just the thing to bring peace.

How to do that? It must be intentional!

Set aside time, whether an hour or several days, where it can be just you and God. Find a space that has little or no distractions. Turn off your phone. Start with gratitude as an act of worshiping the Father.

Be still and listen. Maybe God gives you a word from scripture, or a verse from a worship song, or just an image. Ask Him to speak to you, and then just listen. Write down what you hear Jesus speaking to your heart.

Open the Word. God's word is alive and speaks to us today. Taking the time to really listen and hear Him truly does bring peace that surpasses understanding.

Through a few steps, you can use this time to connect in deeper ways with the Father, Jesus and the Holy Spirit to further train your ears to hear the voice of the Great I Am.

Dig deeper: *Luke 5:16; John 10:27; Revelation 3:20-23*

Laura Watson

February 18

"Trust in Yahweh with all your heart, and don't lean on your own understanding. In all your ways acknowledge Him, and He will make your paths straight." Proverbs 3:5-6

Let's break this down a bit and explore some more of the meaning in these works:

"Trust in Yahweh with all your heart..." When we look at someone as an expert in what they do, it's easy to put our trust in that person. For example, a group of us women entrusted ourselves to a kayak guide for four days on a trip on Lake Superior. It was natural and right that we trusted her, because of her years of experience and knowledge of the lake and the area.

How much more should we trust the Divine Expert of our lives? He created us, has purpose for us, and knows how all the pieces fit together. *"With all your heart"* means with everything that's in us—mind, will and emotions.

"...and don't lean on your own understanding." Don't rely on or support yourself with your own wisdom and know-how. The only time I canoe in the Boundary Waters without a map is when we do our favorite day trip—the one I've been on a couple dozen times. Otherwise, without a map, trying to lean on my own understanding...? Hopelessly lost.

"In all your ways acknowledge Him..." *Ways* is the Hebrew word *derek*. It means a road, way, journey. And *acknowledge* is *yada*—to know Him. It's the same word used for intimacy in marriage! In the various roadways and journeys of our life, know the Lord intimately.

"...and He will make your paths straight." The Lord will smooth out, straighten, make your paths agreeable. That doesn't necessarily mean easy and without any hardship or pain. After all, look at Jesus' life and the life of His disciples.

But He knows which paths to take and how to take them. Like an expert trail guide, He'll lead us along the right trails.

Will you trust Him with your paths?

Dig deeper: *Psalm 1; Isaiah 30:20-21; 2 Timothy 3:16*

February 19

"Finally, be strong in the Lord, and in the strength of His might. Put on the whole armor of God, that you may be able to stand against the wiles of the devil." Ephesians 6:10-11

Every living creature has a God-given way to defend itself.

For a hermit crab and a turtle, it's to retreat into a hard shell, to hide from the threat. For an impala or white tail deer, it's to run quickly and jump high. For a skunk, it's to spray a horribly stinky liquid onto its attacker. A porcupine has quills...a finch has flight.

Each one uses its defense instinctively. And each one can only use the one it's been created with. If a turtle tries to defend itself by running or jumping away, it's a goner! If a deer thinks it can spray a stinky liquid, it'll fail! If a pheasant tries to grow quills instead of feathers, good luck with that!

Here in Ephesians 6, Paul tells us our means of defending ourselves against the only enemy that can really harm us—the devil. This defense is called the *armor of God*. Paul explains this armor in the next several verses, using the armor of a Roman soldier as the metaphor (the Christians of that day were living under the Roman empire):

- The belt of (God's) truth
- The breastplate of (Jesus') righteousness
- The footwear of the preparation of the Good News of peace (the Gospel)
- The shield of faith (in God)
- The helmet of salvation (won for us by Jesus)
- The sword of the Spirit, which is the word of God (the Bible)

This armor used by God's people is effective to protect us *"against the wiles of the devil."* And unlike the physical defenses of the animal world, our armor is spiritual and in our thought life.

How aware are you about "activating" your God-given armor? Only spiritual armor works against a spiritual enemy! The threat is real—just look around you. But our God has given us effective armor to face this threat.

Dig deeper: Luke 4:1-13; Ephesians 6:10-20

February 20

"For the weapons of our warfare are not of the flesh, but mighty before God to the throwing down of strongholds, throwing down imaginations and every high thing that is exalted against the knowledge of God and bringing every thought into captivity to the obedience of Christ..." 2 Corinthians 10:4-5

As we saw yesterday, the main defenses of living things in our world are physical. A parrot flies away. A chameleon camouflages itself. A seal swims. A bull elk faces attackers with its huge rack. A bee stings.

We also know that if a creature doesn't use the defense mechanism it was created with, its defense won't go so well. A duck can fly away, but a penguin needs to swim. A skunk uses its stinky spray, but a porcupine has to use its quills. A turtle hides in its shell, a monkey climbs a tree and a rabbit runs for it.

The same thing is true with us in our defenses against the devil and his army of demons. The only defenses we have—our only weapons—are the ones God has given us. If we try to use weapons *"of the flesh"* like our own cleverness or strength, it won't go so well.

But we still have a part in it—we bring *"every thought into captivity to the obedience of Christ."* Have you ever noticed the main way the devil attacks us is in our thoughts? The battlefield truly is in our mind and heart.

How do we take a wrong thought into captivity? First we ask: Does it line up with God's truth and righteousness? If not, it's a lie from the enemy. Then we entrust our mind to the truth of our salvation through Jesus and put that shield of faith up.

Finally we do what Jesus did when He faced off with Satan in the wilderness—we use the sword of the Spirit, God's word, to counter-attack. That's why it's so key to know His word, to have it embedded in our mind and spirit.

Do you have your spiritual armor on today?

Dig deeper: *Matthew 4:1-11; 2 Corinthians 10:3-5; Ephesians 6:16-17*

February 21

"For there is hope for a tree if it is cut down, that it will sprout again, that the tender branch of it will not cease." Job 14: 7

In the middle of Job's description of the shortness of a man's life, he points out a phenomenon of nature that reveals a deeper spiritual reality. In Peter Wohlleben's book *The Hidden Life of Trees*, he describes this amazing ability of trees to keep on living even after what most would have determined to be death.

Scientists have learned that in the natural forest setting, the roots of trees seek out the roots of other trees and interlock and interconnect. This is helpful for their stability in this life but also is the reason why some trees may go on living for hundreds of years beyond the normal life span.

When the tree "dies" and falls over, or is cut down, the roots beneath the tree are still connected to the roots of live trees. This life source of water and nutrients provides for ongoing life to continue.

Some species of trees have the ability to sprout new shoots that eventually grow up into full size trees. Wohllenben describes an experience of discovering a five hundred year-old stump that was still showing signs of photosynthesis hundreds of years after its "death."

This tree stump had no sprouts but was green. Green only happens in the presence of photosynthesis. This tree was alive and maintained by the surrounding trees photosynthesizing on its behalf.

Is this God's way of revealing the reality of the resurrection? Is it God's way of showing that we are all connected to our past ancestors? Certainly the Native American people have this understanding.

Scripture tells us we were in Adam at the time of the fall and we were in Christ at the crucifixion and resurrection. Indeed, science has proven that we are all blood relatives and as believers we are all one in Christ.

There is great cause for all of us to have hope!

Dig deeper: *Isaiah 40:31; Ephesians 1:15-23; Hebrews 10:23*

Brian Rupe

February 22

"Therefore with joy you will draw water out of the wells of salvation." Isaiah 12:3

The Hebrew word translated *wells* here is *mayan*, which means a spring or fountain.

Natural springs occur all over the world. "They range in size from intermittent seeps, which flow only after much rain, to huge pools flowing hundreds of millions of gallons daily." (*www.usgs.gov*)

Today in most places of the world, certainly in the West, we have access to these springs at the turn of a handle. But in the days of Isaiah and the other Bible authors, these natural springs often meant life or death.

Can you imagine traveling through a desert area or during a drought with little or no water available for days on end? You'd be really careful about how you stored your water to bring with you, and how you rationed it out to be sure you didn't run out.

But then imagine turning a corner and seeing a natural spring gushing out of the rock into a pool. You'd be pretty happy about that! You'd probably take some time to drink as much as you could, refill your water bottles or bladders, and then drink some more. You might even camp out there for a few days just to experience the unending supply of that spring.

That's the joy our heavenly Father offers when we draw water out of the wells (the springs or fountains) of salvation. It's a joy that recognizes, "This water is saving my life!"

Jesus called it *living water*. He said, *"The water that I will give him will become in him a well of water springing up to eternal life."* (John 4:14)

Not only do we have access to this well or fountain of salvation—the fountain is inside us! When Jesus lives in us, His living water springs up in us so we never have to run dry. That's something to be joyful about.

"Therefore with joy you will draw water out of the wells of salvation." Draw on that water today!

Dig deeper: *Isaiah 12; Isaiah 49:10; John 4:1-42*

February 23

"If any of you lacks wisdom, let him ask of God, who gives to all liberally and without reproach, and it will be given to him." James 1:5

This is one of the Bible's most practical verses! Do you lack wisdom? Ask God! He's generous with His wisdom for your situation. I've tried and tested this promise over and over again in my life, and it's really true.

I've asked for God's wisdom when raising our children...when in a relationship squabble with someone...with work issues... computer issues. And yes, I've had to ask God for His wisdom in wilderness situations when we didn't know what to do.

The God who has the wisdom to create all we see and put it all in working order in mystifying, complex and wonderful ways—He's the God who says, "Ask me!"

There are a couple things that need to happen in order for us to do this:

1. We need to recognize our lack of wisdom in this situation. That takes humbling ourself before Him, and maybe before others. It's the opposite of "I can do it myself!"

2. We need to put our faith into the situation and believe God will give us His wisdom when we ask.

Verse 6 continues: *"But let him ask in faith, without any doubting, for he who doubts is like a wave of the sea, driven by the wind and tossed."*

We don't want to be driven and tossed by our doubts, by unbelief. Instead of being like a wave tossed around by the wind, we want our faith to be like a river current—moving forward with purpose to a goal.

Where do you lack wisdom today? Will you humble yourself and ask God to give you His wisdom? He promises to give liberally, freely and *"without reproach"*...without shame or blame.

Believe it!

Dig deeper: *Proverbs 2:6-7; James 1:5-8; 1 John 5:14-15*

February 24

"But He withdrew Himself into the desert, and prayed." Luke 5:16

The Greek word translated *desert* here is *erémos*. It means an unpopulated, uncultivated place—a wilderness area. The word translated *withdrew* is: *hupochóreó*, which means to withdraw, retire or retreat.

Wilderness retreats were modeled for us by Jesus Himself!

One of the best places we can withdraw to connect with God is the wilderness—the lack of distractions, the forced back-to-basics lifestyle. Many wilderness areas have the added benefit of no cell phone service, which reduces distraction even more.

Have you ever withdrawn to the wilderness for a prayer retreat? For Jesus, it was a lifestyle. The Gospel writers wrote of Jesus doing this often. If *He* needed regular communion with His Father through prayer, how much more do *we*?

Jesus sometimes withdrew alone, and other times He took His disciples with Him. Either way, wilderness areas can be a wonderful setting to meet with the Lord for important decisions, prayer needs and potential life changes.

There's something about the world God made that draws us in and closer to Him. So much of what we're immersed in when in nature—especially wilderness—shows us His character.

Being in the wilderness can also bring times of character building or intense training, as it was with the Hebrews between Egypt and the Promised Land. Or with Jesus in those 40 days immediately after His baptism.

In those times it's easy to feel far from God, and spiritually dry. It's easy to wonder why He led us there and not somewhere more comfortable and convenient. Maybe beside those quiet pastures and still waters!

But whether it's an intentional withdrawing for prayer and connection with the Lord, or He leads us out there as a temporary training ground—we can trust He's with us. As He tells us in Deuteronomy 31:6 and again in Hebrews 13:5: *"He will not fail you or forsake you."*

Dig deeper: *Deuteronomy 31:1-8; Matthew 4:1-11; Luke 4:1-15*

February 25

"Happy is the man who finds wisdom...Her ways are ways of pleasantness. All her paths are peace." Proverbs 3:11, 17

When it comes to wilderness trips in an unfamiliar destination, whether a couple hours or several days, we have a few options to choose from.

We can opt for the do-it-yourself version—look at a trail map, research gear to bring and head out. We can ask a friend to guide us who's already been on the route. Or we can hire a guide or an outfitter to take us.

If you decide on the DIY option, you're on your own. You're responsible for your gear, your pace, your route and your risk. Depending on how good your map is and how prepared you are, your adventure may be wonderful or disastrous.

If you ask an experienced friend to take you, or accept an invitation from an experienced friend, you have a much better chance of your adventure landing on the wonderful end of the spectrum. That friend most likely has trail knowledge and the gear needed, and you'll share the risk between you, with you being less responsible.

Hire a professional guide or go with an outfitter and you're likely to have the time of your life. These pros know the best trails, know the best time of day to be on them, when you need to be off, what gear to bring along (and they'll provide it) and often will provide snacks, even full meals. That's a sure way to have both pleasantness and peace on the trail.

It's like the man who finds wisdom in the verses above. Wisdom wants to be your guide on your trek through life. The kind of wisdom Proverbs speaks of is the wisdom of God, which is even better than hiring the best outfitter in the business.

"Her ways are ways of pleasantness. All her paths are peace."

You don't need to be on this journey alone! Find wisdom. It's freely available to you as God's son or daughter.

Dig deeper: *Proverbs 3:1-26*

February 26

"He also chose David His servant, and took him from the sheep-folds; from following the ewes that have their young, He brought him to be the shepherd of Jacob, His people, and Israel, His inheritance."
Psalm 78:70-71

David, Israel's greatest king, was the youngest of several sons and spent most of his formative years caring for his father's sheep. He was anointed king by Israel's prophet, Samuel, when he was still a teenager. And he operated in his kingly anointing in small, faithful ways, long before he was actually the King of Israel.

As David developed his shepherding skills, his heart for the Lord, his courage and faithfulness caring for his father's sheep, God was preparing him for something much bigger. The traits he'd need as a king were developed in the pastures.

He became so skilled with a sling, the Bible says, he defended the sheep from a lion once, and a bear another time, using just a stone. That would give him the confidence later to kill a giant with just his sling and stone, too.

It was with the sheep he developed his heart for worship, learned to play skillfully on the harp, and wrote so many of the songs (the Hebrew word is *psalms*) that are in our Bible.

David had more years of training and development as he led hundreds of (mostly rascally) men and their families from place to place through the wilderness, keeping away from King Saul's attempts to kill him. All the while God kept David in His care and protection, until the right time for him to be king over His people.

Where does God have *you* right now? Does it seem like you're just in the pastures taking care of some smelly sheep? Don't despise anything or any place where the Lord has you. He can use anything in your life, any situation, to train and prepare you for His future plans for your place in His kingdom's work.

Be faithful where He has you now, and trust in His timing and ways for the future.

Dig deeper: *Psalm 33:11; Romans 8:28; Ephesians 2:10*

February 27

"Worthy are You, our Lord and God, the Holy One, to receive the glory, the honor, and the power, for You created all things, and because of Your desire they existed, and were created." Revelation 4:11

When we recognize our Lord and God as the Creator of all things, and realize what kind of wisdom and power it took for that creation to be in existence, how can we not humble ourselves and give Him glory and honor?

How can we not worship Him?

God, Your wisdom is so far above ours. Your power is so far above ours. *Thank You* for this amazing creation! Thank You that You show us who You are through the things You made.

You've filled this world with wonderful things—beauty, power, grace. You made the galaxies, the stars, the universe so big we can't comprehend the sizes and distances. And You've made cells and atoms and molecules so small and yet so complex it's astounding.

You created such beauty that fills us with awe and joy. Such power that thrills and humbles us. Sights, sounds, smells, textures. And You created us to be able to discover and enjoy it all.

Thank You for my life here, now. Because I'm here, I know You've included me in Your creation for purpose. I give You glory and honor. I worship You as the all-powerful, all-wise God. Help me trust You to bring about Your purposes for my life. Give me the grace and strength I need to follow You, Jesus, wherever the path leads.

Remind me every day—when I look at the creation around me—that You, the same God who brought all this into being with Your words, You love and care for *me.*

Jesus, You're the Good Shepherd. Lead me today. Help me hear Your voice. Love people through me. Be glorified in my life today.

Dig Deeper: *Psalm 145*

February 28

"Be strong and courageous; for you shall cause this people to inherit the land which I swore to their fathers to give them." Joshua 1:6

As I look north from the heights over the Boundary Waters Canoe Area Wilderness that forms the border with Canada, I think of the promised land.

The area to the north is the Quetico Wilderness, Canada's equivalent of the BWCAW. I have experienced many fun, difficult and memorable moments in the BWCAW that have developed in me a new level of awareness and ability to trust. I've explored, been challenged, been miserable, learned and triumphed.

But then I look over and see an area at least twice as vast with less than half the people, and trails I've never experienced. I feel a level of challenge mingled with fear about what I would discover if I ventured into it. Could I lead groups there? Would it be too much for my skills?

Joshua saw a new land and was fearless and courageous. He believed the promise and the reasons for taking the land as told to him by God. This stands in contrast to his fellow spies who looked over the promised land and said they could never triumph over such adversity. And so they didn't. They died in the desert.

But Joshua lived out his conviction that God was waiting to go before him to take the territory *He* said Joshua was to possess. He need not be afraid. He could be courageous!

What is the territory I'm called to take hold of? To believe I can be changed? To have hope? To apologize? To move to a new life calling or job that seems less financially secure?

The alternative to these bold "takings" is to return to whatever "Egypt" I feel more comfortable in. To die in familiar places rather than risk the mingled joy and difficulty of being in the new land.

Am I willing to move when called to better place? To be strong and courageous?

Dig deeper: *Numbers 13:26-14:4; Joshua 1:2-9*

Matt White

February 29

" 'Not by might, nor by power, but by My Spirit,' says Yahweh of Armies." Zechariah 4:6

Have you ever tried to do God's work *your* way? How'd that turn out for you? If you're anything like me, it didn't turn out so well! This little passage tucked away in this little book in the middle of the Bible is a key truth for all of us.

Let's break it down:

"Not by might..." The Hebrew word used here is *chayil*. It can mean strength, efficiency, wealth, an army. Our strength, productivity, money, smarts, military force—none of it causes God's purposes to happen.

"Nor by power..." This word is *koach*. Again, it's ability, human strength (like Samson's). Human anything isn't the key to God's will and purpose happening. So what is?

"But by My Spirit..." This is really interesting: the word in Hebrew for Spirit is *ruach*. It means wind or breath. It's the very breath of God that has more force than any kind of human strength or ability. The wind of God.

Here's the thing about wind: it can be a gentle, refreshing breeze. Just enough to lift a feather or a leaf. Or it can be strong enough to cause whitecaps on the surface of a huge lake, to push up waves. Or it can be destructive, like a hurricane. Uprooting trees, flooding coasts.

It's so easy for us to try to take control over the things in our lives—even the good things. To try by our own might and power to make them succeed. It could be our own walk with God. Discipling others. Raising kids. Our work. Our ministry.

But this verse reminds us that it's not by our own efforts, but by the Breath of God through us, in us. You see, the Breath of God has the wisdom of God behind it. The wind of God is so effective because He knows exactly how gentle or how strong it needs to be in any situation.

Are there places in your life where you need to let go of control and let His breath, His wind, His Spirit come in?

Dig deeper: *Isaiah 11:2; John 14:26; Acts 1:6-8*

March

March 1

"I have seen the Spirit descending like a dove out of heaven, and it remained on Him." John 1:32

The mourning dove of North America is one of the most common backyard birds and can be found in every state of the US and in Mexico. Even though it's a game bird and over 20 million are harvested every year, it remains in abundance with an estimated US population of 350 million.

Is it not interesting that there are about the same number of mourning doves as there are people in the US? Could this be a prophetic symbol of God's omni-presence and desire to bring all to a place of restoration?

Observation of the mourning dove is a reminder of the Holy Spirit. There's something about its quiet cooing that reminds us of the still small voice of God—the voice that requires a heart that yearns to listen.

Though there are many species of doves, the mourning dove reminds us of three things Scripture speaks to in regard to our relationship with the Holy Spirit. In Stephen's sermon recorded in Acts 7 we understand we must not resist the Holy Spirit. In Ephesians 5 Paul admonishes us to not quench the Holy Spirit. In Ephesians 4 Paul shares that we're not to grieve the Holy Spirit.

When we resist or quench the Holy Spirit, we grieve the Mourning Dove. The Holy Spirit is grieved when we refuse to listen to His voice, surrender to His will or put out His burning fire that's in us. He mourns over us because He knows there's no peace or rest for our soul when we're not fully surrendered to His loving and gracious plan.

A surrendered life is one that allows the Holy Spirit to be in control of our mind, will and emotions. It's a lifelong process that takes us from glory to glory. When we find ourselves out of sorts with the Holy Spirit it's time to turn around, ask forgiveness and return to a place of sweet fellowship with the Holy Counselor and Comforter of our hearts.

Dig deeper: *1 Kings 19:1-12; John 10:27; John 14:26*

Brian Rupe

March 2

"Be sober and self-controlled. Be watchful. Your adversary, the devil, walks around like a roaring lion, seeking whom he may devour. Withstand him steadfast in your faith..." 1 Peter 5:8-9

The roar of a lion is a frightening sound! According to *Smith-sonianMag.com*, its roar can be as loud as 114 decibels, louder than a rock concert. It can be heard from five miles away. Lions roar for many reasons, but mostly to stake territory and display strength.

So when Peter, here, compares the devil to a roaring lion, think about what his strategy is: the devil is trying to instill fear and stake territory in your life. He can roar through circumstances—your own thoughts, the words of others, adversity. He wants your attention, and will get it through intimidation if he can.

So Peter warns us: *"Be sober and self-controlled. Be watchful."* Just as you would be if you were out in the African bush, in lion country. Know he's out there somewhere and pay attention to his strategies. But you don't have to live in fear of him. Why?

Because there's another Lion the Bible talks about! The Lion of the Tribe of Judah who has overcome (Revelation 5:5).

It's Jesus!

One of the main jobs of male lions is to protect the pride from other male lions. Jesus, the Lion of Judah, is well able to protect His people from the devil, a prowling enemy lion. *"Withstand him steadfast in your faith, knowing that your brothers who are in the world are undergoing the same sufferings."* (all of verse 9)

We can withstand the roaring, devouring devil when we're steadfast in our faith. It doesn't mean we'll escape all suffering. But Jesus, the Overcomer, is in us to make us overcomers through any suffering we go through.

James 4:7 says, *"Be subject (submit to) therefore to God. Resist the devil, and he will flee from you."* First surrender to the Lord, then resist that roaring lion, the devil, steadfast in your faith, and he has to flee. It's a promise.

Dig deeper: *Proverbs 21:31; 2 Corinthians 10:4; Ephesians 6:10-12*

March 3

"For in six days Yahweh made heaven and earth, the sea, and all that is in them, and rested the seventh day; therefore Yahweh blessed the Sabbath day, and made it holy." Exodus 20:11

What's a good day's work for you? For God a good work day was dividing the waters from the dry land on the newly-formed earth. It was speaking existence to the grasses, herbs, trees and flowers. On another day it was creating all the lights of the heavens and dividing light from darkness.

At the end of each day of creation, *"God saw that it was good."* (Genesis 1, in several places) Those were good work days!

Your good days won't be quite as productive, probably! But for you, how do you measure a good work day? By what you get done? By how you treat your customers and co-workers? By your attitude and thoughts? By how closely you walk with Jesus during the day?

A good day can involve all those things. And, thankfully, when we have a not-so-good day at work, we can count on our Father's grace, forgiveness, strength and encouragement to help us cope. And then we can count on His *"new mercies"* the next day (Lamentations 3:22-23).

Working hard and enjoying that work is definitely one of the ways God has made us in His image. But don't overlook the second half of today's verse: *"...and [He] rested the seventh day; therefore Yahweh blessed the Sabbath day, and made it holy."*

I don't think God needed to rest! But knowing we need it, He set a precedent for us. He set the seventh day apart as blessed and holy (separate) from the work week. It was even commanded under Jewish law: keep the Sabbath...or *Shabbat* in Hebrew.

Taking that seventh day to rest physically and mentally from our work, to take time to be with the Lord and other believers—it's not meant to cramp our style. It's meant as a good gift from our good Father!

Dig deeper: *Genesis 1; Exodus 23:12; Lamentations 3:22-23*

March 4

"He said to them, "It isn't for you to know times or seasons which the Father has set within His own authority. But you will receive power when the Holy Spirit has come upon you. You will be witnesses...' " Acts 1:7-8

There's a verse in Ecclesiastes 3 that says, *"For everything there is a season, and a time for every purpose under heaven..."* (verse 1) The writer goes on to list life events like birth and death, planting and harvest, mourning and dancing, war and peace.

The Greek word translated *time* in Acts 1:7 is *chronos*. It means chronological time or seasons. Seasons are something we're used to in our life experience. Some of us live in places where there are four seasons: spring, summer, autumn and winter. Others only experience two seasons: rainy and dry.

While details of these seasons can vary, they're generally pretty predictable. There are prime growing seasons in each climate, and there are seasons of rest and recovery.

We have seasons or times in our life, too: birth, childhood, the teen years and young adulthood, a season where married couples may raise children, career seasons then retirement, and finally old age. These seasons have their differences, but they march on with chronological time.

They're generally predictable, but the specifics aren't—we need to trust the Lord for His hand and timing in them.

Then there's the Greek word in verse 7 that's translated *seasons*, which is *kairos*. It means coming to a head at the right moment. The timely fulfillment of God's purpose.

Either way, Jesus tells us not to get caught up trying to second guess God's timing. *"It's not for you to know..."* He doesn't let us in on all the details of His timing. That's hard! We *want* to know. We want to understand. We want to control, actually.

But He says, "No. That's not for you. This is your role: receive the power of the Holy Spirit and be My witnesses." It's part of our faith walk with Him. That's why the relationship with Him is so important!

Dig deeper: Acts 1-2

March 5

"He built an altar there, and called on the name of Yahweh... There Isaac's servants dug a well." Genesis 26:25

Places hold memories. My life and testimony are marked by certain places where a significant experience changed the course of my life. That summer at camp where I surrendered my life to God. The little chapel where I severed my agreement with resentment and stepped into forgiveness. That special sunrise view where I felt God pulling the pieces of my heart back together. I imagine you have places like that, too.

In the Bible, God also denotes significant places. Throughout the Old Testament when God interacts with His people it becomes a special place.

Mount Moriah is where Abraham had faith to believe God would provide a sacrifice. After Jacob wrestled with God, he called the place *Peniel* to signify the importance of his encounter. Jacob walked out of that encounter not only physically changed forever, but with a new name.

Mount Sinai is where God's presence dwelt and where Moses met with God. That physical location is meant to stand as a testimony to what God has done—a reminder every time we see it. Stunning geographical landmarks can be a historical marker of God's goodness.

While we may not build altars or sacrifice today, we can remember what God has done in us not only through special places, but by being living sacrifices and walking in the identity of the names that He has given us.

How do you remember the work of God in your life? Are there special places that remind you of special moments with the Lord? What do you feel when you go to those places?

I pray today you'll also feel the Holy Spirit abiding in you. That you would see the meaning of your testimony not only in the places you've been, but in the power of carrying God's presence wherever you go.

Dig Deeper: *Genesis 35:7; Deuteronomy 6:12; Psalm 143:5*

Emilie O'Connor

March 6

"The voice of one who calls out, 'Prepare the way of Yahweh in the wilderness! Make a level highway in the desert for our God. Every valley shall be exalted, and every mountain and hill shall be made low. The uneven shall be made level, and the rough places a plain. Yahweh's glory shall be revealed...' " Isaiah 40:3-5

There's no wilderness place in your life where God can't meet you. The enemy of our soul (also called the accuser, or the devil) wants us to think our wilderness is somehow unique. That in some way, our case is special and Jesus wouldn't want to be there.

But this prophetic word from Isaiah says "Prepare the way of Yahweh *in the wilderness!*" In the places of deep valleys and high mountains. In the deserts, the uneven and rough places. That's where the Lord wants to meet us.

These verses are a beautiful picture of the Lord's dominion over the wilderness places, both literal and figurative—the story of our lives. It won't all be made perfect now. Not until Jesus' return and the fulfillment of His Kingdom. But He'll start to make those roads in desert places. He'll raise up some of your valleys and lower some of your mountains. He's able to smooth some of your rough places even now.

His glory is revealed in those times. His power and love and kindness are revealed in those times. Sometimes we have to look for it. And sometimes we find His glory where we least expect it.

A few chapters later in Isaiah it says: *"For Yahweh has comforted Zion. He has comforted all her waste places, and has made her wilderness like Eden, and her desert like the garden of Yahweh. Joy and gladness will be found in them, thanksgiving, and the voice of melody."* (Isaiah 51:3)

It seems impossible that joy, gladness, thanksgiving and singing can be in the waste places. But with God, all things are possible!

Don't wait until you get out of the wilderness to invite Jesus in. He wants in to your wilderness!

Dig deeper: *Genesis 28:15; Psalm 16:11; Hosea 2:14*

March 7

"They overcame him [the devil] because of the Lamb's blood, and because of the word of their testimony...." Revelation 12:11

I never intended to become an alcoholic. I don't know anyone who does. It's not one of those things you say as an eight-year-old, "I want to abuse alcohol when I grow up."

I'd like to say I turned my life around and got help right away. But it wasn't until I started guiding for a wilderness addiction therapy place in the Pacific Northwest. It wasn't until I started hearing their stories that the rose-colored glasses I'd been wearing shattered.

"I'm an addict," I thought. It was a sudden and piercing moment for me.

A long story, but I've now been sober for 7 years and 1 month at the time of this writing and I haven't looked back. Have I been tempted? Absolutely! I still go to AA. I have an incredible faith community. I have an amazing husband who loves me and walks the sober path alongside me. But I'm still young in my sober life and I look forward to celebrating my 30-year anniversary in sobriety someday.

Now, though, I wear this identity as a badge of honor. I can say "Hi, my name is Laura, and I'm an addict," and not feel terrified, but full of hope. I share openly how my struggles are mine, and I overcame them, sometimes at great cost to myself. And I'm thankful every day for the chance to have broken free when I did.

Every breath I breathe is a gift. Every paddle stroke that moves me through the water is a blessing. Every snow-covered slope I rip down on my snowboard is healing. Every agonizing step higher on a trail with a loaded backpack is full of hope. A miracle happened in me—I was able to break the chains of addiction to make my Great Escape into living life abundantly. It's taken a lot of humility, hard work, repentance and complete surrender to Christ Jesus.

And as the song says, "I have decided to follow Jesus. No turning back, no turning back!"

Dig deeper: *Joel 2:13; Romans 6:16; Galatians 2:20*

Laura Watson

March 8

"Suddenly a light from the sky shone around him. He...heard a voice saying, 'Saul, Saul, why do you persecute me?' He said, 'Who are you, Lord?' The Lord said, 'I am Jesus, whom you are persecuting. But rise up and enter into the city, then you will be told what you must do.' " Acts 9:3-6

In this chapter, there are two men who heard the voice of God. One is zealous for what he thinks is right, but is actually working violently against God. The other has been following the truth of Jesus. When the voice of the Lord came, their responses were just as different from each other.

Saul, well known for imprisoning followers of Jesus, accepted His words and instruction, while Ananias' first reaction was to question: "God, how do You not have all the facts on this man? Let me set you straight." Saul's experience may have been more spectacular, but both men knew they were hearing the word of the Lord.

We may not hear God audibly these days, but He speaks even closer to us through His Spirit. How do we respond to His voice? In the busyness and distractions of our world, we're prone to miss Him completely. Walking closely with the Lord will make it easier to hear Him, but won't guarantee we respond the right way. Each day we have another opportunity to listen and obey.

For some reason we have an easier time trusting that God is strong enough to save the entire world, but can question His application to our lives personally.

The same power that spoke the world into existence and raised Jesus from the dead works with us today. God's transformation of Saul should remind us that no matter the current condition of our hearts, God has a plan and has the power to change us. Submitting is all we're responsible for. That is our daily task. It's that simple and that hard. So let's be still and listen, and know that He is God.

Dig deeper: *Acts 9:1-20; Psalm 46:10*

Beth Poliquin

March 9

"If you have run with the footmen, and they have wearied you, then how can you contend with horses...?" Jeremiah 12:5

Jeremiah had a tough life! God called him as a young man, probably a teenager, to be a prophet, a spokesman for Him to his fellow countrymen, the people of Judah. Judah used to be part of the flourishing kingdom of Israel under King David and his son, Solomon.

But a few hundred years later in Jeremiah's time, the people had rejected God. They worshiped idols and lived just like the sinful people around them. Jeremiah's call was to get them to repent and turn back to God—but the people rejected both him and his message. For his whole life.

In this section of the book of Jeremiah, he's complaining to God about how the wicked flourish, even though they're wicked. His sense of justice is offended because God won't judge these people soon enough for him.

God's answer? *"If you have run with the footmen, and they have wearied you, then how can you contend with horses...?"* In other words: If you can't handle this, how are you going to handle it when the going gets *really* tough?

God continues: *"...Though in a land of peace you are secure, yet how will you do in the pride [the floodwaters] of the Jordan?"* (the rest of verse 5)

That doesn't sound very empathic, does it? Well, God has a well-rounded character! He is loving, kind and empathetic...but He's also a righteous, just and wise God who knows what we need when we need it. He knows when a situation demands mercy and when it demands justice.

Here, He's telling Jeremiah to buck up. It's that kick in the pants we all need now and again. How will we receive this kind of word from God? Will we get offended at Him and go pout in a corner? Or will we receive it from Him in humility? Will we ask Him for the help we so desperately need so we *can* run with the horses and survive the floodwaters? Hmmm.

Dig deeper: Jeremiah 12

March 10

"In the beginning was the Word...All things were made through Him. Without Him, nothing was made that has been made." John 1:1,3

What does Jesus have to do with nature? Sometimes we tend to keep certain things in our lives separate. Things that don't seem to go together—like Jesus and nature. But in reality, Jesus and nature are indelibly linked together. Here's what I mean:

1. Jesus created nature. In today's scripture (written by Jesus' closest friend) John recognized through the Holy Spirit that Jesus is eternal. *The Word* he writes of is Jesus. *"Without Him, nothing was made that has been made."*

2. Nature displays Jesus' character. Just as we can learn a lot about musicians and artists by studying their creations, we can learn a lot about Jesus by studying His creation. He's creative, He's orderly, He's powerful, He loves beauty. You get the idea.

3. Nature responds to Jesus' presence. The Bible has many references to nature interacting with God, especially in the Psalms. One of them is Psalm 19: *"The heavens declare the glory of God. The expanse shows his handiwork. Day after day they pour out speech, and night after night they display knowledge."* (Psalm 19:1-2)

4. Jesus will redeem nature one day. When Adam and Eve chose rebellion against God's authority, sin in people wasn't the only result. Nature came under God's curse, too. But when Jesus returns, His promise is to redeem all of creation, not just people.

The Bible tells us: *"For the creation was subjected to vanity, not of its own will, but because of him who subjected it, in hope that the creation itself also will be delivered from the bondage of decay into the liberty of the glory of the children of God."* (Romans 8:20-21)

Just as when people are made new when they come into relationship with Jesus, so one day He will bring *"a new heaven and a new earth"* (Revelation 21:1).

So what does Jesus have to do with nature? Everything!

Dig Deeper: *Genesis 3; Revelation 21:1-8*

March 11

"Happy is the man who finds wisdom...She is a tree of life to those who lay hold of her." Proverbs 3:11, 18

Many cultures in the world have a "tree of life" concept. It's very prevalent in the Bible. The first mention of it is in Genesis 2 when God placed the tree of life in the middle of the Garden of Eden.

When Adam and Eve chose sin by rebelling against God's word, part of the curse was their banishment from the tree of life (Genesis 3:24).

The last time it's mentioned in the Bible is in Revelation 22. This time the tree of life is in a city, the New Jerusalem. This tree grows on either side of the crystal-clear river that flows from God's throne, *"bearing twelve kinds of fruit, yielding its fruit every month. The leaves of the tree were for the healing of the nations."*

What a picture of abundance! A tree that not only bears a dozen different types of fruit—like nothing we see here on earth right now—but it bears fruit all year long. And it's not only the fruit that blesses, its leaves bring healing all over the world.

This verse above in Proverbs 3 is another mention of a tree of life. This time it's not as a real tree, but as a picture of wisdom. When you embrace wisdom in your life, it's like having access to a tree of life. And where do we find wisdom?

Proverbs 9:10 teaches us that fearing God—treating Him with reverence, obedience and awe—is where wisdom starts. The wisdom God gives produces abundance in our lives, like a tree of life. Nourishment comes up from the roots—the rich soil of God—travels through the branches and produces fruit and healing.

The Bible also teaches us that if we search for wisdom like we would hidden treasure, we'll find it. When we ask for it, the Father will give it to us. That's good news!

Dig deeper: Proverbs 2; James 1:5-8

March 12

"But God's love has most certainly been perfected in whoever keeps His word..." 1 John 2:5

What does it mean to "keep His word"? And for that matter, what does it mean to be "perfected"? We'll start with *keep*.

The Greek word used by John here is *tereó*—to guard, watch over, observe. You know what it reminds me of? A mama bear guarding her cubs. It's well-known wisdom to never get between a sow bear and her cubs. Some people have paid a high price for that mistake. It's one of the few reasons why a bear will attack a human.

The other main reason is when a bear believes something or someone is threatening its meal. Again, it's a case of it keeping, guarding, watching over something important to it.

According to John, that's how we, as followers of the Lord, are to be with God's word. That's how God is able to develop His love in us—by watching over, guarding God's word as truth and direction for our lives.

Now let's look at the Greek word translated *perfection*. It's *teleioó*. It's used a bunch of times in the New Testament. It can mean to be made perfect, and also to finish a course, like a race. To reach the end stage of something. To bring to completion.

So God's kind of love doesn't have much to do with emotion or feeling. Rather, it's about keeping His word. Guarding, observing, obeying His word.

The rest of verse 5 and into verse 6 says this: *"This is how we know that we are in Him: he who says he remains in Him ought himself also to walk just like He [Jesus] walked."*

God's love is made complete in us as we actively walk with Jesus on this journey of faith through all of life. To be able to walk like Jesus walked and keep or guard God's word, we have to *know* God's word. *Know* how Jesus walked. And we don't have to guess—it's all right there in the Bible.

Dig deeper: *John 15: 1-17; 1 John 2:1-17*

March 13

"My lips shall shout for joy...all day long..." Psalm 71:23-24

An opening in the tree lot, the transition from bog to forest or from water to woodland is often referred to as *edge*. These edges create areas for sunlight to come in and provide for a diversity of plant species. The diversity of plant species provides, in turn, for a variety of animal species.

This is called the *edge effect* and is a desired condition in nature. Edges are created naturally after a windstorm when many trees have fallen over, or after a forest fire. In proper forest management, edges should be considered part of the strategy to help maintain a balanced and diverse natural community.

Farmers are encouraged to maintain an edge of natural growth on the borders of their plowed fields. This allows habitat for pheasant, fox and other small animals. The diversity of the edge creates an overall healthier environment.

The Hebrew word for *lips* can also mean an edge or a border. In Ephesians 6:17 we're encouraged as part of our spiritual armor to take up the sword of the Spirit, which is the word of God.

We often think of the sword of the Spirit as the Bible, which is certainly true. But perhaps we need to go deeper. Is the sharp word of God, the two-edged sword mentioned in Hebrews 4:12 not also the very words God gives to us that pass through our lips?

These words can come in many forms: a shout of joy when a toddler catches a ball for the first time. A word of comfort to a grieving friend. A powerful message from a gifted speaker. An encouragement from a co-worker for a job well done. A prophetic revelation shared as a word of wisdom.

Should we not consider all of these the very word of God, being spoken through His messengers all day long? This powerful two-edged sword passes through our lips transforming the world around us into the healthy, loving atmosphere of God's presence. This is living on the edge!

Dig deeper: *Proverbs 18:4; Luke 6:43-45; Colossians 4:6*

Brian Rupe

March 14

"In the world you have trouble..." John 16:33

In a recent fellowship time, a friend who had just gone through a major leg amputation was asked to give counsel to another seeking wisdom on finding inner peace.

His response was not all that comforting! He explained that sometimes life is difficult, the pain is intense and there's nothing you can do about it except believe someday it'll pass. Looking back we can see all the good that resulted.

It's true we pray for miraculous healings and sometimes there's an instant healing of body or soul. But more often, the healing is a process God uses to bring a deeper and fuller restoration into our lives. Both the instant healings and the process healings are miracles for which we can rejoice.

The *edge effect is* that amazing condition in nature that's a transition from one ecosystem to another. This place of transition is a place of great health for the natural community.

This edge effect is often first created by tragedy—a mighty storm that destroys the forest or a devastating forest fire causing death and destruction. It's been said, "if you want to experience peace you must also experience tribulation." The contrast and experience of peace and tribulation are essential for our personal development.

Jesus was quite clear in communicating that in this life we would have trouble, or tribulation. But there's a pathway of overcoming in the midst of this trouble. Jesus, who lives in us and through us, said that He has overcome the world and that peace is available: *"Don't let your heart be troubled."* (John 14:1)

In nature, the tribulation of a windstorm or fire is the key to creating the wonderful edge effect that's the paradise of abundance. The same is true in our lives. Living on the edge and in the edge is just the right place to be.

Dig Deeper: *Isaiah 41:10; Romans 8:38-39; Ephesians 3:16-21*

Brian Rupe

March 15

"For we are His workmanship, created in Christ Jesus for good works, which God prepared before that we would walk in them."
Ephesians 2:10

We are His workmanship. That's a completely different way of looking at the world (what's called a worldview) than what the public schools teach, what modern science teaches, what popular culture thinks. We're surrounded by strong voices trying to convince us we're not anyone's workmanship. We're simply products of impersonal forces and random chance.

But if you saw a drawing of a person on a piece of paper, there's no way you'd believe that drawing just happened to show up. I don't care how many years or what kind of random chance was involved. You and I know a drawing—even of a stick person—can't just appear. Someone drew it.

If the drawing was three dimensional with shading, texture and color, and if it looked like someone you know, then you'd realize the person who drew it was highly skilled and gifted.

This body you and I live in started as a single cell. Within 8-9 days it multiplied to hundreds of cells. By the time we were born, we had 100 billion cells in our brain alone, and 3.2 trillion in our body! Each one of them contains a copy of our DNA, mapping out everything about us in precise order.

Science Magazine reported in a 2017 article that a single gram of DNA is capable of storing 215 million gigabytes of information. Those kinds of numbers, the complexity that's present in each of us is mind-boggling.

We don't see our body as a wonder of unimaginable genius because we're so used to it. But when you understand the complexity of one bodily system, even just one cell, you realize this amazing living "machine" couldn't just happen.

We are His workmanship. And the best news—we've been created in Christ for purpose. For good works this amazing God prepared for each one of us. Works that He designed us for. Wow!

Dig deeper: *Psalm 8*

March 16

"For we are His workmanship, created in Christ Jesus for good works, which God prepared before that we would walk in them."
Ephesians 2:10

The common dandelion, to most people, is a weed. Something to get rid of. But dandelions are the workmanship of our wise Creator. Take a look at this list of benefits these perky yellow flowers provide: Vitamins A, C, K, E and some of the Bs. They contain iron, calcium, magnesium and potassium. They can help peoples' liver health, digestion, immune system and skin. They can help lower our blood sugar, blood pressure and cholesterol (source: *biotrust.com*). Dandelions are God's workmanship, created for good works!

Each of us is also *"His workmanship, created in Christ Jesus for good works..."* Good works aren't a ticket to heaven. In fact, the Bible teaches that all of us fall short of God's standard of good when it comes to salvation (Romans 3:23). Only Jesus' blood gives us the way to God's presence through eternal life.

That's not what we're talking about here. The good works Paul refers to in this verse are like the ones a dandelion does—the ones it's been created to do. Provide vitamins and minerals, look cheerful as it blooms, be a food and medicine source.

The purpose of our life is to display the workmanship of the Father, to do the good works He created us to do. Just like different plants have different "works" or properties, colors, smells and benefits...so we each have different good works we're made for.

It could be serving food to the homeless, it could be teaching school. It could be building homes or painting canvases or writing books. It could be preaching in churches, growing food or raising children. No matter what works He's designed us for specifically, all His children have these works: loving, serving, helping, giving. Not to *earn* His love, but to *display* it. To help bring the Kingdom of God to earth where we live every day.

What *good works* are on your heart today?

Dig deeper: Psalm 37:3; 2 Corinthians 9:8; Galatians 6:9-10

March 17

"...but I press on, that I may take hold of that for which also I was taken hold of by Christ Jesus." Philippians 3:12

The Greek words Paul uses in this verse are very dynamic! The phrase *"I press on"* is translated from the word *diókó*, which means to aggressively chase.

It can be either positive or negative. In fact, the same word is used in many places in the Bible and translated *persecuted*. Paul himself uses it in Romans 12:14 when he instructs members of the Roman church to *"Bless those who persecute (diókó) you..."*

In this verse in Philippians, though, we're encouraged to *diókó*—to press on, to aggressively chase, to run after with the intention of capturing something that's positive.

When I read this, the image I get in my mind is a cheetah chasing down its prey, running at full speed, its only purpose to overtake and capture it. It knows by instinct that if it doesn't succeed it'll go hungry. It's not *diókó*—chasing down its prey—for sport, but in earnest.

The next phrase in this verse says, *"that I may take hold of..."* The word there is *katalambanó*, which means to capture, to seize tightly. That's exactly what that cheetah does as soon as possible—it captures and seizes its prey tightly with no intention of letting it escape.

Katalambanó is used twice in this verse: Paul is the one capturing, seizing something in response to how Christ Jesus did the same to him. *"I was taken hold of* (same root word, *katalambanó*) *by Christ Jesus."*

I like the way JB Phillips says this in his New Testament paraphrase: *"...grasping ever more firmly that purpose for which Christ grasped me."* Jesus has already done the work. We're saved by grace alone through Him. But, as *The Living Bible* says another way: *"I keep working toward that day when I will finally be all that Christ saved me for and wants me to be."* We have an active role in this, too!

Dig deeper: *The entire book of Philippians*

March 18

"...but I press on, that I may take hold of that for which also I was taken hold of by Christ Jesus." Philippians 3:12

Yesterday we looked at a couple of the words in this verse translated from the Greek: *diókó* (to aggressively chase after) and *katalambanó* (to capture and seize tightly). If you haven't read it yet, I suggest going back and reading through yesterday's devotional first, then come back to this one.

Remember that *diókó* can be both a positive thing (if you're the hunter) or a negative thing (if you're the prey). Yesterday we took the angle of the cheetah—its intent to pursue and capture its prey is the word picture this verse above should give us.

But in some ways, we're also the gazelle! Even as Paul wrote this letter to the Philippian Church, he was sitting in a Roman prison. He knew taking hold of all Jesus had for him included the other meaning of *diókó*—persecution.

This was no surprise for Paul, or any of the other leaders or members of the early Church. Jesus Himself told them they'd be persecuted: *"If they persecuted Me, they will also persecute you."* (John 15:20)

Doesn't sound very fun, does it? And let's look at this again: Romans 12:14 says *"Bless those who persecute (diókó) you..."* That is *not* fun or easy. It's like the gazelle blessing the cheetah...or the mouse blessing the owl...or the deer blessing the wolf pack.

And not only bless: *"But I tell you, love your enemies, bless those who curse you, do good to those who hate you, and pray for those who mistreat you and persecute you."* Jesus said that in his Sermon on the Mount (Matthew 5:44).

How is that even possible? Only through Jesus! Only by aggressively chasing after all the things Jesus has for us when He aggressively chased after us through His life, death and resurrection. That's intense! Yes. But part of following Jesus.

Dig deeper: Matthew 10:22; Romans 12:17-21; 2 Corinthians 4:8-12

March 19

"...but I press on, that I may take hold of that for which also I was taken hold of by Christ Jesus." Philippians 3:12

We have one more idea to look at before we leave this verse. Another part of the *pressing on*, the aggressively chasing after and capturing.

Yesterday we talked about the persecution side of the word *diókó* (press on). Here's how we can obey Jesus' command to love and bless those who persecute us because of Him—it's Ephesians 6:12:

"For our wrestling is not against flesh and blood, but against the principalities, against the powers, against the world's rulers of the darkness of this age, and against the spiritual forces of wickedness in the heavenly places."

The people who persecute Jesus' followers are the *flesh and blood* this verse talks about. We're in a spiritual battle, and the real enemy isn't flesh and blood people, no matter how cruel they can be. In fact, they're people Jesus died for and invites into His Kingdom, too, if they choose to accept that invitation.

Our real enemy is identified in the rest of this verse: the principalities, powers and rulers of darkness...*"the spiritual forces of wickedness."*

It's sort of like trees in a wind storm. Friends of ours were out in the worst storm the Boundary Waters ever saw when straight-line winds took down some 20 million trees in a few hours. While it seems like the trees were the things that did the damage, they really were just tools of the wind. People could see the trees and the damage they did, but couldn't see the wind—only the effects of the wind.

That's how the spiritual forces of wickedness use people. It's not the people behind the damage, they're just the tools. The damage originates from the unseen. When we look at our persecutors as pawns instead of instigators, we can see them through the eyes of Jesus. We can love and pray for them...through Jesus, with the help of the Holy Spirit.

Dig deeper: *Luke 6:20-49; Ephesians 6:10-18*

March 20

"Yahweh, the Lord, is my strength. He makes my feet like deer's feet and enables me to go in high places..." Habakkuk 3:19

One of my favorite outdoor activities is hiking. Every trail is like a journey to me. The purpose isn't only the destination, but every step along the way and the lessons I learn as I walk. It's worth the hard work to see the beauty of the land and feel connected with the topography around me.

The trails I hike often symbolize seasons of my life. The physical work of climbing a mountain trail helps me process the emotional mountains I'm experiencing. Walking through a valley helps me understand the revelation of God walking with me through my spiritual valleys and times of struggle. Some trails are almost invisible because they're so narrow and rarely traveled. In those hidden places, God speaks. And sometimes it seems the trail just suddenly stops. In those times, God can bring breakthrough where it seems there's no way forward. In the best and worst times of my life, there's been a trail I walked where God spoke to me.

The Bible has many examples of God's people embarking on physical and spiritual journeys, and the ways that God was faithful through all. Jesus and His disciples journeyed throughout the land to teach, minister and bring the Good News. They traveled the miles physically, and grew spiritually, too, as they walked with the Messiah—just as we now journey with God the Father, Jesus and the Holy Spirit daily to grow, learn and share the Gospel.

Through it all, I've learned the journey is for sanctification, purification and God's glory. We may not always see the whole trail, but we take each step by faith. We can trust God to keep us on the right path.

What does your spiritual trail look like right now? How is God speaking to you through the experiences? What is the unique terrain teaching you?

Dig deeper: *Genesis 24, Exodus 40:36-38, Book of Ruth*

Emilie O'Connor

March 21

"By wisdom Yahweh founded the earth. By understanding, He established the heavens." Proverbs 3:19

If you had any doubt before that God's wisdom is infinitely higher than yours, you can have no doubt now, after reading that!

"By wisdom Yahweh founded the earth." The earth with its plant and animal life, thousands upon thousands of them, with new species discovered every year. The earth with its geological wonders and processes. All brought about by God's wisdom.

People's wisdom can go so far. We can learn about all of these species and processes. We can discover what's already there. But people can't create them. We don't have enough wisdom for that.

We can create things made of what we've discovered. For example, very smart people have created complex computers, cell phones and other mechanical and techie inventions. But they still need natural resources to develop them. They have to take what's already there—like copper and nickel—to make something new and useful.

Scientists have been trying to create life in a lab for decades and have failed. They've been able to create things that look similar to life—in a very controlled lab setting. But God spoke life into existence. All life. An astounding variety of life.

In God's wisdom, He created each cell with its DNA strand and tiny but complex structure. He created the various body systems for each animal: blood, brain, nerves, skeleton, reproduction, skin and covering. The various systems for the plant world: roots, stem, leaves, seeds and fruit. They all work together in marvelous complexity.

And by wisdom He created us in His image. Not just with the physical body structure like the animals...but with a thinking mind, with emotions and a will. And, most important, an immortal spirit.

Best of all, we have access to God's own wisdom. Not all of it, of course! But He freely gives us the wisdom we need to live every day in this world He's put us in. What do you need His wisdom for today?

Dig deeper: *Proverbs 2:6; Proverbs 16:16; James 3:13*

March 22

"Ask of Yahweh rain in the spring time, Yahweh who makes storm clouds, and He gives rain showers to everyone for the plants in the field." Zechariah 10:1

For all of humankind's technical advances in so many areas, we can't control the weather. Oh, we've tried. We've tried to make clouds rain or not rain, tried to control the power of hurricanes and tornadoes.

The most our technical advances have been able to do is predict weather. Usually we're pretty accurate, and it *is* very helpful—for those who depend on weather for their livelihood, for those who live in volatile weather areas...and for outdoor recreation lovers who depend on good weather for enjoyment.

This verse in Zechariah isn't a formula. It's embedded in a prophetic word to a specific people for a specific time. But it does give us insight into this principle: God, as Creator of this world has authority over the rain, storms, weather and climate.

Job 38:22-38 is a passage where the Lord is reminding the man, Job, of his place—which is not god: *"Can you lift up your voice to the clouds, that abundance of waters may cover you? Can you send out lightnings, that they may go? Do they report to you, 'Here we are'?"* (verses 34-35)

So, no—we can't call out the lightnings or the abundance of waters. But He can, and does. And as His children we can be assured of His care, in good weather and in bad. And we can certainly ask Him, as His children, for that rain...for snow...for winds or lack of winds.

One of my prayers in the past couple of years has opened up a new way for me of walking with the Lord: "Father, would you give us favor with the weather?" I've been amazed and grateful at how often He's done that!

It's not a formula, but a drawing closer of my heart to His. *"Ask of Yahweh rain in the springtime."* Ask.

Dig deeper: *Job 38:22-28; Psalm 107:29; Psalm 148:7-13*

March 23

"But godliness with contentment is great gain. For we brought nothing into the world, and we certainly can't carry anything out. But having food and clothing, we will be content with that." 1 Timothy 6:6-8

This verse struck me in a whole new way when I read it just after returning from a canoe trip in the Boundary Waters.

Life gets so simple on a wilderness canoe trip! Not easy—there's paddling, portages, wind, waves, rain, cold, camp set-up and tear-down, hanging the food pack(s) in a tree.

But simple. There are only a few things on the agenda: paddle through this lake...carry the packs and canoes over this portage...paddle on the next lake...find a campsite...set up camp...cook our simple meal (the food always tastes great out there!)...tear down camp the next morning, load up and head out.

"But having food and clothing, we will be content with that."

Food and covering are a given in our modern, largely urban lifestyle. But in the wilderness we don't take them for granted. We appreciate them, value them, are thankful for them.

We have to carry our food and covering everywhere we go. So we pack light. Everything we take means something. It has a purpose.

And this kind of break from our harried, hurried "regular" life brings deep contentment. Even though it's hard and inconvenient, it's a wonderful break from day-to-day life.

But this kind of living doesn't just have to be relegated to canoe trips, backpacking trips and other wilderness excursions. Our society is built on *dis*contentment. On always wanting more, or something else, or something bigger. But that's not God's way.

Contentment is possible—but we have to choose it. It's a mindset, it's not circumstantial. Heading into the wilderness every so often is a wonderful reminder of just how possible it is.

"...with these we shall be content."

Dig deeper: *Matthew 6:19-34; Philippians 4:12-13; Hebrews 13:5*

March 24

"He will be like a tree planted by the streams of water that produces its fruit in its season, whose leaf also does not wither. Whatever he does shall prosper." Psalm 1:3

Do you want to be like this? Well-watered, fruitful, vibrant, prosperous? What are the conditions to being like this tree? The psalmist tells us in the two verses that come before:

"Blessed is the man who doesn't walk in the counsel of the wicked, nor stand on the path of sinners, nor sit in the seat of scoffers; but his delight is in Yahweh's law. On His law he meditates day and night." (Psalm 1:1-2)

The kind of person who's anchored like this green, fruitful tree is the one who delights in God's word and God's ways. Who *knows* God's word and God's ways. Notice the verse doesn't say that person won't have any problems. It doesn't say there won't be storms, drought or attack.

No one makes it through life without problems. But one difference between those who walk with Yahweh (the God of the Bible) and His ways, and those who don't is this anchoring. This rooting like a tree that's planted by the streams.

Verse 4 says, *"The wicked are not so, but are like the chaff which the wind drives away."*

Chaff is the dry, scaly covering of a seed, like corn or wheat, that covers the inner, good part of the seed. For centuries, farmers would separate the grain from the chaff by crushing the seeds and tossing them in the air. The light chaff would blow away in the wind, leaving the heavier inner seed behind.

So this psalm gives a picture of the wicked—those in rebellion against God. They're not anchored or rooted. They're driven by the wind. When the same wind blows against those who follow God, they're able to stand firm because they're anchored by good, strong roots. They're watered by the streams.

What a great illustration! Which do you want to be?

Dig deeper: Luke 11:28; 2 Corinthians 10:3-6; James 1:25

March 25

"Yahweh, your Redeemer, and He who formed you from the womb says: "I am Yahweh, who makes all things..." Isaiah 44:24

The formation of life in the womb, whether human or animal, is truly marvelous!

Life is a miracle. Our infinitely wise God designed human life to begin with one cell—the merging of two separate cells from a man and a woman into one new cell. The entire genetic code of a new person is encapsulated in that one cell.

Within 24 hours the cell is quickly dividing, producing more cells. Within three weeks the first nerve cells are already forming in that tiny little human. The mother probably doesn't even know she's expecting yet.

By the end of the first month, this little baby's facial features are developing and circulation has started. The heart starts to beat in the 5th or 6th week.

By the end of the third month (the first trimester) that baby is completely formed. Every organ and limb are there and some systems can already do their job—they just need a few more months of growth and development.

Scattered throughout the Bible are scriptures that clearly indicate the Lord's investment in people as early as pre-birth. One of them is in the first chapter of Galatians when Paul says God *"separated me from my mother's womb and called me through His grace to reveal His Son in me, that I might preach Him among the Gentiles."* (Galatians 1:15-16)

Paul believes his purpose in life was given him while he was still in his mother's womb. That idea is reinforced in other scriptures, too (see the Dig Deeper section below).

And God knew you while you were still in your mom's womb. He didn't just know you, He created you...*with* purpose and *for* purpose.

Dig deeper: *Psalm 139:13-16; Jeremiah 1:5; Luke 1:39-44*

March 26

"...His divine power has granted to us all things that pertain to life and godliness, through the knowledge of Him who called us by His own glory and virtue." 2 Peter 1:3

Every kind of life on our planet has been granted what it needs to exist and flourish. Palm trees, lilies, dragonflies, elephants, tigers, salmon, even one-celled organisms—they all have the information they need to grow, thrive and reproduce through the DNA that's in their cell(s). God's divine power has done that—granted them that ability.

As humans we have that, too—*"all things that pertain to life."* But for followers of Jesus, it doesn't stop there. He's granted us "all things that pertain to life *and godliness.*" Everything we need to walk out this journey of faith is already granted to us.

How? Not through self-effort, but *"through the knowledge of Him who called us by His own glory and virtue."* That word knowledge is important. It doesn't mean just knowing *about* Jesus. The Greek word there is: *epignósis*. It means "knowledge gained through first-hand experience."

It's real relationship with Him. It's knowing His heart, Him knowing your heart. It's spending time with Him like you do with people who are important in your life.

Another important word in that line is *called*. It's the Greek word *kaleó*. It's an invitation. We've been called, or invited by Him into His glory and virtue (or excellence). When we accept His invitation and know Him by experience, we find He gives us what we need for life—physical, emotional, mental, spiritual—and godliness. Becoming like Him.

He puts His DNA in us! How does He do that? It's a mystery. We don't know how He does it, but we see glimpses of the results of it. The more we follow after Him, the more those glimpses become something like habits.

We don't have to work for it anymore than a dragonfly has to work to be a dragonfly. It just *is*...as we walk with Him.

Dig deeper: *Romans 12:2; Philippians 1:6; 1 Timothy 4:8*

March 27

"Have dominion over the fish of the sea, over the birds of the sky, and over every living thing that moves on the earth." Genesis 1:28

This was God's assignment to Adam and Eve and their children—*have dominion over the earth.* That included every living thing, which also includes the environments they live in and on. The song writer of Psalm 8:6 also mentions it: *"You make him (mankind) ruler over the works of Your hands. You have put all things under his feet."*

The Hebrew word translated *dominion* is *radah*—to have dominion, rule, reign, prevail against. We often interpret that as a negative. And people over the centuries—Christians included—have used that as an excuse to treat the natural world without a lot of thought or care.

But when we follow Jesus, the idea of rulership should be modeled after the way *He* rules: with justice, truth and righteousness. And we need to remember He's still the Master of it all—we're to manage it for Him, as *He* would.

Caring for the environment or creation is a huge topic. Whole books have been written about it. There are many differing opinions about it, even among Christians. Maybe you've put lots of thought into it, maybe not so much.

Today, ask the Lord: "What would You have me do—or stop doing—so I can be a good manager of Your creation?"

He may give you an assignment to devote your life to creation care in one way or another. Or He may simply ask you to change some of your personal habits so you don't throw away as much in the trash.

Whatever it is, think of it as helping to manage His world... this wonderful, beautiful world full of things that tell us about Him and display His glory.

Dig deeper: *Genesis 1; Psalm 8; Matthew 25:14-30*

March 28

"All flesh is like grass, and all its glory is like the flower of the field...The grass withers, the flower fades; but the word of our God stands forever." Isaiah 40:6, 8

There are wildflowers that astound us with their beauty. Spectacular blooms in vibrant colors and intricate shapes. Glorious! Other wildflowers seem more common—dandelions, for example. And yet all are temporary. They grow and bloom, then wither and die.

We all hope to live a good long life. We long for purpose and meaning. The average human life span these days is around 70 or 80 years. That seems like a long time when we're in it, but as this verse says, to God it's as short as the lives of the grasses and wildflowers.

We can look at this in two ways. As a rebuke—"Get off the pedestal you've put yourself on and broaden your perspective here...you're not that great! In fact, you'll fade as quickly as the wildflowers do."

And as a wonderful comfort—even though human life is so temporary, when we base our lives on God's eternal word we become part of His eternal Kingdom through faith in Jesus. It then doesn't matter how temporary our life on earth is. In the grand scheme of things—in light of forever—a short life here on earth really is insignificant.

Even though we're transient, *"the word of our God stands forever."* The Hebrew word we translate *word* is *dabar*. It can mean several things—spoken word, a command, a message, advice and counsel, a promise, writings. Those words of God that have been compiled over centuries into what we know as the Bible are rock solid. They stand forever, because God is eternal.

People come and go. Some spend their lives pursuing goodness, others pursuing evil. Others just try to make it through each day until they die.

When we believe God and His word stand forever, we can take our transient life—we can grow and bloom where He's planted us, then age with grace—and honor Him with it.

Dig deeper: *Psalm 12; 2 Timothy 3*

March 29

"We also rejoice in our sufferings, knowing that suffering produces perseverance; and perseverance, proven character; and proven character, hope..." Romans 5:3-4

Isn't it astonishing how trees can grow on a mountainside out of, apparently, solid rock? On a cliff wall, with their roots wrapped around and between the crevices? And not just saplings, but full-grown trees.

Trees like this seem the epitome of perseverance. "I'm not letting go! I'm going to grow here on this cliff wall—I don't care who tells me I can't!"

There's little, if any, soil for nourishment. A tree like this is exposed to wind, rain and, likely, snow and ice. Yet it endures the suffering and perseveres. Its roots are firmly embedded. It hangs on tenaciously to its perch in this harsh environment.

That perseverance gives it proven character, if a tree can have character! It's beaten the odds and has grown into a healthy, mature tree. And where character is proven, there's hope. Hope for life. Hope for fruitfulness.

And *"we also."* Paul speaks from experience when he says *"we also rejoice in our sufferings..."* He had his share of sufferings as he spread the testimony of Jesus throughout the known world in his day (2 Corinthians 11). So if anyone can say "we can rejoice" Paul can!

When we rejoice in our sufferings, the Lord produces perseverance in us. The want-to and the ability to be able to say, "I'm not letting go! I'm going to press on no matter what."

That kind of tenacity produces proven character. We've been tried and tested—refined like precious metals in the furnace. The Lord can trust us to listen and obey His word and His direction.

For those with that kind of proven character, hope abounds. There's purpose. There's vision. There's eternal perspective.

Hope.

Dig deeper: *2 Corinthians 11:24-33; 2 Corinthians 4:7-18*

March 30

"But the path of the righteous is like the dawning light that shines more and more until the perfect day. The way of the wicked is like darkness. They don't know what they stumble over." Proverbs 4:18-19

We're on a journey through this life. The trail can be straight at times, giving us a view of what's up ahead. But it also curves and bends, bringing both pleasant and unpleasant surprises around the next corner. It might be level for a short stretch, but most of the time it either climbs uphill or descends downhill.

Sometimes the trail is quite smooth. But often there are rocks, tree roots, even fallen trees in our path. Sometimes it seems the jungle encroaches around it so much it's hard to see the trail anymore. Sometimes it's muddy or icy, making our footing treacherous.

At times the trail leads through flowery meadows, alongside mirror-like lakes or gently-flowing creeks. But other times it's along mountainsides with thousand-foot drop-offs, or across sketchy bridges that span deep gorges.

Some trails are in civilized parts of our life—where animals are leashed and the biggest threat is rush hour traffic getting back home. Other trails lead into vast wilderness with real threats like grizzlies, rattlesnakes, exposure or lightning.

Tell me—when you're on this trail through life with all its joys and sorrows, its pleasures and risks—what kind of light do you prefer? The dawning light that shines more and more until the perfect day? Or darkness, the absence of light?

We know we can't earn anything by our righteousness, because it's only through Jesus that we're made right before God.

But we can still apply this contrast between those who follow Jesus—who come under the government of the Kingdom of God—and those who reject Him to choose their own path.

Both choices still take us along life's trail. But one of them gets to walk it in the light of day, while the other chooses darkness.

Dig Deeper: *Psalm 89:15-18; John 8:12; Ephesians 5:6-16*

March 31

"Therefore I tell you, don't be anxious for your life: what you will eat, or what you will drink; nor yet for your body, what you will wear. Isn't life more than food, and the body more than clothing?"
Matthew 6:25

In the summer of '96 I had a dream to solo hike the Appalachian Trail. I was young, fit, somewhat knowledgeable... and broke. As I shopped, searched and begged to create my gear kit, I realized almost all of it was purple!

Now I don't mind accent colors. But looking like a grape waddling through the woods wasn't the statement I wanted. I was actually a bit resentful.

Then I came across Matthew 6:25-31 and was convicted of being ungrateful for His provision. A week later I read an article about the color purple in ancient times. It symbolized royalty because it was so expensive. I realized the gear He had chosen for me wasn't only sufficient, but the color of Royalty!

But the process of getting the crown is often unenjoyable. About a week after this revelation, I was offered the role of Interim Director at a camp. I said *yes* and put aside my plans for the trip. The day of my departure, I was woken with a call: I was no longer needed. What?!

It was too late to reclaim my plan for the hiking trip. Since I was suddenly mission-less, I was tapped to help a family member. This lasted all summer and was some of the most discouraging work I've done, both physically and relationally.

But holding onto the idea that God was still getting me ready for royalty, I kept at it. Then I was called out of the blue to serve in Europe for nine months. This very satisfying mission moved and shaped me greatly. And at the end of it I was given a great bicycle with panniers and toured Europe for three months. I didn't see that coming! And yes, I used most of the purple stuff.

Can I trust God to outfit me for this life's needs? Do I see hard experiences as evidence of His absence...or is He equipping me to be part of His plan?

Dig deeper: *Matthew 6:25-31; Mark 15:17*

Matt White

April

April 1

"When I consider Your heavens, the work of Your fingers, the moon and the stars, which You have ordained—What is man, that You think of him? What is the son of man, that you care for him?" Psalm 8:3-4

One of the best ways to cultivate a humble spirit is to go outside on a dark night and look up.

David, who wrote this song, spent many years looking into the night sky. Both in his years as a shepherd and later in his years of hiding from King Saul in the wilderness, he had opportunity to contemplate the vastness and wonder of the heavens.

When we think of the Someone who created all of that with His spoken word—the stars and galaxies, light-years upon light-years in size—and then created you and me...Wow!

"What is man, that You think of him? That You think of her? That You think of me?"

Not only does the Creator of all the heavens think of us—He wants relationship with us!

It's incredible.

It's incredible that this God loves each of us to the point that He would sacrifice His own life to ransom us back to His presence. That's the Good News, the Gospel.

Jesus, the Creator of the heavens, thinks of us. He's always thought of us. He became a man to become the perfect sacrifice so we could be cleaned up from our sin that keeps us from being with God.

Why? Because He—God the Father, God the Son, and God the Holy Spirit—wants us with Him. That's what He thinks of us. Each of us. You. Me. Your parents. Your siblings. Your friends. That person at work or school you can't stand. Your neighbor who drives you crazy. Your mother-in-law (I'm a mother-in-law, so I can make jokes about them!).

As we consider the heavens, let's consider the wonder of God's thoughts toward us, too. And give humble thanks.

Dig deeper: *Psalm 8*

April 2

"Therefore exhort one another, and build each other up..." 1 Thessalonians 5:11

Human friendships—whether in or outside our family—are one of God's greatest gifts. Within the Body of Christ those friendships take on more than just having fun together or working towards something together. It includes exhorting (to urge on, advise, to fill up with encouragement) and building each other up.

One of the most important requirements of friends is that they spend time together. And one of the best ways I've found to spend time with my friends (including friends within my family) is through outdoor activities.

It can be a simple hike in a local park or a walk around our neighborhood. It can be taking out a couple of kayaks on a local lake or river and staying close enough to be able to carry on a conversation. It can be planning a camping, backpacking or canoe trip together to spend a few days with one friend, your family or a small group.

When we do these kinds of things with important people in our life we all get some pretty awesome benefits:

- We get time together. We tighten the bond between us, open up communication, offer counsel or compassion. We can laugh and cry together.
- We get the physical activity. Rather than sitting in a coffee shop, we're moving our bodies. Even people who hate exercise usually enjoy a hike through the woods or a paddle on a beautiful lake. We reap the health benefits of activity while we're also reaping the benefits of relationship.
- We get to be in nature. Call it *nature therapy*, because research really shows that we reap so many health benefits from being in the outdoors.

Put them altogether and we have an unbeatable combination that boosts our health: spending time with people we love...moving our body...in a natural environment. This combination benefits us as a whole person: mind, body, spirit, emotions.

Dig deeper: *Psalm 133; Proverbs 27:9; Ecclesiastes 4:9-10*

April 3

"...let's run with perseverance the race that is set before us..."
Hebrews 12:1

Back when I was in my 40s I ran a half-marathon each year for a while. My most memorable training run was on a morning in early April.

My three companions and I met for this 10-miler in a neighborhood with plenty of big hills (you never want to face your biggest hill in the race itself!). We were looking forward to doing this together and had all been training faithfully for many weeks.

The catch: We had had a snowstorm the night before. There were several inches of fresh snow on the ground. The temps were in the single digits—rare even for Minnesota in April. And there was a biting wind, which, in our climate, means a wind chill factor of 10-15° (F) *below* zero.

It was miserable! The snow made the big hills even harder. The wind was nasty. One of my running mates had been training inside on a treadmill all winter, and that day she discovered that had been a huge mistake. Uneven footing, wind, steep ups and downs—treadmills can't mimic that. Anyway, we survived, but I'll never forget it!

Sometimes life is like that. We wake up expecting to face a daunting task, but suddenly find a few curve balls thrown at us besides. What can we do but face it and move ahead? We have help though...

"Therefore let's also, seeing we are surrounded by so great a cloud of witnesses, lay aside every weight and the sin which so easily entangles us, and let's run with perseverance the race that is set before us, looking to Jesus, the author and perfecter of faith..." (Hebrews 12:1-2)

We know others have faced equally hard things—that great Cloud of Witnesses. We can lay aside entanglements like sin and distractions. And we can look to Jesus for the perseverance we need to finish the race. Each occasion is a "training run" that keeps building that perseverance and experience in us for the next one.

Dig deeper: *Isaiah 40:31; 2 Timothy 4:7; James 1:2*

April 4

"Wherein you greatly rejoice, though now for a little while, if need be, you have been grieved in various trials, that the proof of your faith, which is more precious than gold that perishes even though it is tested by fire, may be found to result in praise, glory, and honor at the revelation of Jesus Christ..." 1 Peter 1:6-7

In my spare time I engage in hobbyist-level blacksmithing. I've had the joy of sharing that craft with many campers over the years, as well as making my own tools for personal use. The concept and reality of refining is put into beautiful practice in this craft, as the extreme heat washes over weary muscles and into the focus of the work.

Peter describes the amazing ways God moves and shapes us through this practice, turning us from ore that is of little use into precious metal, valuable and rich for His purposes. The extreme heat of the fire serves as a strong image of the hardships and testing that happen in life, and also as a beautiful image of what happens in the outdoors as well.

Outside cell phone range, away from running water, away from modern society as a whole—that's what many of us mean by an outdoor experience. And in this setting you really learn about who you are and what kind of heart Christ has built in you. All the joy of being outside couples with tiredness, sore muscles, a serious lack of urban conveniences and a large amount of interaction with animals and insects.

Are you prone to complaining? Are you prone to pride, anger, jealousy, quitting? Or does the good fruit of endurance, trust, playfulness and joy emerge from you despite the hardships?

Peter argues that the entire point of testing times is to result in praise, glory and honor to Jesus, as a result of people seeing and interacting with our faith. What a beautiful call!

Ask yourself: are you willing to endure the fire to emerge more valuable and precious than before? Say yes!

Dig Deeper: *Isaiah 48:10, Zechariah 13:9*

Hogan Brimacombe

April 5

"He gives power to the weak. He increases the strength of him who has no might." Isaiah 40:29

I'm sure I'm not the only one who's gotten partway through an outdoor challenge and thought, "I can't do this!" It could be due to unforeseen circumstances or challenging terrain. As outdoor explorers we've faced moments where we question if we can go any further. Whether it's putting that canoe up on my shoulders to portage it one more time, or pushing through the last and steepest part of the trail to get to the summit.

We encounter these moments in life, too. Moments of being overwhelmed or feeling weakened by life's challenges. It's in those seasons that I've been learning how God wants to partner with me and asks for my weak *yes*.

I've found that in the moments of doubt, grief or struggle, where I can't imagine going forward, my weak *yes* makes a difference. All God asks for is everything I have to give. And while it initially sounds like a contradiction, I've found this to be the most freeing thought. Because when all I can give God is a weak *yes*, He doesn't demand more. In that moment, His strength is there to complete my weakness.

As I look back on my testimony, I see many moments where my weak *yes* allowed God to shepherd me through a season I would otherwise not have made it through. I didn't prevail in my strength alone. And on my weakest of days, that's when God is the strongest. On those days, I've truly learned that my God fights for me.

Where can you give God your weak *yes* today? Where in your testimony have you seen God be your strength? I pray for those reading this who are weary today, that you find rest in our Heavenly Father.

Dig Deeper: *Judges 7; Psalm 18:2*

Emilie O'Connor

April 6

"...whatever a man sows, that he will also reap." Galatians 6:7

It's a law of nature: if you sow (plant) an acorn, you reap (harvest) an oak tree. You get exactly the kind of plant a particular seed produces. If you want to harvest wheat, you have to plant wheat. If you want an orchard of apple trees, you have to plant apple seeds.

It's all around us in the natural world. God created this law of sowing and reaping into everything He made: *"The earth yielded grass, herbs yielding seed after their kind, and trees bearing fruit, with their seeds in it, after their kind; and God saw that it was good."* (Genesis 1:12)

In the above verse from Galatians, Paul is saying that this law of sowing and reaping applies to us and our character and spiritual life, too. In verse 8 he says, *"For he who sows to his own flesh will from the flesh reap corruption. But he who sows to the Spirit will from the Spirit reap eternal life."*

What seeds are you planting in your life? In your walk with the Lord? In your relationships with other people? In your physical health and wholeness? In your future calling and career path? God cares about all of it!

Or you could look at it this way: What harvest do you want in your life? What do you want your relationships to be like? What do you want your relationship with God to be like? What do you want your prayer life to be like?

Do you want to harvest joy in your life? Peace? Patience and the other fruits of the Spirit? Well, we can't harvest what we don't plant! We can't expect the Spirit's fruit in our life if we're not walking by the Spirit.

It goes both ways. We can harvest anger, fear, anxiety, sin. We can harvest kindness, purity, goodness, a sound mind.

"...whatever a man sows, that he will also reap."

What do you plan to sow into *your* life today?

Dig Deeper: *Proverbs 11:18; Matthew 13:31-32; Galatians 5:16-25*

April 7

"You, Lord, in the beginning did lay the foundation of the earth, and the heavens are the works of Your hands." Hebrews 1:10

The belief in Creation by an all-powerful, infinite God isn't just a minor theme of the Christian faith. It's not just confined to a couple chapters at the beginning of Genesis.

God as Creator of the earth and the heavens is a theme that's woven throughout Scripture. It's basic to a biblical worldview and how we look at God. What we believe about Him.

This theme of creating and fashioning, like a golden thread through both the Old and New Testaments, is a beautiful picture of what God's like. He crafts. He builds. He fashions. He designs and creates. He loves detail and beauty and variety.

He works on immense canvases—like the galaxies and the mountain tops. He works on intimate canvases—like plant cells and water droplets. He shows His power through crashing waves, storms and volcanoes. He displays His delicacy through butterflies, wild flowers and snowflakes.

Genesis 1 and 2 are just the beginning of the Bible's description of creation. The basic building blocks.

Job 38-41 is a wonderful account of God's interest and involvement in our world. He brings up the dawn, the seas, light and darkness, constellations, rain and ice, lions, ravens, hawks, horses and sea monsters.

Psalm 139 goes into detail about you and me. How He forms us, knits us together in our mother's womb *when I was made in secret."*

The psalmists, the prophets, Jesus Himself, the disciples and apostles—all the way through to Revelation. The entire Bible assumes and declares that God is the One responsible for everything we see, touch, smell, hear...even what we can't see, but know is there.

That's a pretty great reason to humble ourselves, as Job did, in worship!

Dig deeper: *Genesis 1-2; Job 38-41; Psalm 139*

April 8

"Who despises the day of small things? For these seven shall rejoice, and shall see the plumb line in the hand of Zerubbabel. These are Yahweh's eyes, which run back and forth through the whole earth." Zechariah 4:10

The Mississippi River flows for 2,350 miles. Its watershed covers 1.2 million square miles (3.2 million square kilometers), 40% of the continental US. It's a hugely important international commercial waterway as well as a hugely important migration route for birds and fish. More than 50 American cities rely on the Mississippi for its water supply (source: *nps.gov*).

And yet, you can wade across its headwaters in northern Minnesota. I've stood in them, with the water just up to my knees. Small beginnings. If someone didn't know better, they might scoff at the idea of such vastness and influence coming out of these headwaters, little more than a creek.

Again, the Lord's word to Zechariah: *"Don't despise the day of small things."* Of small beginnings. In this case, it's the plumb line in the hand of a man who was a descendant of King David, and would be an ancestor of Jesus Christ. The plumb line that meant the rebuilding of the temple in Jerusalem was about to start. A work God had assigned to a bunch of refugees.

Don't despise small things. Is God asking you to obey Him in what you think is a small thing? Like *"honor your father and mother"*? Or *"in everything give thanks"*?

It's the small things that lead to the influential, significant things. The Jewish race started when one man obeyed God's invitation to leave his home and go to a new land. Israel's greatest king came from shepherding his dad's sheep in the rural hills. Our Savior was born in a stable and laid in the animals' feeding trough. Jesus' disciples answered the simple invitation to *"Follow Me"* and ended up changing the world.

Our Father specializes in taking unknown people and molding them for His purposes, whatever that may be. Our role? Humility, obedience and faithfulness.

Dig deeper: Proverbs 3:5-6; Isaiah 40:31; Philippians 3:13-14

April 9

"In the beginning, God created the heavens and the earth."
Genesis 1:1

A post from a Christ-following friend of mine said: "I sat on the river bank and cried out to Jesus...and began to study more astrology and energy medicine."

A co-worker wears a rock around her neck for the healing energies it gives off. She doesn't want bad karma so she makes sure she's good to everyone. She really desires to take a trip to Sedona, Arizona because of the spiritual energy vortex. And she wears magnets on her wrists for the living energy they give off.

Not too long ago she shared with me that she's a Christian.

What?? Can these combinations of beliefs be true? Can we be followers of Jesus Christ and read into the stars, focus on the living energies of non-living things, and believe in karma as the force that drives all living actions and reactions?

In our Christian belief, have we forgotten that the God who created everything is in control of everything? Our culture advocates an "accept all" mentality that, in general agrees with our Christian belief to love everyone, but denies the fact that there's an absolute truth found in the Creator God and His Son, Jesus Christ.

Have we begun to worship the creation instead of the God who created it? We must be extremely careful of what the Bible calls *idolatry*—putting any other "god" before Him (Exodus 20:3). God takes it very seriously, and so should we.

Yes, nature is powerful and there's no doubt it refuels our body and soul when we get out and enjoy it. But nature should never be the recipient of our worship. Only God deserves that place.

Dig deeper: Genesis 1; Psalm 135:15-21; 1 Corinthians 10:14

Tracy Blesi

April 10

"For in Christ Jesus neither is circumcision anything, nor uncircumcision, but a new creation." Galatians 6:15

This short verse summarizes Paul's letter to the Galatians. There had been people going into the churches Paul and his team started, telling the new believers they had to follow the Law of Moses (Torah) in order to be true Christians.

Galatians is Paul's response to that—No! You're missing the whole point of salvation. It's not in following the Law of Moses that we're saved (or in our day, following a list of "Do this!" and "Don't do that!"). In fact, the entire history of Israel had been a people chosen by God who tried to live up to that high standard of Law and couldn't.

The point of salvation—the miracle of salvation—is a new creation. The Greek word translated *creation* is *ktisis*. It means *creation out of nothing*, and it always refers to a Divine work. It's the same word used when referring to the creation of the world in Mark 13:19 and Romans 1:20.

When we say *yes* to Jesus, to His saving work in our life and to His authority (lordship) in our life, there isn't anything else we need to add to what He's already done on the cross. At our *yes* the Holy Spirit in us creates an entirely new inner person.

Remember when God created light by saying, *"Let there be light"*? And when He created the entire plant and animal world by saying, *"Let there be..."*? It's the same Creator working in us to make each of us a new creation when we invite Jesus in.

From then on we live as that new creation. As Paul says, *"...it is no longer I who live, but Christ lives in me. That life which I now live in the flesh, I live by faith in the Son of God..."* (Galatians 2:20)

Dig Deeper: *The book of Galatians*

April 11

"In the day that God created man, He made him in God's likeness.
Genesis 5:1

"He made him in God's likeness." Other versions say God's
image. What does that mean?

When an artist draws or paints a likeness of someone we call
it a portrait. A great portrait artist captures an incredible likeness
of the real person on the paper or canvas. The resemblance is
remarkable.

So when the Bible tells us God made man in His likeness (and
by man, we mean mankind—people), it means He made us to look
like Him. Since God is a spiritual Person and not a physical one,
we have to assume that means like Him in spirit, or in essence.

Now there's a huge difference between a portrait of someone
and the real person. The portrait, no matter how excellently done,
is still just a *likeness* of the real person. It's not living or breathing. It *isn't* the person.

So, though we're made in God's likeness, we're not God! The
difference between Him and us is even bigger than the difference
between a drawing on paper and a living, breathing human.

But here's the real kicker. The Bible doesn't say that about any
other living being in creation. Of the thousands upon thousands
of living things created by God, the only one made in His likeness
is us—people. The human.

One of the most demonic lies the theory of evolution produced
was the idea that people are just another step in the random evolutionary chain. If there's no God and people are simply the by-
product of random chance, there's nothing special about us. We're
no more special than polar bears, tree frogs or mosquitoes.

But that's not God's view. Rather than sweeping the human
race into insignificance, the Bible teaches us that the creation of
the first man and woman was God's crowning achievement. From
Genesis on, God's entire universal purpose is for the redemption
of people.

We're created in God's likeness. How does that change your
view of yourself?

Dig deeper: *Psalm 8:3-9; Psalm 139; Romans 8:31-39*

April 12

"Who has measured the waters in the hollow of His hand, and marked off the sky with His span, and calculated the dust of the earth in a measuring basket, and weighed the mountains in scales, and the hills in a balance?

"Who has directed Yahweh's Spirit, or has taught Him as His counselor?" Isaiah 40:12-13

We've separated these two thoughts for emphasis. The *"Who"* in the first section is obviously God the Creator. These created things that seem so big to us—the oceans, the dust of the earth, the mountains—are all insignificant to Him.

Verse 13 then asks: What created being can direct God or counsel Him?

These verses in Isaiah 40 describe God's greatness and our smallness in comparison. *"Behold, the nations are like a drop in a bucket..."* (verse 15)

There are several things we, who are made by this Creator God, can take away here. The fear of the Lord is one of them. This is a theme throughout the Bible, and one that's being questioned in some Christian circles today: "How can you serve a God you're afraid of?"

The Hebrew word we translate *fear* is *yirah*. It means: terror and fear, yes, but also reverence. Reverence isn't a word we use a lot today. It means a feeling and actions of awe and respect, and often love (*American Heritage Dictionary*).

So when we read *"Who has directed Yahweh's Spirit, or taught Him as His counselor?"* it's a question that's not meant to be answered. No created thing can direct or counsel the One Who made it, because the Maker is infinitely above what was made in every way. In wisdom, in morality, in justice, in truth, in ability.

The wonderful thing is that this incredible God who deserves all awe and respect (the fear of the Lord) invites us into His presence through Jesus. The One who requires us to have the proper respect for Him is the same One who sent His Son to die to make a way for us into His family. That's amazing.

Dig deeper: *Isaiah 40*

April 13

"For every house is built by someone; but He that built all things is God." Hebrews 3:4

Do you ever have doubts about God? About our Christian faith? Do you ever ask yourself if this the right path?

If you do, welcome to normal Christianity!

It's normal to have questions. It's okay to wonder about the parts we don't understand.

I was raised in a Christian home by believing parents who, I'm sure, had their own doubts. I'm so grateful for that heritage...but I've had my times of doubt, too. And do you know what always gets me back to a strong belief in God's reality? It's when I look around me to the natural world.

We live in a world that's unbelievably complex and intricate. It's mind-blowingly fine-tuned for life. It's an utterly amazing universe. I simply can't believe it all came into being and continues to function by random chance. I can't.

I'm listening to a Beethoven symphony right now as I write this. I've seen orchestra scores. They're about 17 lines of individual melodies and rhythms for 17 different instruments that are all intricately related. It's not just "built by someone"...it's built by someone who was a musical genius! I don't care how many years you scatter notes on a page, random chance can't produce something as beautiful and powerful as this.

When we see a cabin in the woods, we know it didn't "just happen." Someone built it. Someone with a plan, skill, tools and materials.

How then can we look at a human baby...a flower...even a single cell...and believe that billions of DNA genomes lined up just right and developed entirely by random chance? And that happened over and over again in millions of different species? To me, the most logical explanation is that Someone built it.

I don't need to understand everything in my life or everything about God. But what I see and learn about this world always brings me back to God as Creator. We can go from there.

Dig deeper: *Nehemiah 9:6; Colossians 1:16; Revelation 4:11*

April 14

"When forty years were fulfilled, an angel of the Lord appeared to him in the wilderness..." Acts 7:30

That's a long season of dryness! This story is about Moses. He was a Hebrew who had been raised in Pharaoh's palace. It was part of the Lord's strategy for his life purpose in a time when his fellow Hebrews were slaves.

Moses apparently knew God's purpose for him, *"He supposed that his brothers understood that God, by his hand, was giving them deliverance..."* (Acts 7:25) But when he acted on his own to try to fulfill that purpose, it backfired.

He ended up fleeing for his life into the wilderness, and lived there for forty years before he heard from the Lord again. I wonder how he waited. Did he expect God to show up at any time? Or did he give up on God and his purpose?

What do you think you'd do if you knew God's purpose for you, but then ended up in the wilderness instead? That happens more often and to more of Jesus' followers than we'd like to admit! Maybe that's happened to you.

In Moses' case, he married and had sons. He worked for his wise and wealthy father-in-law. Life was pretty good. He probably would've been content to live out the rest of his days there. But God still had plans for him.

Finally *"an angel of the Lord appeared to him in the wilderness of Mount Sinai, in a flame of fire in a bush."* (verse 30) God was ready to put Moses on the path to his destiny as the deliverer of the Hebrew people from the Egyptians.

What if he would've stayed in the wilderness? In fact, he tried to talk God out of sending him back to Egypt to be the rescuer of his people. But God had a plan, and Moses was key. He did say *yes* eventually and became the most revered of all the Jewish peoples' prophets.

Are you in a wilderness season of life? Disappointed with God? Thought you were following Him, but ended up in the desert? It's not over. Your destiny is still in God's hands.

Dig deeper: Exodus 2-4; Acts 7:18-38

April 15

"But you will receive power when the Holy Spirit has come upon you. You will be witnesses to Me..." Acts 1:8

Sunlight energy is the source of power for all living things. Really, that's quite amazing when you think about it. Whether you think of fossil fuels, solar power, strength to ride your bike or for a wolf to hunt and capture a deer, it all comes from the sun.

Through the process of photosynthesis, sunlight is converted into energy for plant growth, animals eat plants, some animals eat other animals—all the energy we get to live goes right back to the sun as our source.

God designed it this way, and no doubt, it's one clear way to let us know that He's the source of power for life. In pagan religions, many viewed the sun as a god and I can understand why. It's such a mystery!

You can't look at it without going blind, and it carries so much influence over our daily physical lives. But it's not a god.

There's only one God and He made the sun as part of His amazing plan of creation.

"Let there be light." The light of the world is Jesus Christ, the Son of God and He's also the One who is the Baptizer in the Holy Spirit. This baptism is the avenue through which God has blessed us with power to be His witnesses throughout the whole earth.

Power to be a witness means power to live in the realm of the supernatural. Power to hear God's voice and obey. Power to receive a call to go into the world, expect miracles, cast out demons and live in victory.

Jesus not only said He was the light of the world, He also said to His disciples, *"You are the light of the world"* (Matthew 5:14). In other words, Jesus has put His light, His power in us, to testify of His reality to the rest of the world.

Shine bright today! You are the light of the world!

Dig deeper: Matthew 5:14-16; Romans 13:11-14; Ephesians 5:7-14

Brian Rupe

April 16

"The wilderness and the dry land will be glad. The desert will rejoice and blossom like a rose." Isaiah 35:1

One of the most delightful surprises when hiking through desert or desert-like terrain is encountering blooming wildflowers. Those bright petals "rejoice" upon the brown, dusty landscape.

It seems impossible that such delicate beauty can exist in these harsh conditions, yet God created hundreds of varieties of desert wildflowers. And He designed each of them to be able to—not just exist—but thrive in this environment.

Some of them have thick, succulent leaves that store the water it needs. Others take water and store it in their root system. Some are dormant until the rains come, then they come alive.

Do you live in an environment that's spiritually dry or even hostile to your faith? Maybe it's your workplace or school. Maybe there isn't a spiritually-alive church or fellowship near you. Maybe your living situation is less than supportive.

How can you take a lesson from the desert wildflowers to store up the water, the nourishment you need?

One of the best ways is to saturate yourself in God's word by reading or listening to it often—preferably daily. Let His words of life soak into your spirit and mind. Plant those seeds and ask the Holy Spirit to root them deep inside you.

Believe Jesus' promise for the Spirit to *"remind you of all that I said to you"* (John 14:26).

Store His word in your heart for these dry times by memorizing passages that nourish and sustain you.

Then, like the desert flowers, you'll be able to rejoice even in the middle of your desert. Your spirit will continue to blossom and be glad.

Dig deeper: *Isaiah 35*

April 17

"The wilderness and the dry land will be glad. The desert will rejoice and blossom like a rose." Isaiah 35:1

This prophecy of Isaiah's continues in verse 2 and tells us why the desert will rejoice: *"They will see Yahweh's glory, the excellence of our God."*

Do you believe you'll see God's glory and excellence even in the dry land? Even in the wilderness season you might be going through? So much depends on your attitude and what you look for. It's said that in any situation an optimist will always find what they're looking for...and so will a pessimist!

If you hike through a barren landscape just intent on getting through it, you'll miss the beauty, the rejoicing dry land. If you stare at your feet or the trail ahead of you with a gritty determination to forge ahead and be done with it, you risk passing by the patches of bright color that stand out amid the monotonous browns.

Slow down. Look around you. Look for beauty, small as it is. Some of the desert flowers are just in bud—they're not blooming yet. Ask the Lord what He wants you to see and experience on this dry, dusty trail. Don't miss what He's after.

Ask Him to show you His glory and excellence right where you are. If you're alert, watching, listening...He'll show you, He'll speak to you.

And you'll truly be able to be glad and rejoice like the desert roses!

Dig deeper: *Psalm 9:10; Proverbs 8:17; Jeremiah 29:13*

April 18

"The wilderness and the dry land will be glad. The desert will rejoice and blossom like a rose." Isaiah 35:1

There's a difference between traveling *through* the desert and living there.

When you're traveling through, you bring your supplies with you. You have a pack on your back, you carry your food and water. You plan ahead and know how much you'll need based on how long you'll be there. If your trek is long enough, you may even ship some supplies ahead of you.

But sometimes the Lord brings us into a desert and we don't know His time frame. He even calls some people to *live* in the desert.

Then we need a different mentality. A different gear list. Even a different set of skills and knowledge.

And, as followers of Jesus, the most important is sometimes a different level of *trust*. In fact, you'll find this in the lives of mature believers: these desert seasons are what *built* the level of trust they have.

Are you in the wilderness? If it's a season, don't be in a hurry to leave it before the Lord has used it to mature you in a new way. Ask Him to produce fragrant flowers that'll bless those around you. Ask Him to produce the fruit He's after in you and through you for this season.

If you *live* in the desert, learn the skills the Lord has for you to find and store water, find nourishment in Him. Just like He does with the desert wildflowers, He'll give you what you need to thrive in your environment as you lean on Him.

He'll develop life in you—in the desert—so you can partner with Him to further His Kingdom.

Dig deeper: *Psalm 63*

April 19

"Yahweh will guide you continually, and satisfy your soul in dry places, and make strong your bones; and you shall be like a watered garden, and like a spring of water, whose waters don't fail." Isaiah 58:11

While hiking a trail in the Badlands of South Dakota, I saw beauty in the desert. I was reminded of how God tells us that in the desert His voice is tender, and He makes a way where there seems to be no way.

The Badlands look like a wasteland—miles of parched earth, and intense heat that beats down relentlessly. But I found it holds an evocative beauty and is teeming with life in surprising ways. I wanted to learn the secrets of thriving in such an aggressive environment. And I want to learn to have that same thriving in desert seasons of the spirit. God wants to speak to us in places that seem lifeless.

Walking that trail with the heat beating down on my head, I was thankful to have enough water. I could only imagine how much more intense it would be if I didn't have what I needed to stay strong and survive. I was reminded of Psalm 42:1-2 that says: *"As the deer pants for streams of water, so my soul pants for you, O God. My soul thirsts for God, for the living God..."*

In the Old Testament God miraculously made water appear in the desert for His people. In the same way, God brings forth living water in dry places for us. God is our provider at all times, but we see this especially in dry or difficult seasons.

Worship is something that brings to life spiritually dry areas of our lives. When I praise God through hard situations it no longer feels like I'm fighting against the desert. Instead it feels like God is springing forth secret wells of water to sustain me through the hard times.

Where is there desert in your life? How does God want to speak tenderness and life to you today?

Dig deeper: *Psalm 63; Psalm 78:16; Isaiah 32:2*

Emilie O'Connor

114

April 20

"[This is he] to whom our fathers wouldn't be obedient, but rejected him, and turned back in their hearts to Egypt..." Acts 7:39

In this chapter of Acts the disciple Stephan was re-telling the story of the Hebrews' history. Here he told how their ancestors rejected Moses' leadership—and therefore God's leadership—because they were led by God into the wilderness.

The wilderness for them was a literal wilderness—a desert called Sinai. But it also represents a figurative wilderness: a dry, harsh season when God seems absent. It was hard enough for these people that they turned back in their hearts to Egypt. What was Egypt? The land of their slavery.

They were slaves of Pharaoh, living a life so bad they had cried out to God for deliverance. And yet when God delivered them through Moses, with astounding miracles no less, and they came to the wilderness, it wasn't what they had bargained for. They preferred their slavery.

God wasn't absent in this wilderness. Verse 44 in Acts 7 says, *"Our fathers had the tabernacle of the testimony in the wilderness..."* God had moved and kept moving in miraculous ways for these people. They all witnessed His miracles many times...and yet they turned back in their hearts to Egypt.

God's purpose for that generation was to lead them from slavery, through the wilderness where He would train them to be warriors, so they could take the land He had promised them. But because they rejected Him in the wilderness, this entire generation died there instead of inheriting God's promise.

The same thing has happened to many Christians. They experience freedom from the slavery of sin and addiction. But when God brings them into a wilderness season for a time, it's not what they expected...so they bail. They preferred their slavery.

Don't be one of them! Remember—the wilderness is dry and harsh, yes, but God's there, and it's only a season. There's a wonderful devotional book about the Lord's faithfulness through these wilderness times: *Streams in the Desert* by L.B. Cowman. I highly recommend it!

Dig deeper: *Numbers 32:10-13; Psalm 73; Romans 5:1-8*

April 21

"...you heard before in the word of the truth of the Good News which has come to you, even as it is in all the world and is bearing fruit and growing..." Colossians 1:5-6

Fruit-bearing plants and trees are one of God's wonderful gifts to us. They're a major source of food for people all over the world. He designed fruits to have specific nutrients in them that we humans need to be healthy.

But not only are fruits healthy, they're delicious! God also designed them to satisfy our taste buds. And not only are fruits healthy and tasty to eat—the flowers that grow into the fruits are beautiful to look at, and some varieties give off a wonderful aroma. What a blessing!

In Paul's letter to the Colossian Church, he compares the Good News—the Gospel of Jesus Christ—to fruit-bearing plants. Think about it. Only living things can bear fruit and grow, and only those living things that are designed to bear fruit. So when the word of God, the Good News, is said to *bear fruit*, Paul is reminding us that it's alive!

Hebrews 4:12 says: *"For the word of God is living and active, and sharper than any two-edged sword, piercing even to the dividing of soul and spirit, of both joints and marrow, and is able to discern the thoughts and intentions of the heart."*

It's living and active because it comes straight from God. He's put Himself in His word. Remember the first verse of John's Gospel? *"In the beginning was the Word, and the Word was with God, and the Word was God."* John is talking about Jesus.

The DNA of the Good News of Jesus is for fruit-bearing and growth. It'll bear fruit in your own life and in the lives of those you share it with. That's good news!

Dig deeper: *Isaiah 55:10-11; John 1:1-14*

April 22

"...that Christ may dwell in your hearts through faith, to the end that you, being rooted and grounded in love..." Ephesians 3:17

Being rooted is something God designed plant life to do. These roots grow down while the rest of the plant grows up.

The better the environment for each plant's design, the healthier the plant. If we want a plant in our yard to flourish, we take very good care of its root system with the proper feeding and watering. We pull out nearby weeds that would compete for the same nourishment.

A healthy root system contributes to the health of the whole plant. It bears abundant and healthy flowers, fruits and leaves. If the above-ground part of a plant is destroyed, a healthy root system will even cause regrowth.

That's what Paul means here in this part of Ephesians 3. When Jesus lives in us through faith, we're rooted in His love. It's the environment we need to thrive and be fruitful.

Jesus talked about plants, roots and environments, too, in His parable of the farmer and the seeds in Matthew 13 and Luke 8. The farmer's seeds fell on different types of soil in different environments. Only the seed that fell on the good soil was able to grow healthy roots that produced healthy plants.

What was it that made the difference? Jesus explains, *"Those in the good ground, these are those who with an honest and good heart, having heard the word, hold it tightly, and produce fruit with perseverance."* (Luke 8:15) *"...he who hears the word and understands it..."* (Matthew 13:23)

Because of Jesus (called *the Word* in John 1), because of the written word of God (the Bible) and because of the unfailing love of God we can be firmly rooted in our faith walk with Him.

When we nurture our spiritual roots, they become more healthy. They become more able to keep us rooted and grounded no matter what happens.

How are your roots today?

What are you doing to keep them healthy?

Dig deeper: *Matthew 13; Luke 8: 1-15; Ephesians 3:14-19*

April 23

"Yet listen now, Jacob my servant, and Israel, whom I have chosen..." Isaiah 44:1

The desert and canyon country is amazing! It's a place of extremes and opposites. There are large awe-inspiring walls and formations towering in front of you, up and around you. There are dry, desolate places and lush hanging gardens full of life!

The epic grand-scale beauties and the small little details in this world of opposites draw me into this wildness and closer into God's heart.

In August of 2018, I went on a professional development wilderness trip into the canyon country of Utah, unsure of what God would develop in me there. I felt ineffective in what God had called me to do and was honestly doubting whether I was in the right place. The voices of my past and the voice of the enemy kept coming at me from all sides before I even stepped into the van to travel to the trailhead.

But on Day 2 of fourteen days in the wilderness, God gave me the above passage from Isaiah: *"Yet listen now, Jacob [Laura] my servant, whom I have chosen."* The Message Bible says, *"my personal choice."*

He showed me that contrary to the good, the bad and the ugly that I had done before, I am His personal choice. I am enough. I was handpicked by God for this time, this moment and this purpose.

There were days that I felt too weak and unable to hike with the load on my back. He knew that, and kept speaking into me, step-by-step, that I am His personal choice.

So. Are. You.

You are God's personal choice to be the wineskin of heaven to *"pour water on him who is thirsty, and streams on the dry ground."* (Isaiah 44:3) You were created for a time and place such as this. You were chosen to be here. It has always been a part of God's plan that you are here today, reading this, journeying with the amazing people in the communities and places God made.

Dig deeper: *Isaiah 44*

Laura Watson

April 24

"Every good gift and every perfect gift is from above, coming down from the Father of lights, with whom can be no variation, nor turning shadow." James 1:17

I can remember many times in my life when I encountered a "perfect gift" from the Father in the world He created. Many of them have been on hikes in the mountains, overseeing grand vistas. Others have been enjoying a sunrise or sunset from a campsite in the Boundary Waters. Sometimes it's been discovering a wildflower or bird I'd never seen before.

I'm sure you've experienced the same kinds of gifts doing the activities in nature you love. The natural world is an especially amazing gift to us from the Father.

Both people who love and serve the Lord and those who don't get to enjoy these good and perfect gifts. It's often called "common grace." Matthew 5:45 says: *"He makes His sun to rise on the evil and the good, and sends rain on the just and the unjust."*

Some people recognize Him as the Father of lights—the Creator of all these wonderful things. Others don't think about it, they just accept the gifts. Some scorn the idea of a creator, instead giving all the credit to impersonal, random processes.

But everyone gets to enjoy them.

If you or I were god instead, we'd be tempted to let our friends enjoy our good and perfect gifts, but not our enemies. Those who hate us or ignore us? We'd give them the thistles, mosquitos and snakes!

But there's *"no variation nor turning shadow"* with God. His character is consistent across the board. The Father of lights is generous, faithful, good and overflowing with love. He's also wise, just and holy. So someday He'll sit on the judgment seat.

But for now, His light and His good gifts are available to everyone. In fact, He does that purposely so people can look at this good, created world and discover Him through it (Romans 1:20).

Dig deeper: Psalm 145:9; Acts 14:16-17; Romans 2:4

April 25

"'I have made the earth, the men, and the animals that are on the surface of the earth by My great power and by My outstretched arm. I give it to whom it seems right to Me." Jeremiah 27:5

This passage goes on to explain how the Lord appointed a foreign king, Nebuchadnezzar of Babylon, to rule over the known world at that time, including Judah, now present-day Israel.

It's verses like this that remind us how small we are in the grand scheme of things. How little we know. How little we can do. How little control we have over anything.

Have we made any of the animals? Anyone here created a bluebird? Or a tree frog? Or an elephant? We like to say, "We make babies" but in reality, we do our part and the rest is completely out of our hands. 99% of the process is God-created and God-driven. (And what a magnificent, miraculous process it is!)

Have we made anything on the earth that doesn't rely on God-made things? Sure we can build a house, but who made the trees for lumber? Or the sand for cement and glass? Yes, we can make cell phones...but where do we get the copper, gold, silver and platinum that goes into them?

And then there's this part: *"I give it to whom it seems right to Me."* God isn't a bystander in human history. He's been playing an active role—through people—since the beginning. The Bible is full of historical, documented events of His involvement in His world.

So even though we have very little control over anything, our God has vast amounts of control, even unlimited amounts, over it all.

When He stood before Pilate, Jesus knew that: *"Then Pilate said to Him...'Do You not know that I have power to crucify You, and power to release You?' Jesus answered, "You could have no power at all against Me unless it had been given you from above."* (John 19:10-11)

We can rest in that, too—in God's caretaking power.

Dig deeper: *Psalm 2; Proverbs 21:1; Ezra 1:1-5*

April 26

"When He established the heavens, I was there...when He established the clouds above...when He gave to the sea its boundary... when He marked out the foundations of the earth, then I was the craftsman by His side." Proverbs 8:27-30

Proverbs is known as one of the Wisdom Books of the Bible. Chapter 8, where these verses are from, describes wisdom in the first person. The "I" in these verses is Wisdom talking.

If God had Wisdom right there with Him when He created the heavens and the earth, how much more do we need Wisdom in our daily lives?! And the best part: we have access to God's wisdom. That's incredible. How do we know that?

First, He's given us His Word. His Word is full of wisdom for living every day. Not just wisdom for "religious" things, but wisdom for common, everyday practical things like work, business, money, family relationships, church life and more.

Second, when we need God's wisdom—the same wisdom that was with Him when He established the heavens and marked out the foundation of the earth—He invites us to ask Him for it.

"But if any of you lacks wisdom, let him ask of God, who gives to all liberally...and it will be given to him..." James 1:5

What wisdom do you need today for work, for school, for a relationship issue, for your business or ministry? Ask your Father!

Here's something I pray regularly: "God, You are the most creative Person in the universe. I need Your wisdom and creativity for_____. You said if I lack wisdom to ask You for it, and You would give it. So I'm asking You for wisdom, Father. Thank You for giving it to me for this situation."

And then I listen to what He has to say. His answer is usually a thought or impression in my mind.

As Jesus said in His Sermon on the Mount: *"Ask and it will be given you. Seek, and you will find. Knock, and it will be opened to you."* (Matthew 7:7)

What do you need your Father's wisdom for today?

Dig Deeper: *Proverbs 8; James 1:5-8*

April 27

"Immediately the Spirit drove Him out into the wilderness."
Mark 1:12

The wilderness Jesus went to immediately after He was baptized by John was a literal wilderness. The Spirit took Him away from the distractions of the villages and people and into a desolate place.

In our day most of us go to the wilderness to escape life for a little while. It's a break from our daily routine, from the city, from the pressures we face. We usually see it as a place of adventure and freedom. But in Jesus' day the wilderness wasn't an adventurous getaway—it was a harsh life in a harsh environment.

And yet the Holy Spirit took Him there. The Greek word translated *"the Spirit drove Him..."* is *ekballo*. It's the same word the Bible writers used when Jesus drove demons out of people. It's a forceful word.

Why would the Spirit of God *drive* the Son of God into the wilderness?

In those 40 days Jesus was being prepared by the Spirit for the next three years of ministry and, ultimately, His destiny for coming to earth—the cross. Specifically, Jesus faced Satan himself in the wilderness, who squared off with Him with major temptations intended to sideline His purpose.

Later in His ministry, Jesus would often go to the wilderness for a few hours at a time to pray, to spend time with His Father, for a break from the crowds or to get direction. For Him the wilderness wasn't a place to avoid, but a place to embrace.

We often talk about "wilderness times" in our lives when it feels like we're in a desolate place...and it especially feels like God's abandoned us. Like He's silent. Do you think sometimes the Holy Spirit is the one *driving us* to that wilderness time? Is it possible we're there so He can prepare us for the next step of our journey with Him?

Rather than avoid or dread these wilderness experiences, can we tune our ears to hear what the Holy Spirit is saying in them?

Dig deeper: *Isaiah 40:3-5; Matthew 4:1-11*

April 28

"There are three things which are too amazing for me, four which I don't understand: The way of an eagle in the air..." Proverbs 30:18-19

In Proverbs 30 the wise words of Agur references the "book of nature" as seen when watching an eagle fly. Some Bible scholars believe this eagle illustration refers to the Christian life. As we meditate on this verse and what it symbolizes, we should be greatly encouraged.

Agur says this soaring eagle is too wonderful for him to even understand. It's too wonderful because the soaring eagle seemingly defies the law of gravity. With its outstretched wings, the eagle instinctively senses the warm thermal drafts and glides effortlessly higher and higher in the sky. While in the sky, its keen vision realizes the spectacular view of the larger perspective, and has the ability to spot prey at remarkable distances.

As followers of Christ, we have Christ living in us. In the supernatural walk (flight) that should be the *normal Christian life* we have the ability to find victory over the law of sin and death and discover a new law of life and liberty.

This life is symbolized by the eagle defying the law of gravity and embracing the law of lift. The eagle isn't working hard, flapping its wings to find a higher place, a place of vision and victory. It's relying on a natural law of lift. Jesus said His burden is light and His yoke is easy.

As we soar with Christ we gain a greater perspective. Though our view is still clouded as we see dimly through a glass, we're able to trust that Christ in us has everything under control. He sees the beginning and the end. He expands our vision and gives us strategy to live victoriously.

This is also a powerful picture of entering into the Sabbath rest God has provided for us in Christ. The spiritual law of liberty and life implies that the power of Christ (grace) at work in us is the victory over sin and death. It's not human effort that defeats sin and darkness, but Christ Himself and the finished work obtained at the cross.

Dig Deeper: *Psalm 62:1; Isaiah 40:3; Matthew 11:28-30*

Brian Rupe

April 29

"So we, who are many, are one body in Christ, and individually members of one another, having gifts differing according to the grace that was given to us." Romans 12:5-6

Here in Romans 12, Paul is talking about the gifts the Holy Spirit gives His people: prophecy, teaching, serving, giving, etc. While we're one united Body of Christ, the Spirit gives us different gifts—different places of service in that body.

One way to think about this is to look at birds. God created them with certain bird characteristics—beaks, feathers, wings and so on. But these characteristics differ according to each bird's design and purpose.

Raptors have hooked beaks and sharp talons. They're designed to catch, hold and eat animals. Ducks have bills and webbed feet, perfect for life on and in the water.

An eagle will never be able to swim like a duck, though some live near water. A duck will never be able to soar like an eagle, though it can fly. They can't compete against each other in things they weren't designed to do.

Woodpeckers, finches, storks, penguins...they're all birds, but they all have differing "gifts" perfectly suited for the life God means for them.

The body of Christ is like that. If my gift is teaching, given to me by the Spirit, then that's where I'll fulfill my purpose in the body—by teaching. That's also where I'll be most fulfilled and satisfied, because I'm following God's design for me.

What if I try to excel at a gift the Spirit hasn't given me? Maybe out of envy, thinking someone else's gift is better than mine? Not only will I neglect the purpose I was made for, I'll grow frustrated because I'm trying to swim when I was made for soaring. Or I'm trying to soar when I was made for swimming.

It's a wonderful thing to learn what gifts the Spirit has given you and to grow in those gifts! (There are several online places to discover yours. Search it out!)

Dig deeper: *Romans 12: Ephesians 4:7-16; 1 Peter 4:10-11*

April 30

"Of old did You lay the foundation of the earth; And the heavens are the work of Your hands. They will perish, but You will endure. Yes, all of them will wear out like a garment. You will change them like a cloak, and they will be changed. But You are the same. Your years will have no end." Psalm 102:25-27

It's verses like these that help us keep our perspective on the Big Picture.

Psalm 102 is called the *Prayer of the Afflicted*. In the first 11 verses, the writer speaks directly to God and tells Him of his distress and pain. (If you ever thought you couldn't tell God exactly how you feel, reading this will change your mind!)

Then he switches gears. He turns his focus on God. He reminds himself of God's bigness, His faithfulness, His enduring presence. He reminds himself that even things as "permanent" as the earth and the heavens—these things that long outlast human life—will one day *"wear out"* and *"be changed."*

"But You are the same. Your years will have no end."

Our problems can overwhelm us. As the psalmist says, *"My days consume away like smoke. My bones are burned as a torch. My heart is blighted like grass, and withered...My enemies reproach me all day...My days are like a long shadow. I have withered like grass."* (verses 3, 4, 8, 11)

But...*"But you, Yahweh, will remain forever; your renown endures to all generations. You will arise and have mercy..."* (verse 12)

The foundations of the earth...the heavens...and us, His people—all the work of His hands. He's bigger than it all and above it all. We may not always get the answers we want in the way we want them. But we know who holds it all. And we can trust His wisdom and faithfulness in the middle of it.

Dig deeper: *Psalm 102*

May

May 1

"...I count all things to be loss for the excellency of the knowledge of Christ Jesus, my Lord, for whom I suffered the loss of all things, and count them nothing but refuse, that I may gain Christ." Philippians 3:8

So often when looking at the beauty of God's creation I'm moved to a place of praising God for His greatness and holiness. I once stood at an overlook that looked across the Boundary Waters Canoe Area and the Canadian border. This line of the hymn *Give me Jesus* came to mind:

Give me Jesus, give me Jesus
You can have all this world, just give me Jesus

When I heard that song in the past, I'd pictured all the ugly parts of the world I would give away in exchange for Jesus. The questions I have, the sin, the brokenness and darkness that feels too big to fix. And yes, we should give all of that to Christ—the only One who can redeem and restore all things.

But that song means I'd rather have Jesus than the most beautiful parts of the world, too. In that moment I realized I need to desire Jesus more than that beautiful view. I want to be with Jesus more than I want to be in the woods. Nature is a gift to us from our perfect Heavenly Father, but I can't let it become an idol in my life.

In that moment, I prayed and asked God to help me seek Him first. To seek the salvation of the lost more than my own desires. To love His creation rightly. Our love of nature can be a testimony to God's character, provision and faithfulness. It can be part of our witness for why we serve this good and great God.

What part of this world do you need to give to Jesus today? And what part of Himself does Jesus want to give you in return?

Dig Deeper: *1 Chronicles 29:11; Matthew 16:24-26; 1 Corinthians 13*

Emilie O'Connor

May 2

"Keep your heart with all diligence, for out of it is the wellspring of life." Proverbs 4:23

Is water safe to drink from a mountain stream? A northwoods lake? We've dipped our cup off the side of our canoe in the large Boundary Waters lakes and drank. My son was high in the Bighorn mountains and filled his water bottle from the alpine creek flowing by their campsite.

The water looks so pure and clean, and tastes wonderful. And so far we haven't had any issues from it. But I know people who've drank from those pure-looking waters and been very sorry afterwards. Parasites like *giardia* are invisible to the human eye, but can cause months of digestive problems if they sneak in.

There are several good brands of water filters we can bring into the backcountry with us to keep those nasties out of our system. We can take our chances...or we can use a good filter to make sure the water we drink is pure and safe.

Our culture is a big fan of "follow your heart." But here in Proverbs, and elsewhere in the Bible, there are red flags about that. Before we can "follow our heart" we have to know our heart is leading us in the right direction!

Our "heart"—our mind, will, feelings—doesn't always lead us into truth. That's why this is so important: *"Keep your heart with all diligence..."* Guard it. Put a reliable filter on it. *"...for out of it is the wellspring of life."* The things in your heart affect all you are and do.

The spring or lake or creek is only as pure as what's in it. Are there pollutants? Are there parasites? What's there that we can't see? We'd better know before we drink it!

Just so we need to keep our heart diligently. Filter the things we allow into our mind. Filter how our feelings dictate our attitudes and actions. What source of truth are we using as the filter? For followers of Jesus, that has to be His word—the Bible.

Dig Deeper: *Jeremiah 17:7-10; Matthew 15:19; Luke 12:34*

May 3

"...I have learned in whatever state I am, to be content in it."
Philippians 4:11

Contentment is almost a foreign word in our First World society. The entire marketing industry is built on stirring up *discontentment*. The housing industry...the food industry...even politics—they're all built on discontentment.

But that's not God's way. *"I have learned...to be content..."*

Discontentment breeds a grumbling and complaining spirit. It breeds envy, jealousy, striving for what I don't have.

The book of Exodus is full of stories of the recently-liberated Hebrews who quickly became discontent, even within days of witnessing eye-popping miracles: *"So the people grumbled..."* *"And the whole congregation of the people of Israel grumbled against..."* *"But the people thirsted for water and they grumbled..."*

That whole generation lost their inheritance because their complaining, discontented attitude spiraled into self-will, fear and rebellion.

Paul goes on to say in Philippians 4:12: *"I know how to be humbled, and I also know how to abound. In everything and in all things I have learned the secret both to be filled and to be hungry, both to abound and to be in need."*

One of the very best ways to learn and practice contentment is on a wilderness trip—a canoe or kayak trip, a backpacking trip. When you have to pack and carry everything you need for your time out there, you learn to focus carefully on what matters.

We find life on the trail—though hard physically—is so enriching and satisfying partly because of that forced simplicity.

On the last Boundary Waters canoe trip I was part of, every meal tasted good, even if it wasn't food I'd choose to eat at home. Why? Because when you're out on the trail it all tastes good! We're content with it because we don't take it for granted.

That can carry over into the rest of life, too. What really matters? What's my focus? What's my destination and what do I really need in my pack to get there? What can I leave behind because it's not necessary? What will I be content with?

Dig deeper: *Numbers 14; Luke 12:15; 2 Corinthians 12:7-10*

May 4

"The God who made the world and all things in it, He, being Lord of heaven and earth, doesn't dwell in temples made with hands. He isn't served by men's hands, as though He needed anything, seeing He Himself gives to all life and breath, and all things.

"He made from one blood every nation of men to dwell on all the surface of the earth, having determined appointed seasons, and the boundaries of their dwellings, that they should seek the Lord, if perhaps they might reach out for Him and find Him, though He is not far from each one of us." Acts 17:24-27

God doesn't need us. Not the God who made heaven and earth, the rules of physics and mathematics, the creatures of the animal kingdom, the stars and galaxies. He's the author of life. He gives us our very breath.

No, He doesn't need us. But He *wants* us to reach out for Him, search for Him and find Him.

That's amazing! How can this divine Being—who's got an entire universe to pay attention to—care about *me*? About *you*? Or any one of the 7 billion people on our planet today? And yet the Bible teaches us that He not only cares, He loves deeply. He even pursues us.

It's not a trade. We don't serve Him at church, on the mission field or in ministry so He'll reward us with His love. We serve Him because of His love. And because His heart is for *"every nation of men...that they should seek the Lord..."*

Yes, God created and is Lord of heaven and earth. *"He Himself gives to all life and breath."* And He created people—us—in His image (Genesis 1:26) so we can have relationship with Him. He wants relationship with *you*.

No matter how you feel, this is how He feels about you: *"Yahweh, your God, is among you, a mighty one who will save. He will rejoice over you with joy..."* (Zephaniah 3:17)

Dig deeper: *Psalm 139:7-8; Romans 8:34; Ephesians 2:10*

May 5

"To whom will you liken Me? Who is My equal, says the Holy One. Lift up your eyes on high, and see Who has created these, Who brings out their army by number. He calls them all by name. By the greatness of His might, and because He is strong in power, not one is lacking." Isaiah 40:26

Sometimes...well, often...we get an overwhelming sense of helplessness. There's so much injustice in the world, so much hatred, so much impurity and greed. The sin we see at the highest levels of human power can make us feel completely ant-sized. Like there's no hope.

But there *is* hope. Not hope in people. No, we're part of the problem. Even those of us who truly want to live godly lives are part of the problem.

God says, "Don't look down there...look up!" *"Lift up your eyes on high and see Who created these..."* Look at the moon, the stars, the Milky Way galaxy. Modern technology lets us see further than any generation of humans before us, into the reaches of space.

God calls each of these stars by name. Each one is part of His magnificent creation. He knows even the ones we can't see with our most powerful telescope.

Who else can say that? What human—no matter how powerful or influential—can say he or she created *anything*? Even supernatural beings—angels, demons, the devil—can't say that.

When we feel utterly overwhelmed by either our own personal problems or chaos on a national scale—look up! Lift up your eyes and remind yourself who your Father is. Who your Savior is. The One who knows the stars by name knows your name, too.

We know from history—including Biblical history—that life has never been and never will be problem-free. Jesus, in fact, promised we *would* have problems. *"But,"* He said, *"Cheer up! I have overcome the world."* (John 16:33)

"Lift up your eyes on high, and see..." Look at the stars and remember Who your God is.

Dig deeper: *Isaiah 40*

May 6

"Better is the sight of the eyes than the wandering of the desire. This also is vanity and a chasing after wind." Ecclesiastes 6:9

How often are we unsatisfied with what is before us, what is in sight of the eyes, and instead chase after our wandering desires? The grass is always greener on the other side of the fence, or so we think.

Our eyes wander away from our spouse. Our eyes envy what our neighbors possess. We desire more free time, more money, a better job.

Paraglider pilots literally chase after the wind. We watch forecasts closely and learn meteorology so we can better guess what the weather might do. On the evening before a promising day, pilots will plan long-distance cross-country routes. We study to see how high clouds might form. We look for possible convergence lines of colliding air masses, and on and on...

We literally chase after the wind.

Do we ever catch it? Sometimes. Sometimes we're rewarded with a 100, 200, or (rarely) 300-mile flight. But most often, not.

When I finally realized that all this was *"vanity and chasing after wind"* I learned that what is *"better is the sight of the eyes than the wandering of the desire."* So now I choose a mountain, enjoy the climb to the top, and sit waiting for the wind. Sometimes I'm rewarded with a 50-mile flight lasting three or four hours. Other times I just enjoy God's beautiful creation. I no longer strive or chase after the wind. I'm fulfilled and satisfied with the sight of my eyes.

I've learned to apply this throughout my life. I love my wife and desire her only. I'm more than satisfied with my house, my car, my job. I don't need the respect of others, nor honor, nor gain.

As Paul says in Philippians 4:11, *"I have learned in whatever state I am, to be content in it."*

Are you? Or are you chasing after wind?

Dig Deeper: *The book of Ecclesiastes*

Brian Doub

May 7

"...I remind you that you should stir up the gift of God which is in you through the laying on of my hands." 1 Timothy 6:6-8

The Greek word translated *stir up* is *anazópureó*. It means to kindle afresh.

A campfire is a favorite part of everyone's camping trips. Whether we're in a campground or out in the backcountry, or whether it's to cook over or simply for enjoyment.

Our boys used to love the challenge of building the fire when they were young. Laying out the starter, the kindling and the bigger pieces...using just one match to build a roaring blaze.

When the fire has just begun, the challenge is for the flame of the starter and kindling to get hot enough and burn long enough to start the bigger sticks. If it dies out at this point (I speak from experience as a less-talented fire maker!) it can be frustrating to get it going again. That's why we have to be sure we have plenty of fuel at-hand to continue to feed it.

But once the fire burns long enough, the coals are steady and hot. Any piece of fuel placed into these hot coals will catch fire really quickly.

Paul's words in this phrase to his dear son in the faith, Timothy, remind us that our life with God is like a campfire. He reminded Timothy to stir up the coals of his inner fire...kindle afresh. Keep that fire going.

And what is the fire? It's the *gift* of God. The Greek word is *charisma*. It's the gift or operation of Holy Spirit-empowered service we offer Him. It's His life in us that overflows into service to others, both in the church and in our schools or work, or wherever we are.

Note two keys here: One, it's the Holy Spirit's life, breath and work being stirred up. Two, it's our responsibility to do the stirring up, the kindling afresh. We continually add fuel to the fire through worship, prayer, reading the Bible and staying in fellowship with the Lord and with other believers.

Dig deeper: *Philippians 2:12; Hebrews 10:23; Jude 21*

May 8

"But ask the animals, now, and they will teach you; the birds of the sky, and they will tell you. Or speak to the earth, and it will teach you. The fish of the sea will declare to you. Who doesn't know that in all these, Yahweh's hand has done this, in whose hand is the life of every living thing, and the breath of all mankind?" Job 12:7-10

When I read this passage I think of the incredible, complex, intricately-related natural world we're surrounded by—and give glory to God, who I believe created it.

I recently read the book *Undeniable* by Douglas Axe, PhD. In it he explains how biology confirms our "design intuition"—that even young children are able to distinguish between what's random chance and what's been designed by someone.

He gives this example: a folded paper crane—you know, the origami kind. Say one of these is on a tabletop. No one, from a 4-year old on up, will believe that simple little paper crane just happened to be folded that way by chance.

And yet scientific naturalism asks us to believe that *real* cranes are products of random chance. That each system in this magnificently complex, living body that started as a single cell is merely a cosmic accident. Even though a single cell of the real crane is far more complex than the entire paper crane.

But ask the animals...the birds...the fish. Ask the earth. They will teach us. The more we learn about the world around us, the more astounding complexity we discover. And the more convinced we become of the power and intelligence—no, mind-boggling genius—behind it.

That is, unless your mind and heart are closed off to God. The very God who gives *"the breath of all mankind."*

Are you doubting God's existence today?

Ask the animals. Ask the birds and fish. Ask the earth. What are they saying about their Creator?

Dig deeper: *Job 38-39*

May 9

"This is the judgment, that the light has come into the world, and men loved the darkness rather than the light; for their works were evil." John 3:19

Light was God's very first act of creation: *"God said, 'Let there be light, and there was light. God saw the light, and saw that it was good. God divided the light from the darkness. God called the light 'day' and the darkness He called 'night.' There was evening and there was morning, the first day."* (Genesis 1:3-5)

The theme of light and darkness is common throughout both Old and New Testaments.

Light is used as a word picture for God's presence and truth. Darkness represents sin and the absence of God. Let's look at a few more scriptures about light and darkness:

Isaiah 5:20—*"Woe to those who call evil good, and good evil; who put darkness for light, and light for darkness; who put bitter for sweet, and sweet for bitter!"*

Ephesians 5:8-9—*"For you were once darkness, but are now light in the Lord. Walk as children of light, for the fruit of the Spirit is in all goodness and righteousness and truth..."*

John 8:12—*"...Jesus spoke to them, saying, 'I am the light of the world. He who follows Me will not walk in the darkness, but will have the light of life.'"*

Proverbs 2:13-14 talks about people *"who forsake the paths of uprightness, to walk in the ways of darkness, who rejoice to do evil, and delight in the perverseness of evil..."*

Light and darkness are warring inside your spirit, your thoughts and your feelings for control. Behind the light is God Himself. Behind the darkness are *"the spiritual forces of wickedness"* (Ephesians 6:12).

The free will God gives all of us means we choose which we allow to rule us: light or darkness. The more we choose light, the more the light of God's presence and truth fills us. The more we choose darkness, the more darkness fills us.

Where do you need to choose God's light today?

Dig deeper: *Proverbs 4:19; John 1:4-5; 1 John 1:5-6*

May 10

"He will be like a tree planted by the streams of water..." Psalm 1:3

In Psalm 1 we see a beautiful word picture of the believer's life. It describes a person who understands where to walk, to sit and to stand. The result of these choices mixed together with meditating on God's words results in our being like a tree firmly planted by streams of water.

Planted suggests a decision God made in the miracle of creation and in His divine wisdom to place you as a tree by a body of water. You're not there in a casual accidental, half-hazard way. You're firmly and decisively planted. This also suggests your roots are healthy and deep, and you have an endless source of water to satisfy your needs.

When Jesus was talking to the Samaritan woman at the well, He referenced the fact that if she were to drink from His well, she'd have an endless supply (John 4). This living water would fill her up and spill over onto those around her.

The water in a tree is captured deep underground by the tiny root ends. This water mixes with the rich nutrients from the soil and flows throughout the tree like the blood in our veins. It causes growth to happen and then spills out through the leaves in what's called *transpiration*.

The deep tree roots represent a solid foundation. We must rely on the Lord as our firm foundation. Surrendering to His divine purpose we'll find ourselves established by His living word and receiving all the nourishment we need for a healthy spirit, soul and body.

The roots of the tree are the part that's not visible. It's our secret life of prayer, scripture meditation and inward character. Though the foundation can't be seen, it's the part that enables the living water to begin its journey—a journey that results in spilling out, producing fruit and impacting those around us.

Dig deeper: *Psalm 1; John 4*

Brian Rupe

May 11

"But you, beloved, keep building up yourselves on your most holy faith, praying in the Holy Spirit. Keep yourselves in God's love..."
Jude 20-21

I've only been rock climbing once in my life, when I was in college, at the invitation of a couple climber friends. So I'm no expert, but I know there's a big difference between climbing with ropes, a harness and clips...and free climbing.

My brother climbed for years, and I remember him assuring our mom that it was perfectly safe. They were extremely careful about quality-checking their gear every time they started to scale a rock face.

The careful use of that gear keeps rock climbers safe. If they make a mistake, the gear is there to protect them from a disastrous fall. Free climbers, on the other hand, don't have that margin. They may be experts, but one mistake and they don't have a second chance.

Isn't it interesting that in this passage, Jude (who was Jesus' half-brother) says, *"Keep yourselves in God's love."* Have you ever thought about the fact that there are things we can do to stay in God's love? To keep ourselves under His protection, like climbers keeps themselves under the protection of their gear?

Keeping ourselves in God's love is like a climber keeping the gear on. An experienced climber knows what gear is important, how to use it, and when to replace what's worn and unreliable.

So God has provided us with "gear" to keep us in His love, in His protection. The verse just before tells us part of it: *"... keep building up yourselves on your most holy faith, praying in the Holy Spirit."*

How do we keep building ourselves up in our faith? In God's love? By praying in the Holy Spirit. By abiding in Jesus (John 15). By meeting regularly with other believers (Hebrews 10:25) and being an active part of the Body of Christ (Romans 12). By putting on God's armor every day (Ephesians 6).

Keep the gear on! It's an active, daily keeping.

Dig deeper: *The book of Jude*

May 12

"One who walks with wise men grows wise..." Proverbs 13:20

This is really what discipleship is: walking with the wise.

Do you know why there are so many Christian wilderness and outdoor discipleship ministries? It works! It's a wonderful way for children and young people to *walk with the wise*.

We get them away from their everyday lives, away from screens, and some away from a rough home or school environment—and we bring them into nature. While we disciple them in the ways of the wilderness and outdoor activities, we have the chance to disciple their minds and hearts, too.

It's incredibly easy to apply lessons learned through backpacking, canoeing, rock climbing, snowshoeing and other outdoor activities to life itself.

While "the wise" (counselors, older people who are experienced in these activities) spend time with these young folks, it's natural for them to teach along the way. It's natural to bring in life application, spiritual application and heart application to almost any situation.

Whether it's perseverance, coming alongside one another in love, forgiveness, humility, patience, appreciation of beauty, grace, dependence, God's greatness—the opportunities to pass on wisdom are almost limitless.

And you don't have to be a camp counselor or work for an outdoor ministry to include this in your life. One of the best ways is to simply invite them along with you on your own outdoor activities. If you're a parent with children in the home, this will be your own children. Or it could be nieces and nephews, or grandchildren. It could be teens from your church's youth group, neighborhood kids, or young adults you know who'd love to join you on an outdoor activity you love.

Not only is it a super way to build relationships with these younger disciples, it's an extremely rewarding way to use your experience and wisdom to benefit someone else. Discipleship isn't limited to church small groups, to Sunday School or youth groups. Use nature and outdoor activity to pass on wisdom!

Dig deeper: *Matthew 28:19-20; Philippians 4:9; 1 Thessalonians 2:8*

May 13

"Therefore let's...lay aside every weight and the sin which so easily entangles us, and let's run with perseverance the race that is set before us, looking to Jesus, the author and perfecter of faith..."
Hebrews 12:1-2

It isn't easy to run or hike in over-sized, baggy clothes. I certainly don't want anything to make running any harder for me by flapping around, needing to be pulled up, and potentially becoming a tripping hazard.

In our pursuit of following Jesus, why wouldn't we pay attention and diligently cast off those things that trip us up emotionally and spiritually? There are blatant sins we know will keep us from living a Spirit-empowered life, but could it be that other things do, too?

Even good things like relationships and vocation, or neutral things like possessions can entangle us. Obviously focusing on these things to make us happy or give us value is idolatry, sin and a lie. Most of us will readily admit that. But what about my, ahem, very American idea that my stuff is who I am?

We have so much stuff that we think these things tell our story. They tell of where I've been, what I like to do and who has been important to me. Or is my job who I am? Or my relationships or family status?

We allow so many things to tether us to this world that is not our home. The only remedy is to constantly realign our focus back to Jesus. Our God has done such great things for us! We should enjoy His good gifts here to His glory, but always hold them loosely. When we inadvertently find our identity in our relationships, jobs, or possessions, we dishonor the Giver of these good things.

All these things, just like creation, can and should be tools to drive us to worship the one true God, but too often they become the object of our affections. We would do well to regularly question ourselves to see what we hold sacred.

Dig deeper: *Matthew 6:33; Mark 8:34; Colossians 3:1-3*

Beth Poliquin

May 14

"The heavens declare the glory of God. The expanse shows His handiwork. Day after day they pour out speech, and night after night they display knowledge." Psalm 19:1-2

When King David, the composer of this song, looked at the heavens, all he knew was what he could see with his own eyes. To him, the sun, the moon and the brilliant night stars told their story of God's glory. They spoke of His greatness.

Day after day the sun rises to give light and heat to the earth. Night after night we see the beauty of the moon in its various phases. But God created them to do even more than that.

Over the centuries people have been able to tell time and develop calendars around them. To navigate on the open sea by looking at the constellations as they sail.

In our day, as modern technology has replaced the heavens for those purposes, that same technology has given us insight into the expanse beyond anything our ancestors could have even imagined.

3,000 years later we know what King David never could—that beyond the sight of the naked eye is not just this bigness, but breathtaking light shows of galaxies, novas, supernovas, nebulae. Light-years of space that defies comprehension.

(To see about 200 spectacular images taken by the Hubble telescope, go to: *heritage.stsci.edu/gallery/gallery*)

John Glenn, the first American to orbit the earth, said this, "To look out at this kind of creation and not believe in God is, to me, impossible." *

Why not take some time today...tonight...and just look up into the expanse. What kind of mind and power could've created all this with a few words, *"Let there be..."*? Let the wonder of it sink deep inside you.

And thank this God who created the heavens that He also created you. And not only created you, but wants relationship with you!

Dig deeper: *Genesis 1:16; Psalm 33:6; Nehemiah 9:6*

The Washington Post online, 12/8/16

May 15

"One of the elders said, 'Don't weep. Behold, the Lion who is of the tribe of Judah, the Root of David, has overcome...' I saw in the middle of the throne and of the four living creatures, and in the middle of the elders, a Lamb standing, as though it had been slain."
Revelation 5:5-6

Jesus has many names in the Bible. Two of the best known are here in these verses: The *Lion of Judah* and the *Lamb*. The lion, of course, is one of nature's most feared predators—the king of the jungle. Nobody would fear a lamb, though! Lambs are cuddly and cute, and defenseless.

The elder tells John, the author of Revelation, *"Behold, the Lion who is of the tribe of Judah..."* But when John turns to look, he sees a Lamb, not a Lion. A few verses down it's clear the elder is talking about Jesus. But how can Jesus be both a Lion and a Lamb?

When I read this in my Life Application Bible (which I recommend—the study notes help explain a lot!), the notes for these verses helped clear up the confusion: The first time Jesus came to earth, it was as a Lamb. This Lamb looks as though it had been slain, because it *had* been slain—on a cross between two thieves. The sacrifice Lamb.

But the Bible promises Jesus is coming back to earth again, and this time He won't come as a Lamb, but as a Lion. As the Lion of the tribe of Judah—the King.

A few verses down in verse 12: *"Worthy is the Lamb who has been killed to receive the power, wealth, wisdom, strength, honor, glory, and blessing!"*

That slain Lamb isn't dead anymore. He is risen, He's waiting for His time, and He's coming back as a Lion! Do you know Jesus as *"the Lamb of God who takes away the sin of the world"*? (John 1:29) If you do, then you'll joyfully receive Him as the Lion of Judah—the King.

Dig Deeper: *Revelation 5*

May 16

"For the seed of peace and the vine will yield its fruit, and the ground will give its increase, and the heavens will give their dew; and I will cause the remnant of this people to inherit all these things."
Zechariah 8:12

The entire eighth chapter of Zechariah gives a prophetic description of how the Lord wants to someday bless His people in Jerusalem and Israel.

The way He'll show His favor and blessing is through things like the elderly and little children being safe in the streets. He'll bring His people back from the east and the west, and they'll know their God and be His, living in truth and righteousness. People from other nations will want to go there too, to seek the Jewish God.

One way the Lord will show His blessing and favor to His people is the verse above, verse 12. The blessing of abundance in the natural world—their crops, plenty of food, rain and moisture. They won't have to fear drought, storm or natural disaster anymore.

Idyllic nature was part of the original creation, the way it was in the Garden of Eden. And it'll be part of the Lord's return, in new heavens and a new earth.

There are several other places in the Bible that talk about this coming time. Many of these prophecies include a renewed and peaceful natural world: the wolf and the lamb together (Isaiah 65:25), the leopard and the young goat (Isaiah 11:6) and a little child playing peacefully near a cobra's hole (Isaiah 11:9).

Paul, the writer of Romans, talks about how creation longs to be delivered from the curse of sin and death, too:

"Creation waits with eager expectation for the children of God to be revealed...in hope that the creation itself also will be delivered from the bondage of decay into the liberty of the glory of the children of God." (Romans 8:19-20)

What a glorious time that will be! Can you imagine it? How are you living your life in expectation of that time?

Dig deeper: Zechariah 8; Romans 8

May 17

"Be strengthened in the grace that is in Christ Jesus." 2 Timothy 2:1

If you're wise, you'll prepare yourself well for a long distance wilderness trip. If you plan to hike the Appalachian Trail, or go on a 600-mile canoe trip in Canada, or climb Denali you'll strengthen yourself for the journey.

I've personally not done anything that major—not even close! But even for short excursions we sometimes need to draw on inner strength to be able to endure and "conquer" the distance or weather conditions or elevation gain.

One of the hardest short hikes I've done was in Boulder, Colorado at the Flatirons—the hike to Royal Arch. The elevation gain is 1,400 feet in less than 2 miles—which is a lot for this Midwesterner! Especially when the starting elevation was 5,600+ feet. (And I suppose the fact that I had already done a mountain hike each of the previous couple of days might have something to do with my aches and pains after this one!)

You have to call on inner strength for things like this, and especially when it's day after day after day.

It's the same with our journey with God. Day after day after day we're to *"be strengthened in the grace that's in Christ Jesus."* We don't have to—in fact, we can't—do this walk with God on our own. The whole point is to be *in Christ*, to be strong in *His* grace.

And it takes some training, some preparing, just as it does for wilderness treks. We need to take the time and make the effort to know His word, His character, His direction for us. We need to know who we are in Him, His purposes and will for us. We need time in His presence in prayer and worship and praise.

If Jesus needed all those things to complete God's assignment for Him, how much more do we? And the invitation is there: *be strengthened in the grace that is in Christ Jesus.*

Dig deeper: *Deuteronomy 31:6; 1 Samuel 30:6; Ephesians 6:10*

May 18

"Don't withhold good from those to whom it is due, when it is in the power of your hand to do it." Proverbs 3:27

Trees connect with each other in the forest through what are called *mycorrhizal networks*. Research has found that trees communicate within and across species. They share resources like carbon dioxide and sugars, and communicate threats to trees growing around them. Taller trees that get more sunlight will share sugar with younger trees that have less access to the sun. (Suzanne Simard TED Talk: *How Trees Talk to Each Other*)

This is how the body of Christ is meant to function. 1 Peter 2:5 says we're all living stones and that together we make up a spiritual house and a holy priesthood that bring glory to God.

The Bible also explains the interdependence of the church in 1 Corinthians 12 when Paul talks about the body of Christ as a physical human body. We need each other. A forest is not just a tree or the soil, but also the animals and other plants, the sun and water, and so much more.

When walking through a forest, we feel it brimming with life. There's a sense of unity that all parts are working together for balance and survival. This is how the Body of Christ should feel. New believers welcomed into the body of Christ join this network and see the relational connections that are evidence of the fruit of the Spirit.

Jesus said *"I am the vine. You are the branches"* (John 15:5). We do not stand alone. Psalm 68 says we are not orphans but have been set in a family. When I walk through a forest it feels like a living representation to remind us of how the body of Christ should also be overflowing with life and joined together in unity.

What does that mean to you in terms of practical application in your daily walk as a disciple of Christ Jesus? How can you put that into practice today?

Dig Deeper: *1 Corinthians 12, Psalm 68, John 13:35*

Emilie O'Connor

May 19

"But he wanted to justify himself, so he asked Jesus, 'And who is my neighbor?' " Luke 10:29

A certain college student was going down from Ohio to North Carolina to begin a backpacking trip on the Appalachian Trail with eight of her fellow classmates. It finally sunk in that she would be inescapably with this group of people for the next seven days. She would be walking with them, eating with them, sleeping in a tent with some of them, even going to the bathroom near them. She would be hundreds of miles from her dorm room and, soon, dozens of trail miles from any vehicle or civilization. What would happen?

On campus, life was structured and scheduled, food was prepared for you, and everything was clean. It was easy to stay in your own space. You didn't really need to love your neighbor.

The week on the trail was far from easy or comfortable. But as our group hiked together that week we cheered and encouraged each other. We picked each other up when we fell. We warmed each other when we were cold. We cooked for each other and cleaned up after each other. We carried the load for each other when it was too much to carry—literally. We laughed at each other's jokes. We asked each other good questions. We learned about each other's faith journeys. We really listened to each other. We were in each other's space all the time. And we had a great hike and did make it safely back to the van, back to civilization, and back to campus.

Who is my neighbor? That week, our neighbors were the people we saw every day, the people we lived life with, as closely and messily as life is when you're backpacking together. In a new experience, far from the comforts and conveniences of home, we learned to love each other because we needed each other. We learned to love each other in ways we never had nor ever could within the confines of the college campus. We learned to love our neighbors as ourselves because we had to.

Dig deeper: Luke 10:25-37

William Hayes

May 20

"...giving thanks to the Father, who made us fit to be partakers of the inheritance of the saints in light, who delivered us out of the power of darkness, and translated us into the Kingdom of the Son..." Colossians 1:12-13

According to Genesis, God's first act of creation was to speak light into existence and to divide the light from the darkness. (Genesis 1:3-5)

One of the first things we notice about light and darkness is this: light never gives way to darkness, it's darkness that gives way to light. Darkness exists when there's no light. When light arrives on the scene, darkness has to back off.

In several places, including this one in Colossians, the Bible uses light and darkness as metaphors for two kingdoms: The kingdom of light (God's kingdom) and the kingdom of darkness (Satan's kingdom).

The whole point of Jesus' coming to earth and sacrificing His life on the cross was to deliver us out of the power (or kingdom) of darkness and bring us into the Kingdom of the Son (into light).

I remember as a child going on a cave tour with my dad and siblings in South Dakota's Black Hills. I'm sure we saw all kinds of fascinating cave formations. I was in West Virginia's Seneca Caves as an adult with our own kids, so I know how cool they are. But the only thing I remember from my childhood experience was when the ranger shut off the lights! There's no darkness quite like that of the darkness of a deep cave. But those lights came back on, after the ranger proved his point, and he led us out of the cave again and back into the sunlight above ground.

That's what it's like when the Father *"delivered us out of the power of darkness, and translated us into the Kingdom of the Son."* From darkness into light. Two different and opposite kingdoms.

Our inheritance as God's children, as this verse says, is in light. Let's live in that light today!

Dig deeper: *Colossians 1*

May 21

"And Yahweh will guide you continually, satisfy your soul in dry places, and make your bones strong. You will be like a watered garden, and like a spring of water whose waters don't fail." Isaiah 58:11

I've been in several areas of the US that have been through devastating wildfires. One of them is in northeast Minnesota, where a Boundary Waters fire started and spread into Canada's Quetico wilderness in 2007. The fire burned 75,000 acres before it was fully contained.

By that summer, though, fireweed was already blooming in the burn areas and green grass was coming up. Now, as I write this in 2021, there are areas where you can't even see there *was* a fire, the new growth is so abundant.

In the fall of 2020, my husband and I were guests at a ranch in central Colorado where a 138,000-acre fire had swept through in 2002, 18 years before. Granted we were there in October, so things were already brown from the summer...but very little new growth had come up since the fire.

While wildfires are complicated things, there's one major factor that contributes to both a fire starting and the rate of regrowth afterwards: water. In areas of average rainfall like Minnesota, it takes a drought over several seasons to produce prime fire conditions. In Colorado it's much drier on average, so the chances of wildfire in any season is higher.

And once a fire has gone through, rainfall is one of the main factors that affects the rate of regrowth in the forest. Without life-giving water, trees and other plants don't grow as well.

So when God promises His people *"You will be like a watered garden"* that's a big deal! Jesus offers us living water. When we take it and allow that living water to flow out of us (John 7:38) there's less opportunity for circumstances or the devil to produce wildfires in our lives. And if they do come, the restoration comes sooner and more fully.

"You will be like a watered garden, and like a spring of water whose waters don't fail."

Dig deeper: *Isaiah 58*

May 22

"And Yahweh will guide you continually, satisfy your soul in dry places, and make your bones strong. You will be like a watered garden, and like a spring of water whose waters don't fail." Isaiah 58:11

Yesterday we read about how the amount of rainfall in a region has a direct affect on wildfire risk. There's another major factor in how susceptible an area is to wildfire: fuel.

In the Minnesota wildfire of 2007, there was an unusual abundance of prime fuel because of a natural event that had happened eight years before. Devastating winds flattened a million trees over a 500,000-acre swath in Superior National Forest.

Everyone knew it was only a matter of time before a major wildfire would happen, because all those trees would be there drying out and turning into fuel.

Another reason fuel can be abundant in areas where wildfires are common is when people have been suppressing fires there for decades. Fire is a natural occurrence that adds health back into natural areas. When fires are prevented from occurring naturally over a long period of time, the fuel that's there gets drier and drier. It doesn't take much for a fire to spread quickly with that much fuel.

How does all of this apply to our lives? What kinds of things provide fuel for the wildfires that occur in our lives? A wildfire can be outside our control, like a devastating family breakdown or divorce. It can be the loss of someone dear. A betrayal by a close friend. Losing a job you love. Other peoples' sin. Big things like war, terrorism, disease, injustice. Sometimes we provide our own fuel by poor choices we make, a poor attitude, sin in our lives, unforgiveness or resentment.

We can let these things remain in us, suppressing small fires over time, allowing all this dead fuel to build up until a major fire is inevitable. Or we can walk with the Lord through these things and allow His dealings, healings and workings in us.

Dig deeper: *Isaiah 61:3; Hebrews 4:16; 1 Peter 5:10*

May 23

"The heavens declare the glory of God..." Psalm 19:1
"Yahweh's law is perfect..." Psalm 19:7

Psalm 19 should be a nature lover's favorite. What is more inspiring than a perfectly clear night with zero light pollution on the shore of a wilderness lake? I remember one such night when the water was so still the reflection of the night sky was near perfection.

I asked the Lord, "Why so many stars?" The answer came quickly: "I needed an illustration for Abraham." I was shocked and overwhelmed by the answer. Certainly there are other reasons for so many stars! The Lord wanted me to know that His love for Abraham and the calling He had placed on Abraham's life was very important in the grand scheme of His redemption plan. Perhaps the only really important reason for so many stars was to communicate with Abraham the intentions of His plan and covenant.

In Genesis 15:5, God spoke to Abraham: *"Look now toward the sky, and count the stars, if you are able to count them."* Of course, Abraham couldn't number them. In a poetic way, through the book of nature, God was speaking to Abraham of His desire for seemingly countless children. The glory of God is the presence of God manifested in the beauty of creation, including you and me. As we become fully alive, fully redeemed in Christ His glory shines more brightly.

The law of God is perfect and God Himself has written His law in our hearts and is gracing us to follow that perfect law because of the power of Christ living in us. We are blessed to be able to receive His wisdom through the written law and the law of nature, a double witness available to all.

The messages God gives through both avenues are endless. Keep on seeking the glory of the Lord in the majesty of creation and the written word.

Dig Deeper: *Psalm 19*

Brian Rupe

May 24

"Remain in Me, and I in you. As the branch can't bear fruit by itself unless it remains in the vine, so neither can you, unless you remain in Me." John 15:4

While the branch is what bears the fruit, it wouldn't be possible except for the life it gets from the vine. The vine is what puts down roots and draws nourishment from the soil. The life comes up through the vine and into the branches. As long as the branch *remains...stays connected...*many versions translate it *abides...* it'll draw that life and bear fruit.

That's both humbling and encouraging!

It's humbling because we need to be reminded—often—"It's not I who bears the fruit! If I were cut off from the vine, there would be no more life, no more nourishment." When you cut a branch off from the main vine, not only does that branch lose its ability to bear fruit—it dies! There's no life there anymore.

Any fruit we want to bear for the Kingdom—whether for ourselves or others—is dependent on our remaining connected to Jesus, the Vine.

It's encouraging, because bearing fruit isn't dependent on us! It's dependent on our staying in that abiding place in the Vine. Staying connected with Jesus. 1 John 3:24 tells us what abiding looks like: *"He who keeps His commandments remains in Him, and He in him..."*

It's obedience. Obedience is the condition of remaining... abiding...staying connected to Jesus, the Vine.

That doesn't go over well with a lot of people. We value our independence, our freedom to make our own decisions and decide what's right for us. Jesus gives us the freedom to do that—to choose our own way instead of His. But then we also cut ourselves off from the Vine. We lose our source of life and nourishment.

Remain in Him. The fruit He'll bear through you will blow your mind! His ways are beyond our imagination if we'll just trust Him and remain.

Dig deeper: *John 8:31; Galatians 2:20; Colossians 3:1-3*

May 25

"The life of the body is a heart at peace, but envy rots the bones."
Proverbs 14:30

This was written hundreds of years before modern medicine proved its truth! God designed us such that our mental and emotional health directly affects our physical health. Take a look:

"A heart at peace..." The Hebrew word translated *peace* here is *marpe*. It can mean tranquil, soothing, composure, healing. It gives a sense of health, wholeness, settledness. *Heart* is *leb*, or the inner person, will and mind.

"Envy rots the bones." *Rots* is *raqab*, rottenness or decay. The word translated *envy* is *qinah*. It's also translated anger, jealousy, passion, rivalry. This word is sometimes positive and sometimes negative in Old Testament scriptures. Here it's clearly negative. And *bones* is *etsem*, which can mean bones, and also substance and self. So it's not limited to our skeleton.

A positive emotional or mental response taken too far or in the wrong way can become negative, even to the point of causing harm to our body.

The medical world has known this for awhile now. The Mayo Clinic website tells us some of the physical effects of emotional and mental stress: headaches, muscle tension and pain, chest pain, tiredness, stomach issues, inability to sleep well. If prolonged, they can even lead to long-term illness and disease.

But when our heart, mind and emotions are tranquil, at peace and whole it transfers to our physical body as life—*chay*, in Hebrew. Alive, living.

So the state of our mental and emotional health has a huge impact on the state of our physical body. That's practical wisdom from the One who created us!

How to keep our heart tranquil and at peace? Philippians 4:6-7 says: *"In nothing be anxious, but in everything, by prayer and petition with thanksgiving, let your requests be made known to God. And the peace of God, which surpasses all understanding, will guard your hearts and your thoughts in Christ Jesus."* It really works!

Dig deeper: Psalm 4:8; Philippians 4:4-9; 2 Thessalonians 3:16

May 26

"He makes me lie down in green pastures. He leads me beside still waters." Psalm 23:2

Psalm 23 is one of the most famous passages in the Bible. It was written by the shepherd king, David, who himself led sheep in green pastures and beside quiet waters. When he called the God of Israel a Shepherd, he knew what that meant.

"He makes me lie down in green pastures"—full of nourishment, protected. *"He leads me beside still waters. He restores my soul"* (verse 3). Still waters do, indeed, restore the soul. We can be next to it or on it, maybe paddling a canoe or kayak. It's tranquil, restoring, peaceful.

Verse 3 continues, *"He guides me in the paths of righteousness..."* He's our trail guide, leading us safely on our journey through life. But not just through the green pastures and the still waters...

Our life's trail also goes through *"the valley of the shadow of death"* and *"in the presence of my enemies"* (verses 4 and 5). Life isn't a bed of roses. It includes conflict, darkness, death, trial. Jesus promised it when He said, *"In the world you have trouble..."* (John 16:33)

But Jesus didn't stop there, and David doesn't stop there in this beautiful psalm: *"I will fear no evil, for You are with me...You prepare a table* (a feast!) *before me in the presence of my enemies... my cup runs over."* (Psalm 23, portions of verses 4 and 5).

And Jesus said, *"...but cheer up! I have overcome the world."* (John 16:33)

The Bible is clear that following Jesus doesn't mean our life will be easy and painless. In fact, it teaches the opposite—sometimes the waters aren't quiet, they're stormy. Sometimes it's not green pastures but dark valleys we go through.

But the promise is the same: *"Surely goodness and loving kindness shall follow me all the days of my life, and I will dwell in Yahweh's house forever."* (verse 6)

That's our hope. That's what we hang onto—God's goodness and faithfulness...Jesus' victory. Amen!

Dig deeper: Psalm 23; Ephesians 3:14-21; Hebrews 13:20-21

May 27

"The hour comes, and now is, when the true worshipers will worship the Father in spirit and truth, for the Father seeks such to be His worshipers." John 4:23

Worship is a controversial topic within the church. And it's one of the topics within churches that has the most varying of opinions. Some churches stick with a hymnal and others use more contemporary worship styles and sets.

But here's the thing I've learned about worship: it has very little to do with music and everything to do with your heart! There is a specific place and time in a church service structure that we put music, but it's not always worship.

God is seeking true worshipers who worship Him with all of themselves. Their lives. Their resources. Their time. Their bodies. *All* they can give in true worship from a heart's desire to love.

And as much as I love music, to sing and play guitar, it's not about my gifts in music. No, true worship comes from my heart, for it's there that my treasure lies.

So I encourage you to worship from your heart! All you have to give in that moment, let it come from your heart.

Come before Him with awe of who He is and what amazing works He's done for you. Come before Him in humility of the amazing gifts of grace and victory on the cross He gave for you. Come before Him with joy and all the love you can pour into Him, because that's how much (and abundantly more) He has for you!

Give back to the Father in thanksgiving and praise and because He is worthy of our worship and praise.

Dig deeper: John 4:1-42

Laura Watson

154

May 28

"For each tree is known by its own fruit..." Luke 6:44

An apple tree can say all it wants: "I'm an orange tree!" But it'll still be an apple tree. How do we know? Because it produces apples, not oranges. A mango tree can try its hardest to be a cherry tree, but it'll still only produce mangos.

In this passage in Luke, Jesus is using fruit trees to teach us about what's in peoples' hearts:

"For there is no good tree that produces rotten fruit; nor again a rotten tree that produces good fruit. For each tree is known by its own fruit. For people don't gather figs from thorns, nor do they gather grapes from a bramble bush. The good man out of the good treasure of his heart brings out that which is good. And the evil man out of the evil treasure of his heart brings out that which is evil, for out of the abundance of the heart, his mouth speaks." (Luke 6:43-45)

In Galatians 5:16-24, Paul lists the fruits of both walking by the Holy Spirit and walking by our own flesh, or natural desires. These Fruits of the Spirit, as we call them, are the basic level of how a follower of Jesus is *"known by its own fruit."*

Love, God's kind of love. *Joy*, rooted in God's life. *Peace*, the wonderful shalom of God. *Patience*, restfulness in God's timing and ways. *Kindness*, outward expression of God's love. *Goodness*, right actions. *Gentleness*, done with grace and a servant heart. *Faithfulness*, consistent in all these fruits. *Self-Control*, under the command of my spirit and the Holy Spirit, not my sinful nature.

While it's possible for us to wrestle these fruits into our lives on our own occasionally, that's not what being a child of God means. We're to be filled with the Holy Spirit so He works these fruits out in us and through us daily.

Lord, help us! We need You, Holy Spirit. Please have Your way in me today so I can demonstrate Your good fruits to those around me.

Dig deeper: *Matthew 7:15-20; John 15:1-16; Galatians 5:16-26*

May 29

"I heard every created thing which is in heaven, on the earth, un-der the earth, on the sea, and everything in them, saying, 'To Him who sits on the throne, and to the Lamb be the blessing, the honor, the glory, and the dominion, forever and ever! Amen!' " Revelation 5:13

Have you read C.S. Lewis's *Chronicles of Narnia*? One of the unique things about Narnia is the talking animals. And if you've ever had a pet I'm sure you've thought more than once, "I wish I knew what my dog (or cat or whatever) is thinking right now! I wish he could talk to me!"

All created things testify of God's wisdom and glory just by being what He created them to be. But according to this verse in Revelation 5, the animals also talk to Him! I think John was wit-nessing something that goes on around God's throne all the time.

They talk to their Creator and give Him the glory He deserves. And not just the animals, but every created thing. Can you imag-ine the stars...planets...volcanoes...rivers...giant redwoods...wild-flowers...rocks of all kinds—all worshiping God?

Jesus hinted at this when Israel's religious leaders wanted Him to stop the people from giving Him glory. He said, *"I tell you that if these were silent, the stones would cry out."* (Luke 19:29-40)

Don't let the animals and other created things be the only ones that give God glory! As a son or daughter of the Father, you can worship Him every day of your life. It doesn't have to be in church. Worship gatherings are amazing, but our worship to Him can be personal and intimate and alone, too. Sometimes it can just be a few words of thanks and praise.

You can read some of the Bible's wonderful prayers and wor-ship to God in the Psalms or some of the New Testament books. And you can use your own words to give Him glory. When you do that, you join all of creation!

Dig deeper: *Psalm 150; Ephesians 3:14-21; Revelation 4*

May 30

"The righteous shall flourish like the palm tree. He will grow like a cedar in Lebanon. They are planted in Yahweh's house. They will flourish in our God's courts." Psalm 92:12-13

Have you noticed the Bible is full of comparisons with nature? God surrounded us with created things that tell us about Himself. They're a picture of how things work in His kingdom.

In these two verses, the song writer talks about two types of trees he's very familiar with—palms and cedars. The Hebrew word used here for palm tree is *tamar*, which can specifically mean the date palm, the tree that produces dates.

I've had the pleasure of eating fresh dates in Israel, and seeing orchards full of date palms near the Dead Sea and throughout the dry Jordan River valley. Date palms have been central to life there for thousands of years.

"The cedars of Lebanon were the most famous trees in all of antiquity" says an article on *israel-a-history-of.com*. "They defined the economy of ancient Lebanon."

These Lebanon cedars can live for hundreds of years, grow to about 100 feet tall and develop massive trunks. In ancient times they were prized for their lumber. Solomon used them to build his temple.

So here in Psalm 92 the righteous are compared to the date palm and the Lebanon cedar—the two most important and valuable trees in the region. The Hebrew word translated *righteous* is *tsaddiq*. It means blameless, innocent, righteous, just.

And why do these kinds of people flourish and grow like fruitful date palms and valuable cedars? It's in verse 13: *"They are planted in Yahweh's house. They will flourish in our God's courts."*

The word for planted is *shathal*, which means to transplant. What a beautiful picture of our salvation through Jesus. He digs us up from our old life and transplants us into God's house—His life. When He does that and when we choose to live in His ways as the righteous, we'll flourish and grow in that kingdom soil.

Dig deeper: *1 Kings 6; Ezekiel 47:6-12*

May 31

"Let's draw near with a true heart in fullness of faith, having our hearts sprinkled from an evil conscience, and having our body washed with pure water." Hebrews 10:22

I oversee a company that does guided kayak camping trips on Lake Superior. Most of our trips are 3-7 days long. I always try to connect with the guides as they get back from the trip to find out how it went.

As the trip ends, there's a flurry of activity with putting things away, but there is always a great desire to *take a Shower*! There is this amalgamation of campfire smoke (it smelled good when cooking over it, but not now), sunscreen, DEET, neoprene and natural body oils that combine to give a distinctive aroma.

If you've been out in the wilderness for any length of time, you know what I mean! Taking a shower is a high priority. It's times like these when showers never felt so good!

Aren't we glad for such simple pleasures of life!

Realize also, there's a wonderful, refreshing spiritual shower that washes away the grime, odors and stench caused by sin. Because of the sacrifice Jesus made for us on the cross, we're cleaned up and purified, able to be in the intimate, close fellowship with God the Father.

"Having therefore, brothers, boldness to enter into the holy place by the blood of Jesus, by the way which He dedicated for us, a new and living way, through the veil, that is to say, His flesh, and having a great priest over God's house, let's draw near with a true heart in fullness of faith, having our hearts sprinkled from an evil conscience, and having our body washed with pure water, let's hold fast the confession of our hope without wavering; for He who promised is faithful." (Hebrews 10:19-23)

Let Jesus cleanse! Take the shower for soul and spirit. Be free from guilt and shame. Be close to God!

Dig deeper: *Compare Leviticus 16 and Hebrews 9-10*

Neal Schroeter

June

S.BRODIN

June 1

"[Love] bears all things, believes all things, hopes all things, and endures all things." 1 Corinthians 13:7

One of the very best ways to be tested in and live out this verse is with other people in the wilderness!

God has a way of using wilderness experiences in our lives. Not what we sometimes refer to as a "wilderness experience" (symbolism for a hard time), but actual wilderness. He can use them for many different things in our life. This is especially true in very challenging and unexpected situations.

I was on a canoe trip in the Boundary Waters not too many years ago with three other women, all friends I knew well. Two of us were in our early 50s and the other two in their mid-20s. What we thought would be a somewhat easy trip included, as it turned out, 24 of the hardest hours most of us had ever experienced physically.

After it was over and we were looking back on it and laughing, one of the things that stood out to me the most was how selfless those 20-something ladies were. They were just as miserable and just as discouraged...but they both did far above and beyond their share to help us older ladies. They carried more, they carried it more often, they came back to help when they reached the end of the portage first—which was most of the time.

It was a beautiful example of, especially, bearing all things... enduring all things for the sake of others. I'll never forget it.

This is the kind of love the Father offers us from Himself. A love that bears with us, believes in us, hopes the best about us and endures all our mistakes and rebellions. It's also the kind of love He asks us to show to others.

Sometimes that's easy and many times it's not. But He doesn't expect us to strive to love others this way on our own. We're able to love this way when we have the Holy Spirit living in us. He loves others through us.

Dig deeper: *1 Corinthians 13*

160

June 2

"God blessed the seventh day, and made it holy, because He rested in it from all His work of creation which He had done." Genesis 2:3

For six days God created. He spoke our world into existence one system at a time. He created and then filled the earth with all the wonder we see around us. He created the expanse we see in the night skies above us. Then He rested.

The Hebrew word translated here *"made it holy"* is *qadash*. It means to be set apart or consecrated.

God set apart a day for rest. He feels so strongly about keeping a rhythm of rest in our lives that many generations later when He gave Moses the law, a day of rest was an essential part of it.

It was called *shabbat*, or as translated in English, *sabbath*. A 24-hour period each week where His people were called to focus on Him instead of our work.

Our modern culture—even the Church—has pretty much obliterated any sense of a weekly rhythm of rest. And it's been slowly wrecking our lives.

When God rested after He created everything we see, it wasn't because He was tired! He doesn't need rest. He set aside a day of rest for us, because He knows *we* need it. He was setting an example for us.

A secular website, *Inc.com*, writes: "A Day of Rest: 12 Scientific Reasons it Works." The article says that among the benefits of a weekly sabbath are: reduced stress, a chance to be physically active, reduced inflammation and risk of heart disease, stronger immune system, better sleep, years added to your life, restored mental energy, more creativity, and better focus and productivity the rest of the week.

Sounds pretty good, doesn't it?

Our good, good Father knows what He's doing. Since He made each one of us He knows what's best for us. He knows how our integrated body/mind/soul/spirit thrives.

How faithful are you about keeping a weekly rhythm of rest? Something to think about.

Dig deeper: Psalm 23; Matthew 11:28-29; Psalm 127:1-2

June 3

"He will bless those who fear Yahweh, both small and great. May Yahweh increase you more and more, you and your children. Blessed are you by Yahweh, who made heaven and earth." Psalm 115:13-15

Throughout the Bible, especially in the psalms, writers continually remind us that Yahweh (the Hebrew's name for God) is the Maker, the Creator of heaven and earth. It's not just the first couple chapters of Genesis that claim this—it's a golden thread through all of Scripture.

In these verses, and in all of Psalm 115, the writer bases his confidence on God's ability to bless people on this: that as Maker of heaven and earth, God has both power and authority to bless whom He will. As verse 3 says, *"Our God is in the heavens. He does whatever He pleases."*

The writer contrasts that to idols, the gods made by people:

"Their idols are silver and gold, the work of men's hands. They have mouths, but they don't speak. They have eyes, but they don't see. They have ears, but they don't hear. They have noses, but they don't smell. They have hands, but they don't feel. They have feet, but they don't walk, neither do they speak through their throat." (verses 4-7)

Followers of Yahweh through the ages have known Him through many ways: His voice, His actions, His written word, His prophets. He speaks, sees, listens and acts. He sent Jesus in human form to show us even more what the Father is like. *"He who has seen Me has seen the Father,"* He said (John 14:9).

This God who made heaven and earth—as we're so often reminded not just in His word but by looking around us in nature—is ready to bless those who fear (reverence) Him, love Him and walk in His ways (obey Him).

I don't know about you, but I want His blessing! And we'll bless Him back. *"We will bless Yah* [God], *from this time forward and forever more. Praise Yah!"* (verse 18)

Dig deeper: *Psalm 115*

June 4

"Wherein you greatly rejoice, though now for a little while, if need be, you have been grieved in various trials, that the proof of your faith, which is more precious than gold that perishes even though it is tested by fire..." 1 Peter 1:6-7

There's something very special about a campfire. I love staring into the fire in silent contemplation. Fire is a special gift—but not always a welcome gift.

The gift of fire is used to purify precious metals. The hot furnace melts the rock and separates the impurities from the precious gold, silver or iron. So are the fires of life that we must struggle through and find a greater joy on the other side.

A forest fire is a very destructive force. As it rages out of control it seems to destroy almost everything it its path. In the boreal forest of the north woods, though, there's one thing that it doesn't destroy—the seeds of the Jack pine. As a matter of fact, without the fire, there would be no Jack pine.

The tightly sealed cone preserves the Jack pine seed until the day of fire. The fire melts the resin that's sealed the cone and releases the seeds for germination. This amazing tree is one of the fastest to grow and produce seed. Its fruitfulness and toughness can be largely attributed to fire.

No one wants to sign up to go through difficulties in life. Sometimes we bring on our own trouble by poor choices. And sometimes life just happens and the fire is turned up.

Either way, Peter encourages us with an understanding that fire is a gift just as various trials are a gift—to test our faith.

The testing of our faith as we go through the fire is the pathway to fruitfulness, to deepen and strengthen our roots in Him. Though we may not appreciate or see the purpose of a fiery trial at the time, looking back we can rejoice in God's faithfulness in helping us find a purer faith on the other side.

Dig deeper: *Isaiah 43:2; 1 Corinthians 3:11-13; 1 Peter 5:6-10*

Brian Rupe

June 5

"Consider the lilies of the field, how they grow. They don't toil, neither do they spin, yet I tell you that even Solomon in all his glory was not dressed like one of these." Matthew 6:28-29

We know God delights in beauty. It's so evident in the world around us, and particularly in the flowers—*the lilies of the field.*

Our Creator spread them all over the world, in all climates and conditions, shapes, sizes and colors. None of them give their beauty a thought...they just *are.* In His famous Sermon on the Mount, Jesus uses the flowers as an example for us that we can trust in our Father's care.

Even Solomon, the wealthiest man in the world of his day, couldn't compete with the beauty of the wildflowers that just *are.* Not only is their beauty given to them without toil, they reproduce themselves so that beauty is passed on to every succeeding generation of flower—without a thought or care involved.

Just as the flowers are given their beauty from God, so are we. And while outward beauty is part of God's design and is good, it isn't the most important type of beauty in His Kingdom. Physical beauty is often vain, prideful, self-focused. What kind of beauty is on the inside?

Proverbs 31:30 says: *"Charm is deceitful, and beauty is vain; but a woman who fears Yahweh, she shall be praised."*

Our inner beauty—for both women and men—is more important to God than the outward beauty most people focus on. And what He sees the most is how our heart is positioned before Him. Do we "fear" Him? Reverence Him? Honor Him through our trust and obedience?

That kind of beauty—the fear of the Lord—*"is your treasure."* (Isaiah 33:6). The things that make for inner beauty are all part of God's Kingdom—righteousness, peace, joy, kindness, goodness, self-control, gentleness. Does that sound familiar? They're the Fruits of the Spirit listed in Galatians 5.

Consider the lilies...and then consider your own heart.

Dig deeper: *Psalm 112; Matthew 6:24-34; Galatians 5:16-25*

June 6

"Pray for us: for we are persuaded that we have a good conscience desiring to live honorably in all things." Hebrews 13:18

I don't know about you, but this scripture is a stretch for me. I am sure I desire to live this way, but I fall so often. Being sure about a clear conscience is not in my ability. Sometimes I can hardly keep up and my soul overtakes my Spirit.

We just returned from a trip into the Boundary Waters. It was a delight to get away from the pressure and duties of everyday life. One of our favorite places is a waterfall between two lakes that has a "jacuzzi" in the middle of the falls. It's so refreshing to sit under the falls and let it splash all over. It's a deep cleansing in the midst of camping dirt and outdoor life.

The surety of our clean conscience is based on faith and faith alone. Not works! The all-sufficient blood of Christ cleanses us moment by moment. Jesus does not offer us a trickle of forgiveness—He gives us a waterfall of mercy and cleansing. Far more than we will ever need in our entire lifetime.

Using our own standards of measure, seeking to establish our own righteousness, the pure and complete work of the cross is not enough. We need to learn to use the Lord's standards, and accept the righteousness He offers to us freely.

Based on the evidence of the perfect and continual work of the cross *"we are persuaded that we have a good conscience,"* and that even our desires can be cleansed *"to live honorably in all things."* By faith we can *"call the things that are not as though they were."* (Romans 4:17)

The mystery of the faith we participate in is profound. Yet by the help of the Holy Spirit we not only understand this, we live it.

Dig deeper: *Colossians 1*

Tasse Swanson

165

June 7

"You make him ruler over the works of Your hands; You have put all things under his feet..." Psalm 8:6

The "him" the psalmist is talking about here is man...mankind, in Hebrew, *adam*. God, the Creator of heaven and earth, has made us—people—to rule over His creation.

The Hebrew word translated *to rule* is *mashal*, which means: to rule, have dominion, reign, to have charge over, to have authority. When it says *"You have put all things under his feet"* the Hebrew word is *tachath*—underneath or below.

This idea of earthly dominion is also found in Genesis 1:26—" *God said, 'Let's make man in our image, after our likeness. Let them have dominion over the fish of the sea, and over the birds of the sky, and over the livestock, and over all the earth...' "*

Clearly, God differentiates people from the rest of creation. That's part of our Biblical worldview. People were His crowning achievement in His creation process. *You* are part of His crowning achievement.

How different from scientific naturalism that teaches the human race evolved like everything else, from simple organisms to who we are today. No different from any other species. Nothing special. Certainly nothing that deserves special treatment. Just another organism.

These opposite worldviews lead to opposite conclusions... opposite end points in our society. The Biblical view says people are created in God's image by Him, and therefore each one has intrinsic (built-it) value. Naturalism says people are the product of random chance with no more value than a one-celled organism or even a grain of sand.

Which of these do you believe? Why? How does it affect how you see yourself? How you see others?

Dig deeper: *Genesis 2; Psalm 139*

June 8

"The earth is Yahweh's, with its fullness; the world, and those who dwell in it." Psalm 24:1

If we need a reason to care for the planet we live on and the people who surround us, this is it. It all is the Lord's. Why is it His? Verse 2 goes on to say, *"For He founded it on the seas and established it on the floods."*

After He created it all, He gave dominion of it over to the people He created—but didn't relinquish His rule over it. Our task is as managers or stewards for Him (Genesis 1:28, Psalm 8:6-8). What that management looks like can vary widely.

Today we'll look at the second half of Psalm 24:1—*"those who dwell in it." Those* are people. Human beings. From the tiniest to the oldest among us, each person was created by a loving Father for purpose. Especially for relationship with Him.

Unfortunately, through the centuries people have been more interested in *not* caring for each other. Sin has devastated relationships more than any other factor. It's the reason behind slavery, abuse of every kind, abortion, crime, murder, war...you name it.

But God's Kingdom is all about redemption. Our Father wants to redeem people's relationship with Him and with other people.

Lots of people who love nature—especially animals—have a hard time with other people. So they focus on loving their animals, protecting animals and helping animals. And that's great—animals are part of God's creation and we need to care for them. But people are God's highest concern. Only people have been created in God's image, and are crowned with His glory (Psalm 8:5).

Ask the Lord today who He wants you to care for, specifically. It can be someone you know, or someone who serves you at a store or restaurant. Or maybe it's a group of people who are suffering somehow—either across town or across the world.

Those who dwell in the world—all of them—are made in God's image and are loved by Him. Who can Jesus love through you today?

Dig deeper: John 13:31-35; 1 Corinthians 13; 1 John 4:4-21

June 9

"You will show me the path of life. In Your presence is fullness of joy. In Your right hand there are pleasures forevermore." Psalm 16:11

Adventure is a familiar word for nature enthusiasts. The pursuit of the outdoors comes with risks and challenges.

Daily life is an adventure, too. It takes courage to hope and dream, just as it takes courage to spend time in harsh natural elements and wilderness areas where risk is increased.

The last few years I've had a series of experiences where I thought I was on the right path following God's leading and stepping out in obedience. I thought the timing was right and God had led me to that point.

Then at the last moment, those doors seemed to slam closed with no warning or explanation. Has this ever happened to you? It was disorienting. I was blindsided by these changes in direction. These were good things—ministry opportunities and job changes.

I felt lost. Adrift in a sea of confusion. Unable to trust God or myself. This resulted in a timidity towards life and decision making. Could I really hear God's voice in my life? Could I dream about my future? Hopelessness and apathy crept in. Have you ever felt this way?

I heard the Holy Spirit asking me to keep taking chances, and not shut down emotionally to potential change. I felt God encourage me to stay present and continue to be a participant in the journey. In this, I heard the word *venture*.

As I thought about what that word means, I heard God say, "If you'll have the faith to venture, I'll add Myself to your story and it'll become an ad-venture."

Where do you feel God is asking you to open your heart to possibilities, or knock on a door to a potential opportunity? Have you shut down your heart to dreams because you felt like rejection or failure would be too painful? How can you venture today and let God add Himself to create adventure?

Dig Deeper: *Isaiah 58:11; Psalm 32:8; Proverbs 3:5-6*

Emilie O'Connor

June 10

"I have no greater joy than this: to hear about my children walking in truth." 3 John 4

We had just finished a four-day/three-night kayak camping trip in the Apostle Islands—a National Seashore off the coast of Wisconsin in Lake Superior. We were blessed with great weather and an amazing experience due in large part to the knowledge and experience of our lead guide, the co-owner of the outfitter we went with.

She told us of a recent tragedy, though, when a couple friends attempted a crossing without that wisdom. They were in white-water kayaks instead of sea kayaks. They weren't wearing wet-suits as protection against the frigid waters. They didn't have a radio to call for help. When they encountered waves and wind, they capsized and were taken by hypothermia before a rescue crew could get to them.

Tragedies like this are rare, but they happen. The saddest part? They usually don't have to happen. When people set out on the lake with the right kayak, the right safety gear and in the right conditions they can have a wonderful time like we did. When they "walk in truth" about what's needed to kayak on Lake Superior safely.

Walking in truth is even more important in this journey of life. What we believe dramatically affects our choices, our thought life, our mental health, our physical health. And eventually, what we believe affects our eternal destiny.

As with sea kayaking on Lake Superior, some people know the truth and walk in it. Some people know the truth but don't bother with it. Others are ignorant of the truth and must suffer the consequences if they won't heed the warnings. So it is with life.

Why does John, this disciple Jesus loved so much, say his greatest joy is when his "children" (those he's led to faith and discipled) walk in truth? Because he knows their eternal destiny depends on it.

What's your attitude towards truth? Are you walking in what you say you believe? Think about that today.

Dig deeper: Psalm 86:11; John 8:31-32; Galatians 5:16-25

June 11

"...and to know Christ's love which surpasses knowledge, that you may be filled with all the fullness of God." Ephesians 3:19

What is God's fullness? One piece of His fullness is beauty. You can see that by looking around you. It's why we love being in nature, in wilderness, next to a waterfall, in the mountains. Flowers, trees, the animal kingdom, water, canyons, plains—there's beauty in nature everywhere we look.

God created our world, our universe with astounding beauty, and then created us to be able to appreciate that beauty. It fills us up. It gives us life. It gives us enjoyment, satisfaction, peace, hope.

As I was meditating on this idea of beauty, it occurred to me that the presence or absence of beauty has a lot to do with this:

"The mind of the flesh is death, but the mind of the Spirit is life and peace." (Romans 8:6)

Where people are living under a spirit of death, heaviness, crime, oppression, destruction, hate, selfishness—do we see outward beauty as a result? Not so much. There's very little color or beauty in neighborhoods, cities and societies that are under oppression. Outward beauty is seen in areas where people can live with freedom, purpose and hope.

When we set our mind on *"the flesh"*—or the things of this world—we get the fruit of the flesh, which is Satan's domain. He only comes to steal, kill and destroy (John 10:10). When we set our mind on the Spirit, we get the fruit of the Spirit as well as beauty and other parts of God's character.

To be filled up with God's kind of beauty starts on the inside, and then overflows and splashes over to the outside. Where can His beauty splash over in your life today?

If you haven't experienced much beauty lately, do you know and embrace the wonderful love, acceptance and forgiveness of Jesus? It starts there. Then you'll be filled with all the fullness of God, including His beauty.

Dig deeper: Ephesians 3:14-21; Psalm 27

June 12

"For we have become partakers of Christ, if we hold the beginning of our confidence firm to the end." Hebrews 3:14

What does this mean: *"hold the beginning of our confidence"*? Our confidence in what? As the rest of this chapter of Hebrews talks about, our confidence and belief in Jesus as God's promised Messiah.

We're to hold this confidence *"firm to the end."* The word translated *firm* is, in the original Greek, *bebaios*. It means secure, firm, to walk where it's solid, secure and stable footing that can be trusted to give full support.

Have you ever walked through the Upper Geyser Basin in Yellowstone? If you've been there, you'll remember the boardwalks criss-crossing the area. The signs and brochures all warn us to stay on those boardwalks because much of the ground around the geysers and hot springs is unstable.

To step off and walk around on that unstable ground would put you at risk of the ground collapsing under you. Not a pleasant prospect when some of the geyser temperatures reach over 400° F!

So we walk where it's solid. Someone has already done the hard work of placing the boardwalk throughout the geyser areas for us to walk on.

So it is with our faith in Jesus. When we walk where it's solid, we become partakers (partners) with Him. Where is it solid? In His word, the Bible. In God's revelation in the Old Testament...in Jesus' words and His followers words in the New Testament.

God's character is solid, so we walk believing in His faithfulness, love, mercy, grace, justice, power and wisdom. That's solid ground. When we walk on the boardwalk of His character, even when our emotions and circumstances tell us different (the unstable ground around us), we're holding our confidence firm.

The next verse in this chapter quotes Psalm 95: *"Today if you will hear His voice, don't harden your hearts..."* Instead, hold firm your confidence in Him.

Dig deeper: *Hebrews 13*

June 13

"Be imitators of me, even as I also am of Christ." 1 Corinthians 11:1

My favorite camp activity is *Diamond In the Rough*. In this game, participants have to discover a pre-set pattern by stepping on wooden discs arranged in order. No talking is allowed. Once you make a mistake you go to the end of the line and wait your turn. By the end of the game, each one is able to complete the pattern without mistake.

When we debrief, we ask if they could have done it by taking a look at the course on paper: No. We also ask if anyone did it with no error: No. What do we learn from this? We learn how important it is to follow in footsteps.

The common saying is that great people who have gone before us leave "big shoes to fill," and trying to fill those shoes can be overwhelming. My point is that as disciples of Christ, our calling is not to fill big shoes, but to follow in footsteps. To continue on the journey of faith set by those who walked before us in the footsteps of Christ.

In our ministry, we are so blessed by great models and leaders who faithfully and boldly stepped out in faith and opened a path of obedience to the gospel. They served those in need and, not least, have ensured the calling is passed on, impacting generations. Mistakes and errors are to be used for learning and improving, not for condemnation.

Some shoes are too big to fill. But their footsteps are an invitation to persevere, to invest and to trust that God will provide.

Dig deeper: John 8:3-11; Hebrews 11 and Hebrews 12:1-2

Emil Toader

June 14

"...whoever drinks of the water that I will give him will never thirst again; but the water that I will give him will become in him a well of water springing up to eternal life." John 4:14

These are Jesus' words to a Samaritan woman He met at a public well. He knew she had been trying all her life to fulfill her deep soul thirst with things that couldn't quench that thirst.

What is the water Jesus gives? It's Himself! His presence through the Holy Spirit. The Bible compares that presence to a couple different things in nature, one being water, as here.

Isn't it interesting that when God designed the earth and every living thing on it, He designed it to be so water-dependent? This is especially true for us humans. We can live a long time without some things, but only a handful of days without water.

That's a physical picture of what it's like for us spiritually, too. We're designed to exist on the living water Jesus talks about—Himself. His presence is as vital to our spiritual life as water is to our natural life.

The amazing thing about the water He gives is it isn't just temporary, but it'll *"become in him a well of water springing up to eternal life."* The Greek word translated *well* in this verse is *pégé*. It means a natural spring or fountain. Just as these springs and fountains produce a continuous flow of water, so when we drink the water Jesus gives, He supplies a continuous flow of His living water in us.

That living water *"springs up to eternal life"* in anyone who receives it...and it flows out of us to those around us.

The more steady the flow in you, the more it splashes over to those around you.

And just as natural springs are dependent on rainfall, so the spring of living water in us is dependent on the life of God in us. Let's nurture that life...care for it daily through talking to Him, listening to Him and reading His words in the Bible.

Dig deeper: John 4:1-32

June 15

"After it a voice roars. He thunders with the voice of His majesty. He doesn't hold back anything when His voice is heard." Job 37:4

How does God speak? Does the fact that we can explain how something happens take away from how wonderful and majestic it is?

After choosing to follow Jesus at the age of 15, I went to university to study immunology. I learned an incredible amount of science, and my brain was trained to understand things by logical, deductive reasoning about explainable things. I signed up to go on a mission trip teaching Bible study methods to university students in Zambia in my final year, and it was a life changing experience in many ways.

One of the ways I'll never forget was as we gathered on campus ready for door-to-door evangelism, praying in a circle in the main open space. We asked God to bless us, empower us with courage and strength. In the middle of one of the students' prayers, we heard a huge crack of thunder in the distance. We looked up at a blood-orange sky as a white spear thrust down to the earth. The Africans in the circle then dispersed to go out and do their evangelistic work. They didn't even say "Amen"!

I asked one of them in my group what was happening. Why had the prayer ended so abruptly? He said "God answered. So we knew we were done praying."

I saw in that moment how little credit I had given to God, and the arrogance with which I approached the wonder of His works. As if, because I can explain the steps that lead to a thunder clap, it's less valuable as the voice of God speaking and encouraging with His power.

How is God trying to speak to you today? How will you hear His "Yes and Amen"? I encourage you to look, listen, feel, taste and smell for the ways that God's glory may be speaking to you.

Dig Deeper: *Psalm 19, John 3:1-13; Colossians 1:16*

Hogan Brimacombe

June 16

"Take firm hold of instruction. Don't let her go. Keep her, for she is your life." Proverbs 4:13

I've been on many canoe trips in the Boundary Waters. While there's lots of gear I wouldn't want to leave home without when going into this vast wilderness, the most important is the map!

The map is our instructions. A Boundary Waters map tells us where every portage is and how long each one is, every campsite, every entrance point. It shows rivers, bays, points, coves. Without the map, it'd be easy to get hopelessly lost.

The only time we're in the Boundary Waters without a map is on day trips we've done many times. We've memorized the route, know what the portages look like. We could even do it in the dark if we had to.

Otherwise, our map is essential. We guard it extremely carefully! We even bring along a spare in another canoe, just in case.

That's how God's word is for our life! It's our instruction manual. When we take firm hold of it, when we don't let it go no matter what, it gives us instructions for everything we need to know about living.

The most important? It tells us who God is. In fact, the Bible is the way God chose to tell us about Himself. We can learn so much about Him through the things He's made—creation. But we learn specifics about Him through His Word.

Why should we take firm hold of God's word?

"Every Scripture is God-breathed and profitable for teaching, for reproof, for correction, and for instruction in righteousness, that each person who belongs to God may be complete, thoroughly equipped for every good work." (2 Timothy 3:16-17)

That's the short version. You'll find as you take firm hold of God's instruction manual—as you read it, chew on it, believe it and work it into your life—it'll give you life.

(If you're new to the Bible or just find it confusing, there are a couple very helpful websites that break it down for you: *BibleProject.com* and *OverviewBible.com*.)

Dig deeper: *Isaiah 55:8-11; Colossians 3:16; Hebrews 4:12*

June 17

"Yahweh prepared a huge fish to swallow up Jonah, and Jonah was in the belly of the fish three days and three nights." Jonah 1:17

The story of Jonah is one of a man who was God's spokesman (a prophet) who didn't like God's assignment for him. So he ran away rather than obey God. How did that turn out for him?

Well, God being good, wouldn't let Jonah go because of His compassion for an evil city. For a city full of sinful, rebellious people. Throughout this short book—just four chapters—we learn how God used several of His created works to convince Jonah to obey Him, and then to correct his attitude towards his enemies.

First, Jonah recognizes God as *"the God of heaven, who has made the sea and the dry land"* (Jonah 1:9). So when we put two-and-two together, it shouldn't surprise us that He's able to use the natural world to fulfill His purposes. Here's how He did that in Jonah's life:

- *"Yahweh sent out a great wind on the sea, and there was a mighty storm..."* (Jonah 1:4)
- *"Yahweh prepared [or appointed] a huge fish to swallow up Jonah, and Jonah was in the belly of the fish three days and three nights."* (Jonah 1:17)
- *"Yahweh God prepared a vine..."* (Jonah 4:6)
- *"But God prepared a worm..."* (Jonah 4:7)
- *"When the sun arose, God prepared a sultry east wind..."* (Jonah 4:8)

God got Jonah's attention alright! Throughout all of this, though, Jonah only obeyed the Lord grudgingly. He wasn't happy about it. He actually hated the people God had sent him to. They were a cruel people, and Israel's deadly enemies. But God kept bringing the focus back to His compassionate heart for all people—even these (Jonah 4:11).

Has the Lord used His created things in your life to get your attention like He did in Jonah's? For me, it was once a sassy horse God used to teach me patience. He can use anything...keep an eye out! How will you respond?

Dig deeper: *The book of Jonah*

June 18

"See the birds of the sky, that they don't sow, neither do they reap, nor gather into barns. Your heavenly Father feeds them. Aren't you of much more value than they?" Matthew 6:26

Jesus is teaching here about the way God's Kingdom works: *"Don't be anxious for your life: what you will eat, or what you will drink...for your heavenly Father knows that you need all these things. But seek first God's Kingdom and His righteousness; and all these things will be given to you as well."* (Matthew 6:25,33)

Although the curse of sin has wreaked havoc in our world, God's Kingdom is still the authority. His Kingdom principles apply to us, His children.

It doesn't mean a carefree life *"carried to the skies on flowery beds of ease"* like the old hymn reminds us. In fact, Jesus warned us we would have trouble here in this world. But the bottom line: *"I have overcome the world!"* He said (John 16:33).

We have several bird feeders at our home, and we love to watch the birds come throughout the day. Each chickadee, blue jay and cardinal is a reminder that the Father knows how to care for His own. When He created them, He already had a world ready to feed them. And aren't you of much more value than they?

The birds remind us of our Father's wise care of us, too. When we turn our back on anxiety and seek Him, His ways and His Kingdom, His promise is that He will provide our basic needs as well as giving us the Kingdom.

We live in a society that's full to the brim of anxiety. As I read recently (I don't remember where): Anxiety is the sign of a different kingdom. It's not God's way. It's not part of His character or His Kingdom. Jesus was never anxious, and through the Holy Spirit, we can have victory over anxiety.

See the birds and take them as a daily reminder of our Father's care and provision!

Dig deeper: *Psalm 23; Matthew 6:24-34; 1 Peter 5:6-7*

June 19

"Blessed is the man [whose]...delight is in Yahweh's law. On His law he meditates day and night. He will be like a tree planted by the streams of water, that produces its fruit in its season, whose leaf also does not wither. Whatever he does shall prosper." Psalm 1:1-3

"Blessed is the man who trusts in Yahweh, and whose confidence is in Yahweh. For he will be as a tree planted by the waters, who spreads out its roots by the river, and will not fear when heat comes, but its leaf will be green, and will not be concerned in the year of drought. It won't cease from yielding fruit." Jeremiah 17:7-8

What a picture of life and health! Deep roots...leaves green and healthy...fruitfulness. This tree continues green and fruitful even in the times of drought, because it's not dependent on the rain, but on the river.

Remember another river? The *river of water of life* in Revelation 22. That river comes from the very throne of God.

When we trust in the Lord, place our confidence in Him, delight on and meditate in His word—we're that tree planted by the river. Jesus said the river of life would even flow out of *us* as we believe in Him.

How do we receive the many benefits of the river? We delight in the Lord's law, His word. We meditate on it continually. It becomes part of our thinking. Our mindset. We trust in Him. Place our confidence in Him.

That kind of thinking and living and choosing places us in the best position possible: right next to the river of life, to be watered continually.

Do you like the fruit that's in your life? Are your leaves green? If not, maybe you need to check and see how close you're planted to the River.

Dig deeper: *John 15:4; Galatians 5:16-24; Colossians 2:9-14*

June 20

"Blessed is the man who['s]...delight is in Yahweh's law. On His law he meditates day and night. He will be like a tree planted by the streams of water, that produces its fruit in its season, whose leaf also does not wither. Whatever he does shall prosper." Psalm 1:1-3

"Blessed is the man who trusts in Yahweh, and whose confidence is in Yahweh. For he will be as a tree planted by the waters, who spreads out its roots by the river, and will not fear when heat comes, but its leaf will be green, and will not be concerned in the year of drought. It won't cease from yielding fruit." Jeremiah 17:7-8

It's wonderful that we can, personally, be just like that green, healthy, fruitful tree. But the real joy is that the fruit we bear— no matter what dry season we're in—is for others, too, when that water continually gives us life.

As Jesus said in Matthew 20:28 that *"even as the Son of Man came not to be served, but to serve and to give..."* so we are given the water of life as we stay planted by the river, so we can serve and give to others for the Kingdom.

Have you ever tried staying green and fruitful when you've taken yourself away from the river? How often have you tried to serve and minister to others when you're dry yourself?

When the heat and drought come to trees that aren't by the river, their leaves *will* wither, they *will* be concerned. They *will* cease bearing fruit. That's just the way it goes if you're not planted by the source of water...the source of life.

Have you moved away from the river, from your source of life? It's not too late! Plant yourself again. The river is still there!

Dig deeper: *Psalm 92:12-14; John 15:4-5; Galatians 2:20*

June 21

"But we all, with unveiled face seeing the glory of the Lord as in a mirror, are transformed..." 2 Corinthians 3:18

The sun is the source of energy for all of life. Without the sun, we have no light and without light we have no life, no growth, nothing. All green plants respond to the sunlight by turning toward the sun and doing everything it can to capture as much sunlight as possible. The surface of a leaf is full of light-absorbing *chloroplasts*. These organelles are designed to take sunlight and, through the process of photosynthesis, turn it into carbohydrates that cause plants to grow and thrive.

The evidence of this sunlight energy stored in the plant is enjoyed by all who gaze into the mystical campfire. There is something so beautiful and gloriously peaceful about a campfire. The campfire light is pleasant to look at. How many have found themselves at the end of a long day hiking or canoeing, sitting with friends around a campfire under a star-lit night and completely losing track of time.

The sun is too bright to look directly into. Not so the light of a campfire, which is, in fact, sunlight energy manifested in a fire log. It's perhaps one of the most pleasant things to gaze upon.

Is not our Maker calling us to be the campfire in the world? We must allow the light of God's love to penetrate our spirit and transform our character. We must allow the light of Christ to burn in us so that the world will see, and believe. How often do we see the glory of God manifest in a fellow believer? We can see the light that emanates from their eyes and the joy that manifests in their smile. They're like a warm campfire on a cool summer night.

Jesus says He is the Light of the world, and He also says *we* are the light of the world. If you put together a bunch of campfire logs in the beauty of fellowship with one another, you have a good and pleasant campfire that draws in those who are hungry for the light of God.

Dig Deeper: *Matthew 5:14-16; John 1:1-5; John 8:12*

Brian Rupe

June 22

"Show me your ways, Yahweh. Teach me Your paths. Guide me in Your truth, and teach me, for You are the God of my salvation..."
Psalm 25:4-5

When we want to learn skills for wilderness adventures, first aid, paddle trips, archery, rock climbing or any other activity, there are a few different ways we can go about it.

We can try it on our own with the "I can do it myself" attitude. We can read up, do a bunch of research, and ask experienced friends for help. We can take courses from certified instructors in whatever skill area we want to learn. And we can develop enough to become a certified instructor ourselves.

Depending on the difficulty level, each of those approaches can work. We don't need to take a course to hike a trail in a local park. But if we want to do a multi-day kayak trip on Lake Superior, taking a skills course or hiring a guide can make a life-or-death difference.

What's the difficulty level? What are the stakes?

In this adventure trip we call *life*, there are stakes, too. If the Bible is correct, the stakes are eternal life or death.

So how do we want to learn God's ways? Do we follow our own thoughts and feelings about them? Do we follow people in our culture we agree with? Maybe our pastor or other "certified instructor"?

Or do we go right to God and His ways? Do we want Him to teach us His paths? To guide us into His truth?

We can still—and *should* still—do this in the context of a spiritual family...a local church, under ministers who've trained and labored to maturity. But each of us also needs to dig into the Lord ourselves through the way He's chosen to communicate with us—the Bible.

He's already shown us His ways, His paths and His truths in His word. Since He's the God of our salvation, not people and certainly not ourselves, those are the words we want guiding us. After all, God is the ultimate Certified Instructor!

Dig deeper: *Psalm 25; Psalm 32:8; John 14:23-31*

June 23

"He will guide the humble in justice. He will teach the humble His way." Psalm 25:9

The great physicist Albert Einstein once said, "The more I learn, the more I realize how much I don't know."

We can easily apply that to adventuring in nature, especially wilderness. It's often the beginners, the uninitiated, who approach the wilderness with a less-than-humble attitude. Sometimes it takes personal experience to learn about the power of an ocean wave or the nearness of a lightning strike or the unalterable effect of gravity near a cliff's edge.

The more experience we have with the power and often unpredictability of the forces of nature, the more we approach it with humility and care, rather than arrogance. Those who come closest to these forces learn to highly respect them. They realize they don't know everything, but still have much to learn.

It's like that with the Lord. We can easily get arrogant, thinking our spiritual life is greater than it is. Thinking we've figured God out. That we even know better than He does, or care more deeply than He does in our life situation, or in the life of someone we love.

This sentence in 1 Peter 5:5 should make us think twice about holding on to that attitude: *"God resists the proud, but gives grace to the humble."*

We can't come near God from a position of pride—He doesn't allow it. He resists it. But when we come to Him in humility we're offered His grace. He guides us in His justice. He teaches us His ways.

The closer we get to the Lord, the more He reveals Himself to us, and the more we realize how much we still don't know about Him. We can agree with the words of Romans 11:33: *"Oh the depth of the riches both of the wisdom and the knowledge of God! How unsearchable are His judgments, and His ways past tracing out!"*

Dig deeper: *Proverbs 11:2, 18:12; 1 Peter 5:5-7; James 4:6-10*

June 24

"He who sits on the throne said, 'Behold, I am making all things new.' " Revelation 21:5

What if you went on a camping trip but weren't allowed to use any of your gear in the way it was designed and intended to be used? Could you make a weatherproof shelter out of your sleeping bag? Could you stir and eat your food with a tent stake? How would you cook your food? How would you stay warm?

Some of the things you would try would be comical or absurd. Most of them would probably be ineffective or inefficient. And some of them would be downright dangerous or destructive.

I explored this idea once with a group of students at our weekly outdoor club meeting. We had been learning about the four-part story that the Bible tells: Creation, Fall, Redemption and Restoration. One week we put on skits about taking a camping trip like this and the results were indeed comical and absurd.

The intention, though, was to illuminate a key part of the Biblical story.

After entertaining each other by repurposing cooking pots and water filters, we read Genesis 3 and talked about the implications of the Fall. Not only does our sin mean that we're separated from God and in need of a savior, but it means that we don't function fully in the way we were designed to.

Our relationships with God, with ourselves, with others, and with the creation are broken and dysfunctional. This plays out in our lives in a thousand different ways. Sometimes we merely recognize the absurdity of this, and other times we experience the pain and destruction these broken relationships can bring. The effects of sin run deep.

We long for those relationships, instead, to bring life and joy and to function as they were intended to. We yearn for all things to be made new. Camping gear we can handle, but we need God to help us function in the ways He designed and intended us to.

Dig deeper: *Genesis 3; Revelation 21:1-7*

William Hayes

June 25

"After these things I looked, and behold, a great multitude, which no man could number, out of every nation and of all tribes, peoples, and languages, standing before the throne and before the Lamb..."
Revelation 7:9

Aspen trees, with their glorious golden autumn leaves and smooth light bark, are North America's most widespread tree. But did you know they're not individual trees? When you see a grove of aspen, the trees are actually a single, connected organism that spreads through the root system.

The oldest known aspen "clone" (where each tree is genetically alike) is in Utah, and is thought to be older than the sequoias or bristlecone pines—thousands of years old! This massive organism covers just over 100 acres and includes an estimated 47,000 trees. *One* organism! *(Sources: National Forest Foundation and Forbes websites)*

The Body of Christ is like that. Paul says in his first letter to the Corinthian church: *"Now you are the body of Christ, and members individually."*

Individuals, but the same body. The same DNA—the blood of Jesus. Imagine what it'll be like one day to stand before God's throne with our brothers and sisters of every nation, every tribe, every language. Our eyes on the Father and on Jesus, the Lamb, worshiping together with one voice.

How much the Father's heart is for us to act like one body now, here on earth! Connected together by our root system across the divide of country borders, across language barriers, across cultural practices, across racial differences.

The church has a hard time staying connected as one organism even within an individual church, and as churches within the same town. It seems hopelessly idealistic to think we could be one Body across countries and cultures!

And yet that was Jesus' final prayer before going to the cross: *"Holy Father, keep them through Your name which You have given Me, that they may be one, even as We are."*

Let's be part of the answer to Jesus' prayer!

Dig Deeper: *Psalm 133; John 17:6-23*

June 26

"God Yahweh, He who created the heavens and stretched them out, He who spread out the earth and that which comes out of it, He who gives breath to its people and spirit to those who walk in it, says..." Isaiah 42:5

Like this verse, there are several times in this part of Isaiah where God, Yahweh, is about to speak through His prophet. As He does, He begins by reminding His people of His lordship over every created thing, including humans. He reminds us of who He is and what He's made.

Here's another one: *"Yahweh, your Redeemer, and He who formed you from the womb says: 'I am Yahweh, who makes all things; who alone stretches out the heavens; who spreads out the earth by Myself'..."* (Isaiah 44:24)

And: *"For Yahweh who created the heavens, the God who formed the earth and made it, who established it and didn't create it a waste, who formed it to be inhabited says: 'I am Yahweh. There is no other.'"* (Isaiah 45:18)

The enemy of our soul has been working tirelessly for centuries to convince people that God isn't needed to explain the origins of the world, animals or people. That message has been repeated so often that most people believe it, even when the evidence doesn't support it.

But this theme of a Creator God who made everything in the heavens and the earth is woven throughout the Bible, from Genesis to Revelation.

It's this that I, personally, always fall back on when I've had doubts about my faith. This amazing, intricate, complex, beautiful world we live in—I just can't believe it came from nothing. It had to have come from, not just an intelligent mind, but a brilliant, genius mind. An incomprehensible mind.

The more science learns about every part of this creation—from the microscopic to the galactic—the more astounding we find it. And this Creator keeps reminding us of it all though His word. There's no one like Him!

Dig deeper: *Genesis 1:1; Nehemiah 9:6; Revelation 4:11*

June 27

"For you, brothers, were called for freedom. Only don't use your freedom for gain to the flesh, but through love be servants to one another." Galatians 5:13

Paragliding means *Freedom* for me.

I feel so free whenever I fly in the upwind over the Alps, past crevasses or at sunset on the rock faces of the Dolomites. On the other hand, flying for me also means taking *responsibility*. Once I have taken off, there is no turning back. I am responsible for my own safety. I need to assess situations and the weather realistically and know my own limits.

Freedom and *responsibility* is a pair of words that also plays a big role for me in my faith. The letter to the Galatians is about exactly that.

We are called into the *Freedom* in God. We are invited to freedom. But how do I experience this freedom? In order to experience freedom while paragliding, I need to hang on to my paraglider. Freedom in God means exactly that: I hang myself onto the love of God. I make myself completely dependent on Him. I let myself completely be carried and loved by Him.

In a healthy faith, enjoying freedom and living responsibly go inseparably together. Paul cannot think of the freedom that God offers us without the responsible lifestyle. For him it is clear: Whoever experiences the enormous freedom that God offers must develop an impact on his lifestyle. Otherwise something does not fit.

But what does it mean, now in the 21st century, to live responsibly? To live responsibly as a Christian means to live in such a way that other people start to ask questions.

Paul mentions two timeless things in the text: To serve one another in love, that is, to love one's neighbor. And secondly, to question oneself again and again: In which spirit do I live and act? To whom and what do I orientate my life? Do I orient my life to what is important to God or to the principle: *Me, myself and I?*

Dig deeper: *Galatians 5*

Timon Weber

June 28

"Where were you when I laid the foundations of the earth?" Job 38:4

Talk about getting put back in your place!

Job was about to get a lesson from the Creator of the universe: *you* are not God. You don't know it all. In fact, you know hardly anything!

"Have you commanded the morning...caused the dawn to know its place?" (verse 12) *"Can you bind the cluster of the Pleiades, or loosen the cords of Orion? Can you lead the constellations out in their season?"* (verses 31-32) *"Can you send out lightnings, that they may go? Do they report to you, 'Here we are'?"* (verse 35).

It's so easy for us to be caught in our limited world of self—either in insignificance or self-importance. We can be overwhelmed by our weaknesses and circumstances. Or we can err on the side of arrogance, thinking we have all the answers.

God reminded Job of his place, and at the same time reminded Job of *His* place. We need to understand both in order to walk with God humbly and yet with boldness. Surrendered to Him and yet stepping out in the authority He's given us.

The most amazing part of it all is that this God who laid the foundations of the earth...who commands the morning and leads the constellations...this God calls us His beloved children! This God longs for fellowship with us.

"Where were you when I laid the foundations of the earth?"

We weren't there. But He was, He is and He will be. We can trust Him even if we can't always understand Him.

He never explained Himself to Job—He just reminded Job of who He is and who Job was. And that was enough for Job to choose worship.

Is it enough for you?

Dig deeper: *Isaiah 14:27; 2 Corinthians 4:7; Ephesians 1:15-23*

June 29

"Count it all joy, my brothers, when you fall into various tempta-
tions, knowing that the testing of your faith produces endurance.
Let endurance have its perfect work, that you may be perfect and
complete, lacking in nothing." James 1:2-4

The Greek word translated *temptations* here can also mean
trials or *hardships*. All of them are a test of our faith. Will we
continue to trust the Father through them and let them bring us
closer to the goal of becoming complete and mature in Jesus?

There are so many personal goals we can have that are set in
the wilderness. We can aim to through-hike the Appalachian
Trail. We can aim to climb the granite cliffs of Yosemite. Or we
can aim for less ambitious goals: getting through a 3-day backpacking trip in Glacier or a weekend canoe trip in the Quetico.

Have you noticed that with outdoor adventure goals we willingly put ourselves through hardship and "trial" to both train for
and take us towards these goals? We can even say we *delight* in
these hardships, and *count it all joy* because the challenge is part
of the adventure, fun and experience. Part of the goal.

Just as we willingly endure hardship to reach our wilderness
goals, so we should willingly endure all the various temptations
and hardships of life that help us reach our goal of becoming
more and more like Jesus!

Isn't it interesting that we invite some hardships into our lives
but resent others? If it's about fun, adventure, challenge—"Yeah,
bring it on!" No problem counting it all joy. But have you ever
resented a hardship in life, something you thought God should've
prevented? *Not* counted it all joy because you didn't choose it, or
it even blindsided you?

Just as hardships on wilderness adventures produce all kinds
of positive growth in us, so life's hardships can produce the same
kind of growth in us...if we let it.

"...the testing of your faith produces endurance," so *"Let endurance*
have its perfect work" in you!

Dig deeper: *Deuteronomy 31:8; John 16:33; Romans 8:35-39*

June 30

"Count it all joy, my brothers, when you fall into various temptations, knowing that the testing of your faith produces endurance. Let endurance have its perfect work, that you may be perfect and complete, lacking in nothing." James 1:2-4

When a climber tackles Half Dome at Yosemite, it's not his or her first climb! He or she has faced scores of previous climbs of various levels, and endured plenty of grueling hardships to get to this level.

Through-hikers of the various continental trails in North America (Appalachian, Continental Divide, North Country, etc.) don't just get up one day and decide to start hiking. They've prepared, studied, trained and equipped themselves to be able to go the distance—a couple thousand miles or more.

Smaller, less ambitious outdoor adventures train us for the big ones. We develop endurance by enduring things. We learn to overcome hardships by overcoming things. It's not theory—it's real life.

That's what James is saying here in his letter. Our goal in Jesus is *teleios* in Greek—completeness, maturity in character. It takes many encounters with hard things to train us and work in us the endurance we need to become that complete, mature believer.

That's how we can experience various temptations, hardships, trials, tests and count it all joy. We know they test our faith, and our faith can't grow unless it's tested. We know tested faith produces endurance. And endurance gets us closer to being made *"perfect and complete, lacking in nothing."*

How can you *"let endurance have its perfect work"* in you today? Can you choose joy in a hard situation you're in right now? Or rather, *will* you choose joy? It's a paradox (contrary to expectation) of the Kingdom—to choose joy when faced with things that aren't that joyful.

The Holy Spirit is right there ready to help us do that: *"The fruit of the Spirit is...joy..."* (Galatians 5:22). Ask Him to develop the fruit of joy in you. It's His joy to do that!

Dig deeper: *Psalm 16:11; Romans 5:3; 1 Peter 4:13*

July

July 1

"Jesus said to them, "My food is to do the will of Him who sent Me and to accomplish His work." John 4:34

All living things have to eat to survive. The higher the quality of food and the more abundant it is, the more a living thing grows and thrives—not just survives. This is true for plant life, for animal life, for bacterial life, for human life.

The quality and abundance of food—or lack of it—also impacts a living thing's ability to reproduce healthy offspring. A healthy, thriving apple tree produces healthy, abundant apples. An apple tree that goes through drought and is rooted in poor soil doesn't produce apples well.

Humans are the only beings in all creation that can "feed" their soul and spirit as well as their body. Just like our body needs high quality food in the right amounts for optimal health, so our mind, emotions and spirit need high quality food in the right amounts for optimal inner health.

What did Jesus mean when He said: *"My food is to do the will of Him who sent Me..."*? It means Jesus was as fulfilled in His inner person by doing God's will as His physical body was fulfilled by eating.

We have to feed our spirit and soul with godly food in order for our spirit and soul to thrive, grow and spill over to others (reproduce).

Have you ever done something you knew was God's will for you, and afterwards were filled with this sense of peace and "right-ness"? That's what Jesus meant—doing God's will does for our spirit and soul what food does for our body. It satisfies us. We're full. It brings health.

Jesus said, *"I am the Bread of Life. Whoever comes to Me will not be hungry, and whoever believes in Me will never be thirsty."* (John 6:35) He wasn't talking about physical hunger and thirst, but spiritual hunger and thirst.

What food are you depending on for the health and growth of your spirit and soul?

Dig deeper: Isaiah 58:6-11; 1 Timothy 6

July 2

"The heavens declare the glory of God. The expanse shows his handiwork." Psalm 19:1

Seeing the beauty of the Lord's creation in nature is one of the most spiritually compelling things we can experience. The majesty of mountains seems to shout that God's character is glorious and magnificent. The power of God is in the roar of waterfalls. Summer forests brimming with a harvest of berries, flowers, and mushrooms remind me that God is our provider. This world was intentionally designed by the omnipotent Creator.

It brings to mind the hymn *For the Beauty of the Earth*:

> *For the beauty of the earth,*
> *For the glory of the skies*
> *For the love which from our birth*
> *Over and around us lies*
> *Lord of all, to Thee we raise*
> *This our hymn of grateful praise*

The hymn writer continues to extol the praises of God for the wonders of creation throughout this entire beautiful song.

God uses His creation to speak to us of His presence and the reality of the spiritual world around us. He paints sunsets every evening. He's so limitless that no two snowflakes are the same. The glory of God's creation is part of what witnesses to us of His existence and character.

Martin Luther is quoted as saying "God writes the Gospel not in the Bible alone, but also on trees, and in the flowers and clouds and stars." Romans 1:20 says: *"For the invisible things of Him since the creation of the world are clearly seen, being perceived through the things that are made, even His everlasting power and divinity; that they may be without excuse."*

Because of nature, we can know that God is real. And through nature we can get to know His character and understand our Creator better. What a blessing, that through the beauty of the world we can grow in intimacy with our Heavenly Father!

Dig Deeper: *Job 38, Psalm 19, Jeremiah 32:17*

Emilie O'Connor

July 3

"Now to Him who is able to keep you from stumbling, and to present you faultless before the presence of His glory in great joy..." Jude 24

In the context of this verse, Jude is warning his readers about false teachers. So when he talks about stumbling, it's not sinning he's referring to so much as it is stumbling over false teaching.

How can we recognize false teaching? The best way is to know what the truth is. The word of God—the Bible—is our most reliable source of truth. It's hard for false teachers to dupe people into believing falsehood when they know the truth. On the flip side, it's easy for false teachers to dupe people who don't read the Bible or know what it says.

It's like trekking through the unknown wilderness with an experienced guide. The more treacherous the environment, the more valuable the guide! The guide knows the conditions, the terrain, the weather patterns and potential hazards.

The more risk involved, the more important the guide is. It's much more important to have an expert guide if your goal is to summit Mount Everest than it is to summit our tallest peak in Minnesota, which is under 3,000 feet. It's more important to have an experienced guide if you want to kayak Lake Superior than to kayak a small local lake in your neighborhood.

The risk involved in knowing the difference between truth and falsehood in teachings about God, Jesus, salvation, the Bible—it's immense. In fact, it's a matter of life and death. It's a matter of where you'll spend eternity.

The Holy Spirit is our great Counselor—our Guide—in this. Jesus said, *"When He, the Spirit of truth, comes, He will guide you into all truth..."* (John 16:13) He'll guide you into truth through the word of God, the Bible. And He can guide you personally through an inner impression, through other people, through circumstances.

Invite Him today to show you if there's anything you've been believing that isn't part of the truth of His Word and character. He's faithful to keep you from stumbling!

Dig deeper: *The book of Jude*

July 4

"He said to all, 'If anyone desires to come after Me, let him deny himself, take up his cross, and follow Me.'" Luke 9:23

Humans are the only beings God created with moral choice.

To the animals He gave instincts. They don't have choice, they follow instincts. Migration, nesting, defending territory, competition for mating, caring or not caring for their young, what they eat, what kind of home or shelter they have. None of it is a matter of choice for them, but of the way they were created and the instinct God put in them.

Not so with us! When God decided to create people *"in Our image"* (Genesis 1:26), that included moral choice. The ability to choose right or wrong thoughts, attitudes and actions. The entire Old Testament is the story of how people chose to follow God or not, and what happened when they did or didn't.

The idea of "sin"—something being wrong, a wrong choice—is very much out of style in our culture now. Oswald Chambers, the author of the classic devotional *My Utmost for His Highest*, explains why:

> *"The disposition of sin (which is the sin nature in each of us) is not immorality or wrong-doing, but...self-realization—I am my own god...my claim to my right to myself."*

The main issue isn't actually sin. The main issue is authority. We've probably all heard a little kid say (and maybe said it ourselves): "You're not the boss of me!!" When we choose our own way instead of obeying the Father, what we're saying to Him is: "You're not the boss of me."

We all like to emphasize the love of God, and rightly so. His nature is love, His character is love. That love is the strongest force in the universe. But along with that love comes the surrender to His authority over our life.

Jesus said it to His disciples many times: *"Let him deny himself...and follow Me"*... *"If you love Me, keep My commandments"* (John 14:15).

Who's the boss of you?

Dig deeper: John 14:21; Luke 9:23-26; 1 John 3:21-22

July 5

The Story of Enoch Part 1

"As an eagle that stirs up her nest..." Deuteronomy 32:11

The fledgling bald eagle was named Enoch. He was an only eaglet and grew up in a large nest carefully prepared by both his mother and father. The nest had been in the family for several years and its size had been added to every year, growing to six feet across and eight feet deep.

As all baby eagles, Enoch really loved his nest and his life. The soft feathers placed for his bed made sleeping a pure delight and the daily menu of sushi, fresh from the Mississippi River, couldn't have tasted better.

Both mom and dad had helped to build his home and sat on him as an egg to keep him warm. He loved looking up into the blue sky watching their amazing soaring flight patterns as they effortlessly circled higher and higher on the warm thermals.

Life could not have been any better until one day it was clear that mom and dad both wanted Enoch to begin to discover the world for himself. You see, life had become too comfortable for Enoch. They knew that in order for him to find success in life, he would need to learn how to fly. They showed up less frequently with meals and Enoch's growling stomach was motivating him to find food on his own.

Have you ever been uncomfortable with your life? Have you ever felt hungry for something but uncertain as to what it was? The stirring of the nest mentioned in Deuteronomy can also refer to helping someone wake up.

The seasons of discontentment can be opportunities to wake up to a new understanding of who God is and who you are as His child. Take advantage of discomfort as a gift. The danger is filling that hunger with things that are harmful.

Go after God and allow Him to satisfy your deepest desire.

Dig deeper: *Psalm 36:5-12; Jeremiah 29:11*

Brian Rupe

July 6

The Story of Enoch Part 2

"Why do you spend money...and your labor for that which doesn't satisfy?" Isaiah 55:2

Our fledgling bald eagle friend, Enoch, had become increasingly hungry and uncomfortable. The sparse meals from mom and dad weren't enough to satisfy his taste buds so he hopped up to the edge of the nest, spread his wings and jumped. Unfortunately, Enoch was not quite ready to fly. Though it was almost his eight-week birthday, he hadn't stretched his wings enough. He hadn't flapped them up and down to strengthen his muscles. He hadn't studied the methods of flying his mother and father had tried to demonstrate for him. He was unprepared for flight.

The result was a long fall to the bottom of the forest and a near-death experience. Fortunately, his spread wings and the soft leaf bed below protected him from major injury. Enoch stood himself up, shook off the dry leaves and began to walk through the forest to find some satisfaction for the hunger he felt deep inside. It was both a sad and comical site to see a nearly-grown eagle walking through the forest. An eagle's taloned feet aren't designed for walking—but for landing on branches and capturing fish. Enoch should've known this but he wasn't thinking straight. So off he went looking for a juicy fish meal in the middle of the forest.

God has designed us in every way—physically, mentally, emotionally and spiritually—for a purpose and a way to live. When we wander from His ways we find ourselves in the wrong habitat, looking for something that's impossible to find. Our natural desire for fulfillment turns into a lust for something that destroys.

God created us to be fully satisfied with Him alone. His home is in our hearts and His unfailing love satisfies our deepest longing. It's easy to blame others or our circumstances for the messes we find ourselves in. It's time to wake up, turn around and take responsibility for our actions. God is ready and willing to feed us the good food and the good drink that truly satisfies.

Dig deeper: John 4:1-42

Brian Rupe

July 7

The Story of Enoch Part 3

"To a hungry soul, every bitter thing is sweet." Proverbs 27:7

Enoch the fledgling eagle continued on his journey through the deep dark woods. As he wandered, he became increasingly hungry and tired. He couldn't find any fish or anything that even resembled fish.

Off in the distance, a gang of turkeys carefully observed Enoch and followed quietly behind. The turkey gang leader, Biff, talked with his fellow turkeys. They decided Enoch must be a misfit turkey who had lost his way and was, perhaps, a little slow with the gobble.

Biff approached Enoch and startled him with a gobbling question: "Who are you and what's your name?" Enoch, though half startled by the strange looking creature, blurted out, "I'm Enoch the eagle and I'm very hungry!" After considerable gobbling discussion the turkeys gave Enoch the happy news—they'd be willing to take him into their gang. They shared with him some of the acorns they'd collected for their evening meal.

Enoch was very hungry. When you're really, really hungry, you'll eat almost anything. Enoch had a very hard time properly breaking the shell, but after much encouragement from his new turkey friends, he managed to consume his very first acorn. It was awful! It tasted nothing like the sweetness of the walleye his mother had brought him. But his hunger was stronger than his senses and he ate several more, ending up with a terrible stomach ache but a full stomach nevertheless.

What are you eating? Healthy food is very satisfying and good for our bodies. Even more important, what is your spirit eating? Where are you going to satisfy your hunger? There are an exorbitant number of turkeys willing and ready to feed garbage to your spirit. Too often we surrender our soul to eating junk food. God wants to fill us with rich milk and spiritual meat from His word. Taste and see that the Lord is good!

Dig deeper: *Psalm 34*

Brian Rupe

July 8

The Story of Enoch Part 4

"Be careful that you don't let anyone rob you through his philosophy and vain deceit..." Colossians 2:8

Enoch's new found "friends" began to question him about his life. He explained his eagle past, his parentage and desire for fish. The turkeys were very troubled. They had never met a turkey so deeply confused. They informed him of his turkey identity, explaining he wasn't an eagle, as there was no such thing as an eagle. There's no such thing as soaring high in the sky or eating fish or growing up in a nest high in a tree. Enoch was pretty sure they were wrong, but it was difficult for him to prove or explain his story.

The next day, Biff, the turkey gang leader began to train Enoch in the ways of turkeys. He showed Enoch how to walk like a turkey, how to talk turkey talk and eat turkey food. All of these turkey behaviors were critical for Enoch to learn if he was going to be a respectable turkey. It was clear to Biff that Enoch had been neglected as a chick and had to learn how to live properly. Enoch needed to be turkeyerized.

Enoch wanted to fit into the gang so he tried his hardest. His feet weren't designed for walking but the turkeys said he must walk in order to find food. His bill wasn't designed for cracking acorns but the turkeys told him he must eat the acorns. Over time Enoch became more and more convinced he must, indeed, be a turkey. Of course, he always knew he would never be a good turkey but he would try his best.

Who are you as a believer in Christ? Christ is in you and you are in Christ. You are created by God and you've been bought with a price. This isn't a fairy tale—it's reality. And yet, there are so many turkeys in this world, dead set on turkeyerizing you. Their false philosophy and deceit bombard us with messages determined to destroy our true identity. Christ in you, the hope of glory!

Dig deeper: Colossians 1

Brian Rupe

July 9

The Story of Enoch Part 5

"...the sheep follow Him, for they know His voice." John 10:4

Many weeks passed in Enoch's life and it seemed the harder he tried to be a good turkey, he was simply not able to succeed. He became more and more discouraged and depressed. One day he decided to go to a turkey bookstore and purchase a best selling self-help book on how to succeed as a turkey. He put all the ideas into practice. It seemed to help a little, but something was still not right.

Biff encouraged him that he was seeing improvement. Enoch was happy to be accepted by the turkey gang and assured Biff he would keep trying his best. Biff explained that trying harder was the key to his future as a great turkey. With Biff's encouragement Enoch went back to the bookstore and bought many new titles: *How to Turkey Trot in 6 Simple Steps*, *How to Influence Others with Great Gobbling* and *How to Fit in With Rich and Famous Turkeys*.

As we continue to follow Enoch on his life journey toward fitting in and being happy as a turkey, it should be painfully clear that Enoch is working hard going in the wrong direction. He's headed for disaster. The story certainly applies to the unbeliever who has never been awakened to the joy of following Christ.

For believers, though, this story is also applicable. All too often we lose our way and drift from listening to the Good Shepherd. Many believers arrive at a comfortable place, partway toward understanding their identity in Christ. But then they camp out and never go further.

Like the children of Israel, they find freedom from some level of slavery. But in the wilderness they neglect to go deeper with God and refuse to hear his voice. They may try hard to be good people but they don't understand that God has a much greater breakthrough for their lives.

Of all the voices to listen to, remember you are God's sheep. You can listen to His voice and press deeper into your true identity as a child of His love.

Dig deeper: *John 10*

Brian Rupe

July 10

The Story of Enoch Part 6

"There is a way which seems right to a man, but in the end it leads to death." Proverbs 16:25

Enoch read all the self-help books and listened to Biff's advice, but something still wasn't right. Every now and then he'd stretch out his wings and feel the power of something he couldn't quite understand.

One day he heard a voice from above hoot down at him. An owl called out to Enoch: "Hey, what are you doing walking around on the ground with your head down?" Enoch explained he was looking for acorns, as this is what a proper turkey eats for lunch. The owl began to laugh so hard he nearly fell out of the tree. Enoch didn't understand what was so funny. The owl apologized for his abrupt response and introduced himself as Amos the Wise.

Amos asked Enoch if he really believed he was a turkey. Enoch exclaimed, "Of course I'm a turkey! That's what my friends told me!" Amos said he had some very good news for Enoch if he was interested in hearing it. He told Enoch he wasn't a turkey but an eagle. He was designed by God to soar in the sky, nest high up in the trees and eat fish from the river.

Now it was Enoch's turn to laugh. This couldn't be the case! He'd invested all his growing up years into learning how to be a turkey! Amos assured him that he was, indeed, an eagle. He advised him to look up in the sky, keep stretching his wings and listen to God's voice.

Sometimes it's difficult to hear the truth. Enoch had been so convinced of his turkey identity that he wasn't yet ready to face a different reality. He knew something wasn't right—he wasn't yet complete—but how could he trust this new voice?

Are you ready for a fresh start? Are you excited about learning something new about God and about yourself? God is ready to share some great news with you today. Are you ready to listen?

Dig deeper: Joel 2:25; Romans 6:4; 2 Corinthians 5:17

Brian Rupe

July 11

The Story of Enoch Part 7

"...the god of this world has blinded the minds of the unbelieving, that the light of the Good News of the glory of Christ...should not dawn on them." 2 Corinthians 4:4

As Amos the Wise flew off into the sky, Enoch knew he had some serious thinking to do. Owls are wise, and this must be a voice to consider. He stretched his wings, looked up at Amos soaring in the sky and felt a sense of joy he hadn't felt before. It was impossible to describe the joy and it came as a surprise, but it felt very good.

Enoch stretched his wings and began to move them up and down. He was surprised to discover they actually lifted him off the ground. He had hopped around with the turkeys in low branches before, but never considered it truly flying. As he tested his wings in a clearing on the edge of the forest, he began to take off along the ground and use his wings in a new way.

Biff, his turkey mentor, had noticed Enoch was not with the gang and went looking for him. This was a common occurrence as Enoch was always slow and falling behind the group. When Biff finally found Enoch at the edge of the woods and saw what he was doing, he let out a loud gobble: "ENOCH, stop that behavior right now! That is NOT how turkeys fly!" Enoch quickly pulled in his wings, plunked to the ground and apologized profusely to his dear leader, Biff. He was sternly scolded for his misbehavior and promised to do better.

Something was happening in Enoch's heart, but the pull of the world was very strong. We must be aware that we live in a world where Satan is the prince. He's established systems and carefully crafted messages to keep us down. Everything Satan touches and influences turns us away from our God-given potential and the intimate relationship God wants us to have with the Holy Spirit. Be aware! Be alert to the prince of this world and his deceptive schemes.

Dig deeper: Matthew 13:19; John 8:44; Ephesians 6:11

Brian Rupe

July 12

The Story of Enoch Part 8

"Therefore, if anyone is in Christ, he is a new creation." 2 Corinthians 5:17

Enoch felt bad that he'd disappointed his dear leader, Biff, but something inside had shifted. A few days passed and, taking Amos's advice, he looked up and saw a beautiful soaring raptor. Even though Enoch believed he was a turkey, his true eagle eye sight had a very good view of this soaring eagle. He looked at the eagle and he looked at himself. He looked again at the eagle and looked again at himself.

That same sense of pure joy once again surprised him. Maybe he was an eagle. Maybe he was meant to soar. He walked back to the forest edge where he had space to practice. He began to exercise his wings. He lifted off the ground and began to move gracefully along the surface. With a few more flaps he turned toward the sun and upward. Enoch thought, "Oh boy, does this feel good!"

Suddenly, he heard the voice of the Biff gobble screaming at him to stop—but it was too late. Enoch felt the warm thermal air lift him higher and higher. He could see the mighty Mississippi River off in the distance. He soared that direction, and to his delight viewed many menu options swimming near the surface. He swooped down, stretched out his talons, grabbed a walleye and gracefully landed in the nearby branch of a dead oak tree.

Enoch was free! He had tasted of the turkey world and found it greatly wanting. He had finally found his way back home where he belonged.

There's an Enoch in all of us. The Enoch of the Bible soared so close to God that the Father invited him to come on up the rest of the way (Genesis 5:24). Even in the midst of difficulties and the storms of life we can find a place of soaring. By the power of the cross we defy the law of sin, death and the ways of this world and discover the law of life and liberty in Christ Jesus.

Dig deeper: *Romans 8*

Brian Rupe

July 13

The Story of Enoch the Eagle

"The thief comes only to steal, kill and destroy. I came that they may have life, and may have it abundantly." John 10:10

Over the west bank of the Mississippi River I spotted Enoch the eagle soaring in small circles a short distance above the shore. Around him were three crows screaming annoying caws and trying to disrupt his flight. I was too far away to notice the fish in his talons, but it would be safe to assume the menacing crows were attempting to steal a tasty morsel.

The crows had a strategy—take turns harassing Enoch until, hopefully, he would give up the fish.

Jesus said, "The thief comes only to steal, kill and destroy." You can be sure the only reason the crows were hanging out with Enoch was to steal his meal. Crows can be a major menace to a bald eagle. They're clever in their ways. And by teaming up on an eagle they often frustrate this mighty bird of prey and steal its provision.

Enoch took off at top speed and I cheered, believing he'd left those crows in a cloud of dust. A few moments later, he flew just above my head as if to show off his superior speed. A lone crow flew as fast as he could, attempting to chase him down. You see, Enoch was winning, but the crows didn't give up.

We must be wise and aware of the enemy's tactics. Satan understands our weaknesses and knows how to steal our life, our joy, even our provision. He's not going to give up. Though the victory is sure in Christ, we have an adversary.

The good news is this adversary can be the very tool to strengthen our wings, motivate us to soar higher and reach the overcoming freedom provided in Christ. Be alert and don't give in to the tormenting crows. Soar higher and receive the abundant life God has for you today.

***Dig deeper:** 1 Peter 5:8-11; Ephesians 6:10-18*

Brian Rupe

July 14

"And when you turn to the right hand, and when you turn to the left, your ears will hear a voice behind you, saying, 'This is the way. Walk in it.' " Isaiah 30:21

Rock cairns are stacks of rocks created by trail maintenance and park staff and used on mountainous trails to show the path. They are guides along the route in places where the trail is difficult and may be easily lost. Navigational cairns can even have messages embedded in them.

I used rock cairns to help guide me to the summit of Cloud Peak in Wyoming, and saw a close connection to how God guides us in daily life.

Often when climbing through the boulder fields, only one cairn was visible. When I got to that one, I could see the next one. This reminded me how God guides us one step at a time. I knew we were going generally in the right direction because I had the topographical map and compass. That's like the Bible. It gives us a heading and points us in the way forward.

But we often lean on specific guidance that aligns with scripture to know where to go next in our life. So cairns are like God's guidance in the day-to-day and throughout seasons. God asks us to have faith in the journey. We can't see every cairn from the start.

During that hike I found myself praying for God to highlight the next cairn as I searched for it. That reminded me of seeking God's guidance when discerning which direction to go next in life. It reminds me of the stories in the Bible where God led His people step by step, and they followed in trust not knowing where exactly the trail would lead, but knowing they were following a good God who would take them to places of peace and promise.

Are you looking for your next step? How can the Bible give you general direction as you seek God's guidance in specific steps?

Dig Deeper: *Psalm 25:4-5; Psalm 119:105; John 16:13*

Emilie O'Connor

July 15

"One thing I have asked of Yahweh, that I will seek after: that I may dwell in Yahweh's house all the days of my life, to see Yahweh's beauty, and to inquire in His temple." Psalm 127:4

We don't have to wait until heaven to see God's beauty—did you know that?

We can look around us every day and see His beauty everywhere. Sure we also see the ugliness of sin, despair and oppression, which is the work of our enemy, Satan. But as poet Sara Teasdale wrote:

"Look for a lovely thing and you will find it.
It is not far—it never will be far."

The beauty of God is evident in the things He created. In this world He gave us to live in.

When you see the deep blue-green of a lake or sea...the glorious reds, oranges, pinks and purples of a sunrise or sunset...the bright greens, deep greens and blazing autumn colors of trees...the myriad of brights displayed by wild flowers.

All of these are on display and represent an aspect of God's beauty. He put Himself in these colors.

When you hear the birds sing...the wind blow through the treetops...a brook trickling over rocks or waves crashing on the shore...rain on a summer night. These sounds all exhibit an aspect of God's beauty.

When you stand on the summit of a mountain to survey peak upon peak around you, that's God's beauty on display. Then look down to see a delicate alpine flower blooming, just a few inches tall. That's God's beauty, too.

The brilliance of a peacock's feathers. The glossy coat and long mane of a horse. The power of a tiger or bear. The grace of a leaping deer. The soaring of an eagle high above. These all display something of the beauty of the God who formed them.

So look for those lovely, beautiful things in the natural world around you. They won't be far. And know you're witnessing the beauty of their Creator.

Dig deeper: *Psalm 104*

July 16

" 'I am the Light of the world. He who follows Me will not walk in darkness, but will have the light of life.' " John 8:12

Wilderness and backcountry areas can be so dark at night. When there's no moon or in overcast skies it's hard to take even a step without a headlamp or flashlight. But turn on that headlamp or flashlight and your path is lit for many feet ahead of you and around you.

The light from your battery-powered gadget pushes back the darkness of the night so you can see where you're going, and not have to stumble along blindly.

That's what it's like following Jesus.

Our world is dark—not with the absence of physical light, but because of spiritual darkness...sin. Things like confusion, depression, anxiety, fear, despair, hatred, bitterness, resentment, rage, selfishness...these produce spiritual darkness around us.

These words of Jesus, that He's *"the Light of the world"* means He pushes back the spiritual darkness around Himself like your headlamp pushes back the physical darkness around you at night in the wilderness.

And when we follow Him, we follow in His light. As we stay close to Him, we stay in His light. Instead of being surrounded by spiritual darkness, we're surrounded by spiritual light. Jesus calls it *"the light of life."*

Things like unconditional love. Inner joy and peace that can't be disturbed by circumstances. Patience and kindness—from Him, through us, to others.

Can you imagine living like that? It's possible by following Jesus close enough to walk in His light. That means when He heads straight out, we head straight out with Him. When He turns left, we turn left. When He turns right, we turn right.

That's following pretty close! And that's the idea. We won't see too far ahead of us, but we can be confident in His leading.

"He who follows Me will not walk in darkness."

Dig deeper: *Psalm 119:97-105*

July 17

"I will bring the third part into the fire, and will refine them as silver is refined, and will test them like gold is tested. They will call on my name, and I will hear them. I will say, 'It is my people;' and they will say, 'Yahweh is my God.' " Zechariah 13:9

Silver and gold aren't inventions of people, they're natural resources. God created them and put them in the ground for people to discover, value and learn to use. The way these precious metals are refined is through heat—intense heat.

The melting point of gold is 1,947.52° F. The melting point of silver is 1,763° F. That's *Hot* with a capital H! Compare that to the boiling point of water, which is just 212° F, yet can cause serious burns on human skin.

So when God speaks through Zechariah here and says he'll refine His people as silver and test them as gold, He's talking about a seriously intense process! He's "turning up the heat."

Another prophet, Malachi, wrote about this process, too: *"He [Yahweh, the Lord] will sit as a refiner and purifier of silver, and He will purify the sons of Levi, and refine them as gold and silver; and they shall offer to Yahweh offerings in righteousness."* (Malachi 3:3)

This refining process can be confusing, inconvenient and downright painful. But the Lord has one goal in mind: Our purification. Our turning to Him and calling Him "Lord." Changing our stubborn, rebellious hearts to be softened and open hearts that respond to Him, love Him, surrender to Him.

It's His love that causes Him to purify us like silver and gold. He's not angry with us...He's after our heart. He knows what'll get our attention and cause us to look to Him.

Have you experienced God's purifying "heat" in your own life? Maybe you're going through it right now. Rather than focus on the heat, turn your gaze to God's purpose—the refining and purifying. Cooperate with Him so your purpose matches His: for you to be more like Jesus.

Dig deeper: *Romans 5:3-5; 2 Corinthians 4:17; 1 Peter 4:19*

July 18

"A cheerful heart makes good medicine, but a crushed spirit dries up the bones." Proverbs 17:22

The way our wise Lord created us is as whole, integrated people. Our mind and emotions are integrated with our physical body in such a way that they affect one another, either for good or ill.

This proverb was written almost 3,000 years ago, way before medical science could prove how accurate it is! And yet, research shows exactly what it says:

"A cheerful heart makes good medicine..." When the Bible talks about our heart, it refers to our mind, will and emotions. So...

A cheerful heart, a grateful and thankful heart, a heart that chooses joy, that chooses a good attitude makes good medicine. Here's what researchers know about joyful, grateful people: they're less stressed (and stress is responsible for up to 90% of what sends us to the doctor!), they have a stronger immune system, better cholesterol levels and lower blood pressure.

That is, indeed, good medicine! *"...but a crushed spirit dries up the bones."*

Bone density is really important for bone health. When bones lose their density, they're more susceptible to fractures. But guess what researchers now know is one factor in bone loss? Depression...a crushed spirit. It literally dries up the bones. Along with a healthy diet and weight-bearing exercise, good mental health is important for bone health.

We are whole organisms, in the broadest sense of the word. In His great wisdom and understanding, the Lord fashioned us so our moral, relational and attitude choices affect our physical body, along with our emotions.

And, knowing this, the Bible is very clear about what choices we're to make in order to live in harmony with how He's created us. These include choices for a cheerful heart: *"Always rejoice...in everything give thanks..."* (1 Thessalonians 5:16-18) *"Rejoice in the Lord always...In nothing be anxious..."* (Philippians 4:4-6).

Dig deeper: *Psalm 100; 1 Corinthians 13; Philippians 4:4-9*

July 19

"Yahweh's voice strikes with flashes of lightning. Yahweh's voice shakes the wilderness..." Psalm 29:7-8

This psalm was written by David, Israel's greatest king. David didn't grow up in a palace, though, but in the fields taking care of his father's sheep. He knew all about wilderness life. He also knew God—Yahweh. In fact, God called David *"a man after My heart."* He had plenty of flaws, but he loved and pursued God his whole life.

It's very likely David was in the wilderness with his sheep while he wrote this psalm, as seven of its nine verses refer to the natural world:

"Yahweh's voice is on the waters. The God of glory thunders, even Yahweh on many waters. Yahweh's voice is powerful. Yahweh's voice is full of majesty. Yahweh's voice breaks the cedars. Yes, Yahweh breaks in pieces the cedars of Lebanon. He makes them also to skip like a calf; Lebanon and Sirion like a young, wild ox. Yahweh's voice strikes with flashes of lightning. Yahweh's voice shakes the wilderness. Yahweh shakes the wilderness of Kadesh. Yahweh's voice makes the deer calve, and strips the forests bare..." (verses 3-9)

These verses talk about God's voice being as powerful as thunder and lightning, as an earthquake (shaking the wilderness). When God speaks, things happen!

This shouldn't surprise us, as way back in Genesis 1 we learn that God used His voice to speak everything we see into existence: *"God said, 'Let there be light,' and there was light."* (verse 3) *"God said, 'Let there be an expanse...' "* (verse 6) *"God said, 'Let the waters under the sky be gathered together to one place, and let the dry land appear...' "* (verse 9) *"God said, 'Let the earth produce living creatures...' "* (verse 24)

God's voice is infinitely powerful. Are you hearing His voice, His words in your life? David ends this 29th psalm like this: *"Yahweh will give strength to his people. Yahweh will bless his people with peace."*

God's voice is power in nature. It's also power and strength in our own lives, ultimately bringing peace.

Dig deeper: *Genesis 1; Psalm 29; Luke 3:21-22*

July 20

"Without faith it is impossible to be well pleasing to Him, for he who comes to God must believe that He exists, and that He is a rewarder of those who seek Him." Hebrews 11:6

There's a temptation to think it isn't a good "Christian" motivation to work for a reward. Don't we teach our children to obey for the sake of the relationship and doing the right thing rather than just trying to get something out of it for themselves?

There's much about our fallen human nature we must be careful not to embrace, like laziness and selfishness. But God seems to expect us to be motivated by rewards. He talks about them a lot.

We serve a God of promises, and He's pleased by our faith. Part of our faith is in who He says He is, and things He's already done for us. But a lot of our hope and faith are in what God's promised to bring about. The entire eleventh chapter of Hebrews is stories of God's people who looked forward to a reward.

What motivates us today? What makes us endure the hard times? Don't we all love the feeling of getting to the overlook at the summit after a long hike? What makes the struggle worth it?

Like our heroes in the *Hall of Faith*, our ultimate reward isn't to be experienced completely in this world, but we do have more now than they did! They weren't just looking forward to Heaven, they were looking forward to God's redemption story in Jesus.

In Jesus, we have many rewards that are both already and not yet. We can have peace with God knowing our sins are forgiven. We can be empowered to say *no* to sin and *yes* to faithfulness. We can have fellowship with God through the Holy Spirit to guide and comfort us. Even more, we have the hope of these gifts completely and eternally.

God has revealed Himself in His creation, through Jesus Christ and through His Word. Seek Him and His reward!

Dig deeper: *Hebrews 11*

Beth Poliquin

July 21

"I will instruct you and teach you in the way which you shall go. I will counsel you with My eye on you. Don't be like the horse, or like the mule, which have no understanding, who are controlled by bit and bridle, or else they will not come near to you." Psalm 32:8-9

I was one of those horse-crazy little girls growing up. I never had my own horse, but got to ride quite a bit at summer camp or with friends. Later in life I was able to take some riding lessons from a friend of ours. It was at that time I realized how amazing it is to ride a well-trained horse.

Jack was trained with leg cues and an "active seat" which meant he would change direction on a dime, go forward or stop without needing a bit or bridle. Since Jack, I've ridden other horses who had a mind of their own. A bit and bridle was absolutely necessary to "instruct them in my ways"!

I can tell you it's much more enjoyable for both rider and horse when that horse submits to the instruction of the rider. Both are more relaxed. When you look at working horses—whether show, farm or ranch—the best ones have been well-trained under their riders. It's a joy to watch and, I'm sure, a joy to ride like that.

Here in Psalm 32, the psalmist is speaking for the Lord: *"I will instruct you...I will counsel you...don't be like the horse, or like the mule, which have no understanding, who are controlled by bit and bridle..."*

Don't be untrained, stubborn, independent, willful in God's dealings and training with you. Imagine the joy we give our Father when we cooperate with Him instead of resist. When we turn on a dime when He nudges us to. When we move ahead, stop or back up when we get His gentle cues.

Then *"...loving kindness shall surround him who trusts in Yahweh. Be glad in Yahweh, and rejoice, you righteous!"* (verses 10-11)

Dig deeper: Psalm 32

July 22

"For by Him all things were created in the heavens and on the earth, visible things and invisible things, whether thrones or dominions or principalities or powers. All things have been created through Him and for Him." Colossians 1:16

Who is the *Him* referred to by Paul here? Verse 15 tells us: *"He is the image of the invisible God, the firstborn of all creation."* It's Jesus of Nazareth, also called the Christ the Messiah.

How can it be that Jesus, *Yeshua* in Hebrew—who was born on the earth about 2,000 years ago to real parents and walked on the ground—created all things visible and invisible? It can only be because Jesus is eternal, like the Father and Holy Spirit.

Jesus' disciple, John, wrote about this in his gospel, too: *"In the beginning was the Word, and the Word was with God, and the Word was God...All things were made through Him."* (John 1:1,3)

What a mystery! Paul refers quite often to *the mystery of Christ* in his letters to the churches.

So this Jesus created all things in heaven and earth. Visible things, of course, includes all we can see with our physical eyes. Invisible things are the things in the spirit realm—thrones, dominions, principalities, powers. Those things are a mystery, too.

But think about that Someone who has the power and wisdom to create all of that, everything we see and even what we can't see.

Microscopic organisms that scientists have discovered are amazingly complex. The wonderful array of wild flowers, each designed for its own environment, whether jungle or mountain top. Towering trees that can live for thousands of years. An animal kingdom of mind-boggling variety. Stars of incomprehensible sizes and distances that are arranged in the heavens in predictable patterns we call constellations.

Who thinks of these things?!

Jesus does! Jesus did, in partnership with His Father and Holy Spirit. Wow! It's all been created through Him and for Him. And He asks us to partner with Him to share it. Wow.

Dig deeper: *Genesis 1; John 1:1-18*

July 23

"The wind blows where it wants to, and you hear its sound, but don't know where it comes from and where it is going. So is everyone who is born of the Spirit." John 3:8

"So is everyone who" flies a paraglider! The Greek word for *wind* and *Spirit* is the same word.

Paragliding flights are very similar to a child blowing on a feather to keep it afloat. We only go up when there is rising air. Though we can fly in any direction relative to the wind, to fly cross-country we generally can only fly with the wind.

As we fly downwind, we lose height and must find rising air—thermals—so we can gain height and glide further downwind. We're always in search of this uplifting, sustaining, invisible wind. The more our wing is filled with this rising wind (Spirit), the further we can fly. The higher we can *"mount up on wings as eagles,"* (Isaiah 40:31) the more our physical bodies and spiritual souls are sustained through the journey.

Paul writes, *"For who among men knows the things of a man, except the spirit of the man, which is in him? Even so, no one knows the things of God, except God's Spirit."* (1 Corinthians 2:11)

In our journey through life, if we're not filled with God's Holy Spirit, we won't survive. We'll lose altitude and perspective, then sink down and crash to the ground. But with the filling of the Spirit we are raised up to new heights.

The higher we rise, the further we can go and the more we can accomplish for His kingdom. But rising air can be very rough and turbulent. Therefore we must seek the Spirit and a way through the turbulence to get to the heights that God offers us in order to accomplish the journey He's set before us.

Be filled with the Holy Spirit and be lifted up to new heights each day!

Dig Deeper: *Isaiah 40:28-31; John 3:5-8; 1 Corinthians 2:10-12*

Brian Doub

July 24

"Don't let your heart be troubled..." John 14:1

What thoughts came into your mind when you read that? Anything like this: "Yeah, that's easy for you to say!" "Are you kidding me?" "How can my heart *not* be troubled? You don't know my life!"

We live in a troubled, anxious, fearful, often-angry world. And yet Jesus is the one talking here: *"Don't let your heart be troubled"* (we'll deal with the second half of this verse tomorrow). How is that possible? Let's look at the deeper meaning.

Culturally, when we hear the word *heart* we think of *feelings*. So when someone says, "What does your *heart* tell you?" they mean, "What do your *feelings* tell you?" That's not what Jesus means here, though. The Greek word translated *heart* in this verse is *kardia*. That word is talking about the inner life of our mind, will, intentions, desires and decisions. Our feelings are part of that, but the *heart* isn't driven by our feelings.

The Greek word translated *troubled* in this verse is *tarassó*—put in motion, agitate, stir up, shake. So Jesus is saying we have control—decision-making power—over our heart. *"Don't let your heart be troubled..."*

Animals can't do that—they're controlled by instinct. A deer can be at perfect peace until it senses a threat. Then it won't be at peace again until it senses that threat is gone.

Water is like that, too. A lake in an atmosphere of calm is calm. When there's no wind, the surface of the lake is glasslike—calm enough to see a perfect reflection. But when the wind comes, the surface of the lake gets stirred up, agitated, troubled. The stronger the wind—the outside circumstance—the more it's stirred up.

Most people are like that, too. Their inner life is at peace if everything around them is at peace. But Jesus is saying it doesn't have to be that way for those of us who follow Him. 2 Corinthians 10:5 says we're to bring *"every thought into captivity to the obedience of Christ."*

That's powerful! And possible.

Dig deeper: John 14

July 25

"Don't let your heart be troubled. Believe in God. Believe also in Me." John 14:1

When we read Jesus' entire statement we get a clue as to how we're able to keep our heart (our mind, will, decision-making inner self) from being troubled—it's by believing in God the Father and in Jesus our Savior.

The Greek word translated *believe* here is *pisteuó*. It means to have faith in, to entrust, trust in, believe. We can't have an untroubled heart in troubled circumstances without that. And it's not just a "Sure, I believe in God" kind of trust. It has to be a deep down, entrenched, committed kind of trust.

Even Jesus' disciples—the ones He's talking to here—got very troubled in the next few days as Jesus was arrested, tried, whipped and crucified. They were still troubled after He rose from the dead. It wasn't until a few weeks later when He sent the Holy Spirit to them that they were able to truly not be troubled.

Remember the lake in yesterday's devotion? Without wind, a lake is calm enough to cast a perfect reflection. When the wind picks up, the surface becomes agitated, troubled. The greater the wind, the more the surface gets stirred up.

But like Jesus did in the storm with His disciples that night (Mark 4:35-41), when He lives in us, when we live in Him, we can say to the storm—the trouble—in our heart: "Peace! Be still."

2 Corinthians 10:3-5 gives us more insight into this. We can't do this in our own strength or ability, but because we're in Jesus. *"The weapons of our warfare are not of the flesh, but mighty before God..."* (verse 4).

This isn't easy! Even Jesus' disciples weren't able to really get a hold of this until they were filled with the Holy Spirit a few weeks later. That's also the key for us—the filling of the Holy Spirit, abiding in Jesus (the Vine), a true entrusting of ourselves to the Father. Not easy...but possible!

Dig deeper: 2 Corinthians 10:3-5

216

July 26

"Peace I leave with you. My peace I give to you; not as the world gives, I give to you. Don't let your heart be troubled, neither let it be fearful." John 14:27

Jesus said it again: *Don't let your heart be troubled.* In this verse He gives us even more hope, more insight into how this is possible for His followers—He leaves us with His peace.

The Greek word translated *peace* here is *eiréné.* Beyond a sense of quietness and rest, it implies a "joining together into a whole." A wholeness, an inner security or assurance. Jesus had that because of His relationship with His Father. And the Holy Spirit makes it available to each of us.

The picture that comes to my mind about this kind of peace was one I witnessed on a visit to Niagara Falls. Millions upon millions of gallons of water rush over these falls. We were walking along the edge of the very brink (New York's state park service did a fantastic job of providing walkways for an up-close-and-personal experience).

Out there on solid rock, surrounded by the rushing torrents on both sides, a small purple flower had bloomed. This natural picture gave me such a sense of beauty and peace in the midst of very tumultuous circumstances. That little flower was able to grow and thrive there.

I love how the Living Bible paraphrases Jesus' words in the verse above: *"...the peace I give isn't fragile like the peace the world gives."* Jesus' peace—available to all His followers through the infilling of the Holy Spirit—is a vibrant, living peace. It's a peace that's powerful enough to displace agitation and fear in our hearts.

It's a peace that's not dependent on whether things around us are peaceful—that's the fragile peace of the world. No, it's an inner assurance of our Lord's reality, sovereignty and love. This peace is a fruit of the Spirit in our lives.

Because of this peace we can obey Jesus' instruction: *"Don't let your heart be troubled, neither let it be fearful."*

Dig deeper: *Psalm 4; John 16:33; Romans 5:1-11*

July 27

"The words of a man's mouth are like deep waters. The fountain of wisdom is like a flowing brook." Proverbs 18:4

One of the coolest experiences is kayaking or canoeing on a deep, clear lake when it's calm. You can see down to the rocks below, then the shoreline slips away and it's just the dark blue-green depths of water.

What's down there? How far does it go?

And a flowing brook. You can sit next to it for hours...days. It never stops flowing. Water keeps going past you. The source feeds it and it just continues.

Proverbs talks a lot about wisdom. It treats wisdom as more valuable than gold or silver or precious gems. Why? Because it gives so much life! Like the way the earth's water—the deep waters and flowing brooks—gives life to everything on the planet.

Wisdom gives life to our soul and spirit the way water gives life to our body. It's what makes everything else work properly.

But not just any wisdom. Proverbs also makes it clear where this kind of life-giving wisdom comes from: *"The fear of Yahweh is the beginning of wisdom."* (Proverbs 9:10)

Have you been helped in your life by others who have spoken that kind of fountain of wisdom to you? Maybe your parents, a youth pastor, a teacher or older, wiser friend? I know I have. When we take in the wisdom of others from their life experiences, their study of God's word and their walk with Him—whether in person, through their writings or their spoken words—it gives life to us.

We can also be that kind of life for others, that flowing brook or those deep waters! When we *"seek her (wisdom) as silver, and search for her as for hidden treasures: then you will understand the fear of Yahweh, and find the knowledge of God. For Yahweh gives wisdom. Out of his mouth comes knowledge and understanding."* (Proverbs 2:4-6)

Be blessed. Be a blessing. Go after that flowing brook of wisdom from others, and develop it in yourself!

Dig deeper: *Proverbs 8*

July 28

"Yahweh of Armies, the God of Israel...You are the God, even You alone, of all the kingdoms of the earth. You have made heaven and earth." Isaiah 37:16

That's quite a claim. Back in Isaiah's day, that meant differentiating between the God of Israel and the gods of the surrounding nations—Baal, Dagon, Ashtoreth, Marduk and others.

In our day there are rival gods, too—Allah of Islam, the thousands of gods of Hinduism, and even the "god" of naturalism, to name a few. You can't read the Bible and read the texts of these other religions and conclude that the God of the Bible is the same as these others, just with a different name.

And if you've been paying attention while reading through this devotional, you've noticed *God as Creator* is a theme throughout the entire Bible. Not just in the first few chapters of Genesis, the Creation Story.

To get into how we know *our* God is the one who really did create heaven and earth is way beyond the scope of this devotional. But have you looked into it yourself? Do you believe the God of the Bible is who He says He is? If you do, that includes that He is, indeed, the Creator of heaven, earth and all life, including *you*.

To believe this has profound implications. It means, contrary to evolutionary and current cultural thought, there *is* an absolute moral standard—God's. It means there's an eternal afterlife in both heaven and hell. It means there's purpose...redemption...calling...healing...accountability. It means there are right and wrong ways to live our life.

To not believe it also has profound implications. If the Bible is wrong and God isn't the author of heaven, earth and all life on it, where does that leave us? What else in the Bible is wrong?

Thankfully we're not alone in this. Many very smart people have written and spoken about Creation and how we can know beyond a reasonable doubt that it's the result of the God of Israel. You'll find suggested resources at: *brodinpress.com/devotional* (scroll down to find them).

Dig deeper: *Isaiah 37*

July 29

"Deep calls to deep at the noise of Your waterfalls. All Your waves and Your billows have swept over me. Yahweh will command His loving kindness in the daytime. In the night His song shall be with me—a prayer to the God of my life." Psalm 42:7-8

Standing on the shore of Lake Superior, the Spirit of God seemed to be saying these love words to me:

As the roar of the water—so is My acclaim of My children in heaven.

As you see the volume of water before you, this and far beyond is My love for My own.

Confess freely; emptying yourself of that which binds and limits you.

Confess fearlessly; become empty of sin and shame.

As you pour out, so I pour in the deep secure richness of My love, My cleansing water, My redeeming blood that now flows in your veins is your Victory.

My Victory has become yours; My Victory installed in your very being.

Let Me transform your body, mind and spirit to align with My Truth.

You are to live as one cleansed, redeemed, able, secure, doing My will, speaking My truth, and trusting moment by moment in your redemption and My Power.

It's hard to imagine that the Lord acclaims us in heaven, much as He did with Job when Satan asked permission to test Him.

His deep love knows no earthly limits, and helps us make earth-sized attempts to understand. Our Heavenly Father speaks in our language and on our terms to impart His love. What a gracious Lord!

He invites confession, not as a shame to us, but as a cleansing release of our spirits, making room in our hearts for His Presence to dwell. Claiming and reclaiming His victory over sin, a daily washing of truth.

Dig deeper: *Job 1:6-8; Psalm 42; Ephesians 1:7*

Tasse Swanson

July 30

"The fruit of the righteous is a tree of life..." Proverbs 11:30

The natural world around us is full of examples of fruit and fruit-bearing. God uses these natural examples all the time in His Word, the Bible, to teach us about life. About life *with* Him and life *without* Him.

The fruit of a plant is what it lives for: the apples from an apple tree, the wheat grains from a wheat plant, the berries from a blueberry bush. The fruit both provides food for people and animals, and has the seeds to make more fruit-bearing plants.

The fruit of a plant is only as healthy as the plant itself. We were in northern Minnesota in late July hoping for some good blueberry picking. In "normal" years—with a healthy mix of sun and rain—the blueberries there are fantastic. But this year it was disappointing. Severe drought in the area meant a very poor blueberry season. Either the bushes were fried by too much sun with no rain, or the bushes that still looked healthy produced very little fruit, and what was there wasn't very tasty.

Not only is that disappointing for us hobby blueberry pickers, it can be disastrous for the bears and other animals that depend on those berries for some of their food supply leading into the long winter.

We're like that tree of life—that healthy fruit-bearing plant that gets plenty of sun and rain—when we're righteous. That's a word we don't really use anymore. The Hebrew word is *tsaddiq*. It means righteous or just, blameless, one in the right. It's the term the Bible uses for people who walk with the Lord, who obey the Lord's instructions, who live in the way the Lord commands.

When we accept Jesus' sacrifice for us, stop living for ourselves and live for Him and in His ways, then we develop good fruit. That fruit benefits both us and everyone we relate with. What a blessing! What an amazing way to live.

Dig Deeper: *Proverbs 15:4; John 14:6; Revelation 22:1-2, 14-15*

July 31

"The fruit of the righteous is a tree of life..." Proverbs 11:30

Who is the righteous? How do the righteous produce the kind of fruit that makes them a *tree of life*?

If you go to culture for the answer about who's righteous you'll be completely confused. This group says this is right, that group says that's right. These people over there say no, you have to do this to be right. Everyone wants to decide what's right for themselves...and often for others, too.

Has that produced the kind of fruit in our culture that's a *tree of life*? If so, we wouldn't have the highest rates of anxiety, depression and suicide in our history. We wouldn't have the addiction problems, the crime problems, the poverty problems.

The Bible makes it crystal clear what it means to be righteous, just and good according to God, the One who created us in His image. And He designed us in such a way that when we choose to follow Him, to obey His instructions, to love Him—we bear healthy, abundant fruit. We can actually become like a *tree of life*. A healthy, vibrant tree that grows healthy, tasty, nourishing fruit. It's life-giving to us and it's life-giving to those around us.

Romans 8 is key for us in understanding what it means to walk righteously before God, so we can have this kind of life-giving fruit in our lives. The bottom line is this:

"For those who live according to the flesh [living for myself, not in faith] *set their minds on the things of the flesh, but those who live according to the Spirit, the things of the Spirit. For the mind of the flesh is death, but the mind of the Spirit is life and peace..."* (verses 5 6)

How do you get the mind of the Spirit? That's the divine miracle of new birth in Jesus! All who believe He's the Son of God and choose Him as both Savior and King get the Spirit. Then we work that out with Him every day for the rest of our lives.

Dig Deeper: *Romans 8*

August

August 1

"Don't you be afraid, for I am with you. Don't be dismayed, for I am your God. I will strengthen you. Yes, I will help you. Yes, I will uphold you with the right hand of my righteousness." Isaiah 41:10

One way God speaks to us is through connecting revelation with simple aspects of physical life. We see Jesus do this in His ministry through parables. These connections allow our mind to have a deeper understanding of the practical applications of spiritual principles. That allows us to live out our faith in new ways.

Fear is a common experience for everyone, a symptom of the fall. We're promised victory through our faith in Jesus.

God has spoken to me about spiritual fear through connecting it with something I'm afraid to see in nature—snakes.

The first time God used this comparison with me, I was hiking Stone Mountain in Georgia. I walked toward the edge of the mountain top to find a quiet place. As I walked, I heard the Holy Spirit whisper to me, "On the less-traveled path, there are more likely to be snakes."

I interpreted the practical application of this to be that going after my dreams and the places in life where it takes courage, these may also be the places where it's more likely I'll need to face my fears. This is especially true if I say *yes* to walking a less traveled path—maybe pursuing a unique calling, or how I live my life boldly as a Christian in a world that's opposed to those beliefs.

Saying *yes* to the unknown takes boldness and requires stepping into places where we'll be challenged to grow. Jesus says, "Follow Me" and promises provision along the way.

How is God challenging you to grow today? Are there paths you feel God is asking you to walk that will require you to face fears? How does God want to be with you as you say *yes* to that?

Dig Deeper: *Isaiah 43:2; John 14:27; Revelation 12:11*

Emilie O'Connor

224

August 2

"For God didn't give us a spirit of fear, but of power, love, and self-control." 2 Timothy 1:7

We have experiences that shape how we respond to the world around us. Not all of them teach us truth that aligns with God's mind. That's why the Bible tells us to *"bring every thought into captivity to the obedience of Christ..."* (2 Corinthians 10:5).

Yesterday I shared how God used a metaphor to challenge me to choose courage over fear. Here's another conversation about fear where God addressed my thought life.

I was camping in northern Minnesota. I saw a snake in the grass by the lake, and from then on was skittish near the tall grass, where I'd been bold before. I felt the Lord say to me that fear was working in my life like that snake.

Fear keeps me living a partial life. It makes me believe lies about myself, other people and about God's character. It may keep me from entering territory that's my spiritual inheritance—just like in Numbers 13, when fear kept the Israelites from trusting God and entering their Promised Land. Fear holds us back from fully being who we're called to be in Christ.

I then felt the Holy Spirit challenge me: "Why are you afraid of snakes but not afraid of flies? The flies bite you, fly directly at your face, attack with ferocity. They give you no peace and yet you don't fear them. You know the snakes in this region will only run from you—yet your life is disrupted with fear of them."

That made me realize there are things I fear in my life that have no real power over me. But there are very real areas of sin in my life that I tolerate and think lightly of the damage they could cause.

Where are you holding onto lies about yourself, God or other people? Are there things you fear that aren't in alignment with God's truth? Is there sin God is telling you is more damaging than you think?

Dig Deeper: Numbers 13, Matthew 17:20

Emilie O'Connor

August 3

"He has said to me, 'My grace is sufficient for you, for My power is made perfect in weakness.' Most gladly therefore I will rather glory in my weaknesses, that the power of Christ may rest on me."
2 Corinthians 12:9

God continued to speak to me through my fear of snakes...

I was backpacking in the Black Hills in South Dakota. The visibility on the less-traveled trails was limited with tall grasses on both sides. I got the idea in my head that there could be a snake on the path. I was hiking in front of my two friends, and so I started jogging through the high grass doing this funny looking jump/run/kick thing to get through it. I refused to turn around or take another trail.

Even if it looked weird, I wanted to do what it took to face my fears in that moment. I could feel God strengthening my heart and my desire to overcome my fears. I wanted to prove to myself that this fear wasn't connected to logic or reality, and that I could be strong enough to reach the other side for the sake of growth. Having my friends there to laugh with me and encourage me helped so much! And I knew God was with me.

Most strongly in this experience, I felt the Lord speaking to me that despite the situation or my feelings, if I'm walking with my Heavenly Father, I'll be protected from all harm. God is in control and that will always be true over any fear I may have.

God will continue to use our fears and weaknesses to challenge us, teach us and bring us closer to Him. He knows what we need to be able to walk through uncomfortable situations and face our fears—and we're not meant to do it alone. Conquering our fears will look different for each of us, but let's do it, and let's do it together.

Dig Deeper: *Psalm 139, Isaiah 11:8, 1 John 4:18*

Emilie O'Connor

August 4

"He has made the earth by His power. He has established the world by His wisdom. By His understanding He has stretched out the heavens." Jeremiah 51:15

The power, wisdom and understanding of our heavenly Father, wow! With them He set the stars in galaxies. He filled the oceans with thousands of different species. He created mountains, valleys, deserts, forests, jungles, rivers, lakes, plains.

With His wisdom and understanding He set up guidelines for the universe to function: gravitational attraction, thermodynamics, genetic mutation, cellular automaton and other things I don't understand!

The Bible tells us we're made in God's image (Genesis 1:26-27, Genesis 5:1-2, Genesis 9:6, 1 Corinthians 11:7, Colossians 3:9-10, James 3:9). Part of that is the ability to create, establish, to be filled with wisdom and understanding and apply it to our life.

Of course, we can never equal God's wisdom. His ways are as high above ours as *"the heavens are higher than the earth"* (Isaiah 55:9). But we can have a measure of God's wisdom and understanding simply by going after it. Asking for it.

In the book of Proverbs wisdom is a major theme. It promises *"those who seek me* [wisdom] *diligently will find me."* (8:17) *"If you see her* [wisdom] *as silver, and search for her as for hidden treasures..."* (2:4)

What do you need wisdom and understanding for today? It's part of our inheritance as followers of Jesus. We're not on our own—not in our family life, not at work or school, not at church or on the mission field.

We have access to God's divine wisdom and understanding. James 1:5 says: *"If any of you lacks wisdom, let him ask of God, who gives to all liberally and without reproach, and it will be given to him."* That's quite a promise! And it's for you.

Dig deeper: *Read through the scriptures in paragraph 3 above*

August 5

"By Yahweh's word, the heavens were made, all their host by the breath of His mouth." Psalm 33:6

The wilderness—away from the light of cities—is the best place to fully see the night sky with all its host of stars, planets, our own Milky Way galaxy. Especially in seasons and places where the air is dry and clear, they're absolutely brilliant.

The extraordinary distances and sizes of these heavenly hosts are beyond comprehension for us...and yet the psalmist reminds us they were created by the very breath of God.

To even come up with the idea of such things as stars and space is one thing—to be able to create them by speaking them into existence is something else altogether!

It reminds us that *"...as the heavens are higher than the earth, so are My ways higher than your ways, and My thoughts than your thoughts."* (Isaiah 55:9)

Every time we look up into the night sky and marvel at the beauty and wonder of a full moon, northern lights, constellations, our galaxy...they can remind us of His ways, His thoughts. Just as we can't match His mind or creative power, so we can't hope to match His ways and thoughts.

They humbles us, the heavens and their hosts. They remind us who God is and who we are. And they call us to worship this Father of ours who has this mind and power so far beyond our own.

It causes gratitude, that a God like this wants relationship with us, His children. He wants to share His beauty and creativity He's shown in the heavens. He's created us with the ability to appreciate it, want to discover more about it, glory in it.

What a wonderful heavenly Father we have!

Dig deeper: Psalm 33; Isaiah 55:8-13

August 6

"But we have this treasure in earthen vessels, so everyone can see....this power is from God and is not our own." 2 Corinthians 4:7

My husband had such a gift to use visible things to help illustrate the ways of God.

He used a canoe paddle to share about the "j-stroke" in paddling. It's a stroke you use to make a course adjustment as your canoe moves forward. A *j-stroke*, from the stern on either side, moved the front of the canoe right or left just a bit.

He was encouraging all of us to heed the course corrections of the Lord in our lives.

The Lord gave me a course correction the other day when He helped me see I was focusing too much on the things I *couldn't do*. He helped me see I needed to focus on the things I *can do*. When the *can't do* things present themselves in my life, I need to focus on His face. A j-stroke for me.

A *Streams in the Desert* reading also added to this perspective, and gave me a new way to appreciate what God might be saying to all of us in hard seasons:

"God may send you, dear friends, some costly packages. Don't worry if they are done up in rough wrappings. You may be sure there are treasures of love, and kindness, and wisdom hidden within. If we take what He sends, and trust Him for the goodness in it, even in the dark, we shall learn the meaning of the secrets of Providence." (*Streams in the Desert* by LB Cowman, original version, Cowman Publications, ©1950)

O Father, please keep on with each of us as we surrender to Your ways in our lives in this season of trusting You, though we don't see down the road. Help us to surrender to the j-strokes You show us in our lives, that You might receive glory through us, Your earthen vessels.

Dig Deeper: *Job 5:17; Ephesians 2:10; 2 Timothy 3:16*

Nancy Patten

August 7

"Your word is a lamp to my feet, and a light for my path." Psalm 119:105

One of the most wonderful things about being out in nature, especially in wilderness areas, are the dark, dark nights. One of my favorite things is looking into that clear night sky—the stars and moon are absolutely brilliant.

I can still remember the first time I was able to see the Little Dipper. It was in the far north of Minnesota on the edge of the Boundary Waters. A place dark enough to see those faint stars.

But when the sky is clouded over in these dark wilderness places, it can be inky dark! Can't-see-your-hand-in-front-of-your-face dark. The only way to make your way into that kind of darkness is with a flashlight or headlamp. Then it's no problem.

Our life is like that. We live in a world with growing spiritual darkness. As we get closer and closer to the end, the darkness is getting darker. Jesus predicted that would happen, so it's no surprise (Matthew 24 and Luke 21). We can see it every day on the news, on social media, talking with people.

So how are we able to make our way through that kind of darkness?

There are two ways. The first way is with the Bible, God's divinely-inspired word (we'll look at the second way tomorrow). The verse above says: *"Your word is a lamp...a light..."* The Bible is our headlamp, our flashlight in dark places.

Do we need to use a flashlight in the daytime? Since there's plenty of light from the sun we don't need flashlights to make our way around. We take light for granted. But in the darkness we realize how vital light is. We can't make our way without it.

God's word as a light for our path is absolutely vital in these dark times. And it'll get more vital as the days get darker. Now is the time to dig into His Word—the Bible—as we never have before. Don't be caught in the dark without it!

Dig deeper: *Psalm 119*

August 8

"In Him was life, and the life was the Light of mankind. The Light shines in the darkness, and the darkness hasn't overcome it."
John 1:4-5

Have you been in a wilderness area at nighttime, maybe camping or backpacking far away from city lights? It's amazing, isn't it? It's when the sky is the darkest that we can really see the stars. The Milky Way is spread across our view. Constellations are easy to pick out. If there's a full moon, its light will even cast shadows.

No matter how dark it is, those stars and that moon overcome the darkness with their light.

Here in the Gospel of John, Jesus is that Light. We don't just live in a physical world that we can see, taste, smell, hear and touch. It's a spiritual world, too. In these first few verses, John isn't talking about physical darkness, but spiritual darkness.

Jesus—the Light—shines in the darkness—the spiritual darkness. And the darkness hasn't...and can't...overcome His light.

Yesterday we looked at how the spiritual darkness in our world is getting darker as time moves forward. There are two ways we're able, as followers of Jesus, to make our way through that darkness. The first way is with the Bible, the Word of God.

The other way is Jesus Himself—the Light of mankind. He called Himself *"the Light of the world"* (John 9:5). Jesus isn't on earth in human form anymore, but He's sent the Holy Spirit to fill us, live in us, guide us, comfort us and teach us.

We can know the Bible inside and out. But unless we also know Jesus, the Father, the Holy Spirit as a Person we don't have His light. It's the presence of this three-in-one God that makes the written word come alive to us and be that light on our path.

When we have this Light we don't have to fear the darkness.

Dig deeper: *John 1:1-5; John 12:44-46; 2 Corinthians 4:1-6*

"The mouth of the righteous talks of wisdom. His tongue speaks justice. The law of his God is in his heart. None of his steps shall slide." Psalm 37:30-31

Mountain goats and mountain sheep are designed for mountain slopes. Even the babies are sure-footed.

One morning my family was driving through Badlands National Park, and stopped to watch a herd of bighorn sheep. There were several young ones in the group. It was amazing to watch them scamper along the edges of steep drop-offs as if it were the most natural thing in the world. Which it was for them, of course!

On another trip we were hiking at Logan Pass in Glacier National Park. We looked over to the face of the mountain next to us and could see tiny little white specks ambling along. They were mountain goats—a nanny and her two kids, as we could see with our binoculars. Again, they made their way with ease and confidence along the steep cliff edges.

Psalm 104:18 says, *"The high mountains are for the wild goats..."* Their feet don't slide in their mountain home because God designed them for that habitat.

Psalm 37 assures us that we can be sure-footed like that on the steep mountain slopes of life! Yes, there are drop-offs, steep cliffs, slippery spots, places we'll need to jump across. But when we live by God's wisdom, by His justice, with His ways in our heart we don't need to fear falling off.

Just as the mountain sheep and goats have no fear in their mountain home, we can live with confidence when we live by God's ways. It's how He's designed us to live. It's what we're made for.

Dig deeper: Proverbs 3:5-6; Romans 12:1-2; 2 Timothy 3:14-17

August 10

"They will never be hungry or thirsty any more. The sun won't beat on them, nor any heat; for the Lamb who is in the middle of the throne shepherds them and leads them to springs of life-giving waters. And God will wipe away every tear from their eyes."
Revelation 7:16-17

This is the life we all long for. It was the life Adam and Eve had in the Garden of Eden at first, before sin entered the world (that story is in Genesis 1-3). A life of walking with God in the cool of the day. Of tending a garden that produced fruit and beauty with no weeds. Of sweet relationships with others.

But it's not what we experience here and now. Not since this world came under the curse of sin and death all those years ago.

We sometimes get glimpses of this kind of life now and again. Glimpses of heaven on earth. Without hunger or thirst. When the weather is perfect—not too hot, not too cold, not too rainy or dry. When it's a joy to be with others. When we experience the Lord's presence in a real way.

But usually we get mosquitoes in the cool of the day...and sunburn in the heat...and weeds in the garden. We tend to argue with each other, get impatient and want our own way.

What this and other Bible passages do, though, is give us hope. This is the way God always intended us to live. When sin came in, that way was sabotaged. But He promises one day it'll be this way again all the time for those whose names are written in the Lamb's Book of Life (Revelation 20:11-15).

So don't let your heart stop longing for this kind of reality. Our Heavenly Father has put that longing there because we were made for more than this broken world. We were made for life with Him.

Dig Deeper: *Isaiah 11:6-9; Isaiah 65:17-19; Revelation 22:1-5*

August 11

"Then Jesus was led up by the Spirit into the wilderness to be tempted by the devil." Matthew 4:1

There's a huge difference between hiking a wood-chipped path in a city park and hiking a wilderness trail up the side of a mountain, or in heavy forest with tree roots criss-crossing the trail. Biking a paved trail in your local city park is very different from biking a challenging single-track trail with obstacles.

In one scenario you can move along the trail without thinking too much. In fact, your mind can go in many directions during your hike or ride, and you may not even notice how far you've gone before you focus back on the trail.

In the other scenario, if you don't focus intently on the trail you're likely to end up tripping, or rolling down a hill. Both my brothers mountain bike in Colorado where they live. I have no doubt they keep their mind focused on the trail! There's not much room for mental sight-seeing if they don't want to careen off the mountainside.

When the Spirit led Jesus into the wilderness, it wasn't to amble along a wood-chipped trail in a city park. The harsh environment was for focused purpose. This was part of His preparation for His coming three years of public ministry. He met the devil head-on and faced temptation.

God does that with us, too. When we're coasting through life, our mind wandering here and there, not too worried about our footing, it's easy for us to lose focus on Him and His purposes. But when He leads us into the wilderness, that changes the game. It forces us to key in on the trail, the hazards, the elements... sometimes even our spiritual survival.

He does this with us, with you, because of His love, mercy and faithfulness. He knows what you need to grow and become more like Jesus. Allow the Spirit to lead you where He will, including into the wilderness. It's there you learn to focus on the trail He has you on.

Dig deeper: *Matthew 4*

August 12

"My soul, wait in silence for God alone, for my expectation is from Him. He alone is my rock and my salvation, my fortress. I will not be shaken. My salvation and my honor is with God. The rock of my strength, and my refuge, is in God." Psalm 62:5-7

When I read these verses I think of being carried down a river along with the rapids. Fighting to keep my head above water, I spy a rock rapidly drawing closer. I kick my feet and reach out with my arms to grab ahold of it.

As I pull myself up on it, that rock has become my salvation—my rock of strength. My fortress in the middle of this river that's trying to carry me along to an uncertain end.

Imagine sitting there and suddenly the rock grows until it's over the river, above the rapids and the danger.

That's what it's like when we put our trust in this God! He is our rock, our fortress and refuge even in the middle of the swirling river. When my expectation is from Him, my eyes are fixed on Him, He grows and becomes bigger in my field of vision.

His stability and strength make the river seem small and powerless. It's still there...but compared to the strength of the Rock, it's now insignificant.

What does David, the psalmist, mean by *"wait in silence"*? Maybe he was telling himself: "Quit complaining and look to God!" It'd probably do us all a whole lot of good to tell ourselves the same thing!

Quit complaining. Quit talking out of fear, out of the *what ifs.* Quit talking and wait for God's answer. And in the meantime, remember He's the Rock that can't be moved. He's a strong fortress, a refuge. *"I will not be shaken."*

Stand on it. Believe it.

Dig deeper: *Psalm 62*

August 13

"Yahweh, who makes a way in the sea, and a path in the mighty waters [says]...'I will even make a way in the wilderness, and rivers in the desert.' " Isaiah 43:16, 19

People have done extraordinary things. They've scaled the earth's highest mountains. They've paddled thousands of miles in boats. They've biked across continents. They've backpacked entire mountain ranges.

There's something in us that wants to "conquer" nature using our own strength and wits. It gives us such a sense of accomplishment and fulfillment. And yet we can never really conquer it. We can use all the resources we muster together to do our best, but in the end we're just created beings along with the rest of creation.

But if there's anything we learn about God—Yahweh—by reading through the whole Bible it's that seas, mighty waters, wilderness and deserts can't stop Him!

We read about Him opening the sea for a million people to walk through, and then closing it to destroy an entire army in a matter of minutes. We read about Him creating a brand new food source in the middle of the desert for those same people. That food the Hebrew people called *manna* (literally "what is it?") lasted for the entire 40 years they wandered the wilderness.

Because God is the creator of the physical world, He has authority over it. He can make a path through the sea. He can make a river in the middle of a desert, in the physical sense.

But He also is the creator of you and me, and has authority over our circumstances.

Like the Israelites did so often, we can rebel against that authority and reject Him, which will give our enemy room to attack. But when we stay under His authority, connected to Him in relationship (Jesus called it *"abiding in the Vine"* in John 15:4-11) we can expect Him to move on our behalf, too.

It often seems like we're in the middle of a wilderness or drowning in mighty waters. God will make a way for our rescue.

Dig deeper: *Isaiah 43*

August 14

"It is written, 'You shall worship the Lord your God, and you shall serve Him only.' " Matthew 4:10

Not too long ago a friend of mine shared with me how God revealed to her that her worship is louder than the lies of the enemy.

I was blown away! With all the planning, stressing, and strong emotions I feel sometimes, I have to go to God in worship and song when I feel emotions so hard that I can't even pray. It settles my heart and my soul in ways that sitting down and praying doesn't do.

During my time alone with God one morning I was reading in Matthew chapter 4 where Jesus goes into the wilderness, and all the tests Satan puts before Him.

At the end, it hit me where Jesus tells Satan to beat it and quotes out of Deuteronomy (6:13), *"It is written, 'You shall worship the Lord your God, and you shall serve Him only.' "*

So Jesus has all these tests, but then goes and says to worship God and only Him. What about worship in the midst of incredible testing helps us? Well, for me, when I'm worshiping, I'm not thinking about anything else. There's no room for anything else in my brain other than connecting with God.

But...I definitely do *serve* first and *worship* second. That, I think, is a huge reason why I get so agitated in the first place! I wait to worship Him until after I feel empty and fully drained from my "single-minded" service.

This verse reminded me very clearly that I have it backwards. If I'm putting anything first before God, I'm doing it out of my own pride and strength rather than being a vessel for His amazing goodness and grace.

After all Jesus went through in the wilderness, He chose to worship God first, before stepping into His ministry and serving the people. After all those tests, God sent the angels to take care of Jesus' needs, and He will for us too!

Dig deeper: Matthew 4:1-24

Laura Watson

August 15

"That we may no longer be children, tossed back and forth and carried about with every wind of doctrine, by the trickery of men, in craftiness, after the wiles of error; but speaking truth in love, we may grow up in all things into Him who is the head, Christ..." Ephesians 4:14-15

What does it look like for an object to be *"tossed back and forth and carried about with every wind"*? I'm sure you've seen it—a leaf that's being tossed around in a stiff breeze. It has no control over its destination because that breeze is strong enough to carry something as light as a leaf. It flits around, sometimes endlessly.

There are stronger winds that can toss around heavier objects. Gale force winds can take off branches, and even take down trees. Winds cause waves of various heights on lakes. The strongest winds—tornadoes and hurricanes—rip buildings apart, grab mature trees up from their roots and carry them through the sky. These winds cause a crazy amount of destruction.

In this passage in Ephesians, Paul is warning us about *"every wind of doctrine"* and *"trickery of men."* False teachers. He tells us: don't be like little children who are vulnerable and tossed around by these winds, trickery and error.

When we don't know who Jesus really is, what He came to do, what He said...when we don't know what God's word says...then we're vulnerable to every wind in our culture that says this or that. That tells us to think or do this or that.

Paul says *No!* Be mature. Grow up in Jesus. Stay under His authority. Know His truth and speak it, always in love. Then you won't be tossed around by these cultural winds.

Ever since the church began a couple thousand years ago, the enemy of our soul has sent his false teachers—*every wind of doctrine...the trickery of men*—to try to blow Jesus' followers around. That's still true today.

How are you doing standing against those winds?

Dig deeper: *Ephesians 4 (really the whole book of Ephesians!)*

August 16

"Let's therefore draw near with boldness to the throne of grace, that we may receive mercy and may find grace for help in time of need." Hebrews 4:16

Our family has had a lease campsite at a wilderness ministry in northern Minnesota for many years. We keep our small camper there through the summer and into the fall and get up there from the city whenever we can. One of the many blessings about it is the wildlife we've gotten to see over the years.

Of all the birds up there, there's one that's unique. The Canada jay, also known locally as the whiskey jack. This bird doesn't have the same fear of people the others do. We've been able to feed them out of our hand many times.

In fact, as I'm writing this devotional I'm sitting here at the camper and have been feeding bits of pecans to one of the jays. What a delight to have him land on my hand, grab the pecan, look me in the eye, sit there for a few seconds and then fly off. He's come back probably a dozen times, at least.

That's how our Heavenly Father wants us to approach Him! Expectant. Confident. Repeatedly. *"Let's therefore draw near with boldness to the throne of grace..."*

What gives us that confidence? The author of Hebrews has been telling us in the verses leading up to this one: Jesus our High Priest (verse 14). Verse 15 says: *"For we don't have a High Priest who can't be touched with the feeling of our infirmities, but One who has been in all points tempted like we are, yet without sin. Let's therefore..."*

It's not that we deserve to come to that throne of grace, or have done anything to earn it. No, "Jesus paid it all, all to Him we owe"... as the old hymn says. Because of His willingness to be that once-and-for-all sacrifice, we can come before the Father boldly for the mercy and grace we need.

Hallelujah! What an amazing gift. Will you draw near with confidence today?

Dig deeper: *Luke 15:11-24; Revelation 22:17*

August 17

"Yahweh, the Lord, is my strength. He makes my feet like deer's feet, and enables me to go in high places." Habakkuk 3:19

This verse closes out a passage that's an extraordinary statement of faith by someone facing the destruction of his nation by an enemy army.

After a dialogue with Yahweh, the God of heaven and earth, about justice, judgement and mercy, Habakkuk says:

"Rottenness enters into my bones, and I tremble in my place, because I must wait quietly for the day of trouble, for the coming up of the people who invade us." (verse 16)

This is real life for him. It's not metaphor or allegory—it's a historical event in the history of the small country of Judah. It happened in 588 BC, and Habakkuk was there. He would experience the destruction. And though he's afraid of what's coming, he's able to stand firm in his faith:

"For though the fig tree doesn't flourish, nor fruit be in the vines; the labor of the olive fails, the fields yield no food; the flocks are cut off from the fold, and there is no herd in the stalls: yet I will rejoice in Yahweh. I will be joyful in the God of my salvation! Yahweh, the Lord, is my strength. He makes my feet like deer's feet, and enables me to go in high places." (verses 17-19)

That's pretty amazing! How does he get to that place of faith in the Lord? The same way everyone else does—by connection, by relationship with Him. By trusting in God's ultimate plans and purposes for His people. By accepting His ways, even though he can't understand them.

Through it all, Habakkuk knows he has to rely on God's strength to get through this. And not just to get through it, but to *"go in high places"* in the middle of it. *"He makes my feet like deer's feet..."*

Have you seen deer run and leap? They're pretty great at it! Our Father can give us that ability as we face troubled times, too.

Where will you look for your strength today?

Dig deeper: *The book of Habakkuk (it's just 3 chapters long)*

August 18

"For a day in your courts is better than a thousand (elsewhere)..."
Psalm 84:10

In paragliding, if you want to fly long distances you regularly have to regain your altitude. We are able to do so through thermals. These are bubbles of warm air that raise up until they condense and form into clouds.

It's a beautiful feeling to be lifted up by this force of nature. The more you stay within the core of the thermal, the faster you get back up to the cloud base. With every vertical meter, your perspective gets wider and you will be able to glide further. If you don't take time to thermal back up or don't find the next thermal, you won't be able to fly long distances. You will soon "be grounded."

I think in many ways, faith is like a long distance flight. Our faith needs to take time to stop and "regain altitude." Times "in the core" with ourselves and with God. Times that lift us up. Times to gain new perspectives. Times where we don't move forward, where we don't plan or organize things. Time only to *be* with ourselves before God.

In the Bible we read that Jesus took these times. Mostly He hiked up a mountain to be alone and searched out times with His Father. The psalmist also experiences that being near to God is the biggest treasure in his life, helping him to regain strength for his life and faith.

If we don't take these times, our faith will lack strength and deepness. Soon our faith journey will "be grounded," too. Quality time with God is the core of our faith journey.

When do you want to take time in the coming week to be in the core with yourself and God?

Dig deeper: *Psalm 84; Matthew 14:23; Luke 6:12*

Timon Weber

August 19

"Now may the God of peace...make you complete in every good work to do His will, working in you that which is well pleasing in His sight, through Jesus Christ..." Hebrews 13:20-21

We're using the World English Bible translation for this devotional because it's a public domain translation—we don't need anyone's permission to use it. But in this case, there's one phrase I like better in the translation I normally read, New American Standard. Instead of *"make you complete in every good work"* the NASB reads: *"equip you for every good work."*

The Greek word is *katartizó*, which can mean several things, including equip and complete.

When we use *equip*, it makes me think of the way we equip ourselves for a wilderness excursion—or the way we're equipped by an outfitter for a specific area or activity.

As I write this, a group of women friends and I are just three weeks away from a 4-day kayak camping trip in the Apostle Islands. This world-class kayaking destination along Lake Superior's south shore in northern Wisconsin is definitely something we need to be equipped for.

Most of us have some paddling experience. But kayaking on Lake Superior takes a certain kind of kayak, it takes knowledge of the lake itself, it takes special gear to cope with the hypothermia-inducing water temps, and it takes experience with the area to make it the best trip possible. We knew we needed to hire an outfitter to equip us with their gear and experience.

The big difference between being equipped for outdoor adventures and being equipped for *"every good work to do His will"*? We never get past the point of needing God's equipping!

We can choose to get trained, certified and experienced enough to someday kayak Lake Superior without hiring an outfitter. But we don't get certified out of needing God's equipping to do His will through Jesus.

He continues to equip us, make us complete, throughout our lifelong journey with Him.

Dig deeper: *Exodus 4:10-12; Isaiah 61:1-2; 2 Timothy 3:16-17*

August 20

"For we all stumble in many things. Anyone who doesn't stumble in word is a perfect person, able to bridle the whole body also."
James 3:2

In northern Minnesota where our family loves to spend time, the ground is rocky and the many trees there have shallow root systems. Because of that, the hiking trails and canoe portages have lots of rocks and tree roots on them.

If you don't pay attention while you're hiking or portaging, it's easy to stumble. In fact, sometimes it gets frustrating. When I hike I want to be able to enjoy the surrounding beauty. But to enjoy it at a brisk pace means risking a stubbed toe, a twisted ankle or a wipe out.

I've learned to slow down, keep an eye on the trail, and stop when I want to enjoy something that's especially eye-catching. Even then, I still stumble once in awhile, although I usually manage to avoid anything serious.

Our conversations with others can be like that—full of rocks and roots, sometimes a downed tree, mud or loose gravel. When we rush forward it's really easy to stumble with our words. To let words out before we think about what we're saying.

Sometimes that only causes a bit of a trip, but other times it can cause a full-on wipe out. We've hurt someone by our words. Or we've been critical and gossipy about a friend or co-worker. Or taken our anger out on a parent, sibling or child simply because they were within earshot.

The entire third chapter of this letter of James is on the subject of our words, our speech. He says: *"Anyone who doesn't stumble in word is a perfect person..."*

Have you ever thought of that? Have you ever wished you had said something that would've helped a situation? Or wished you could un-say something that didn't help at all, or even made it worse?

Do we ever need the Holy Spirit's help with this! Invite Him to help you today to carefully choose the words that come out of your mouth.

Dig deeper: *James 3*

August 21

"Sing, you heavens, for Yahweh has done it! Shout, you lower parts of the earth! Break out into singing, you mountains, O forest, all of your trees, for Yahweh has redeemed Jacob, and will glorify Himself in Israel." Isaiah 44:23

It's so fascinating how often the natural world plays a part in the words of the Old Testament psalms and prophets, isn't it?

In these verses, God is corralling the heavens, the earth, the mountains and forests to rejoice with Him for the redemption of His people, Israel. They're witnesses to what He does and what He'll do.

It reminds me of Jesus' words in Luke 19. The Pharisees told Him to rebuke His disciples for praising Him and calling Him a king during what we call His triumphal entry into Jerusalem. Jesus told them, *"I tell you that if these were silent, the stones would cry out."* (verse 40)

In places like this in the Bible, the text places *anthropomorphism* onto these non-human, created things—giving them human traits and behaviors. Sing, shout, break out into singing, cry out.

What's the significance? Is it just poetic form? I don't know. But when I read these words about these natural creations I love, it causes more joy and gratitude to well up inside me for God's awesomeness!

When I'm in the mountains, when I look into the night sky, when I hike in a forest and look around me—I'm filled with wonder. If these created things have so much beauty and bigness, how much more so the God who created them?

Verses like this expand our view of things beyond just our own life and experience. God is always at work in the Big Picture as well as in life's intimate details. In this case, He's concerned with the entire nation of Israel.

If the mountains and heavens are called to rejoice with Him, how much more are we, His children?

How much do we know of what He's doing in the world today so we can rejoice with Him?

Dig deeper: Psalm 19:1-2; Isaiah 44; Isaiah 55:12

August 22

"Most certainly I tell you, unless a grain of wheat falls into the earth and dies, it remains by itself alone. But if it dies, it bears much fruit." John 12:24

Seeds are miracles! We take them for granted because they're all around us. But when we stop for a real look—wow.

An acorn is the seed of an oak tree. Acorns provide food (in our Minnesota neighborhoods, where there are oak trees there are sure to be thriving squirrel families!). But that's not their main purpose. The main purpose of an acorn is to produce another oak tree.

If an acorn was only interested in surviving and remaining intact as an acorn, it might stay whole for a short time. But then it wouldn't do what it's been designed to do. When that acorn falls to the ground it eventually splits open (dies) and a shoot comes out of it. That shoot grows, develops leaves and grows for several decades. In the DNA of that one acorn is an oak tree that will produce 10,000 more acorns. That's fruitfulness!

That's what Jesus meant when He said, *"If it dies, it bears much fruit."* In the context of John 12, Jesus compared His own purpose in life with that of a seed. He could hang on to His life instead of obeying His Father and fulfilling His purpose. It would've saved Him intense pain and suffering. But He would've abandoned His main purpose for coming to Earth.

And He was speaking to all of us who follow Him: *"He who loves His life will lose it. He who hates his life in this world will keep it to eternal life."* (verse 25)

The Greek word for love here is *phileó*—to have an affection for. The word for hate is *miseó*, which also means to love less or esteem less...to renounce one choice in favor of another.

Not surrendering completely to Jesus will likely mean a more comfortable, and maybe even safer life. But if we value His purposes for us more than comfort or safety, that's where Kingdom fruitfulness comes.

Dig deeper: *John 12*

August 23

"Now the God of perseverance and of encouragement grant you to be of the same mind with one another according to Christ Jesus..."
Romans 15:5

We see in all of nature a magnificent harmony. Though there's competition and the survival of the fittest is prevalent, it all points to a greater principle of balance and harmony that keeps a wonderful world healthy and prospering.

As believers we're called to live together in harmony. A favorite illustration of this harmony is found in the experience of paddling a canoe. There's something very special about paddling a canoe across a clear wilderness lake or down a winding river.

The person in the back, or stern, is primarily responsible for steering. The person in the front, or bow of the canoe, is responsible for power. The stern paddler can see everything that's going on including the paddling of their partner. The person in the bow can see what lies ahead a little bit closer, but isn't steering and can't see the person paddling behind them.

The exercise of canoeing can be a real test of a relationship. It requires skill, strength and trust. The ability to go straight is the sign of a team of paddlers working together in harmony.

The bow paddler needs to communicate danger to the stern; the stern paddler needs to be prepared to switch sides at any moment to paddle opposite the side of the bow paddler. The stern paddler needs special skills to balance with their partner and perform efficient steering strokes. The bow paddler needs to be strong and provide the majority of forward motion.

When the team is working together and fulfilling their responsibilities, a pleasant and harmonious experience results. This is also true in life. It can be seen in a married couple that have understood one another's strengths and weaknesses and found joy and comfort in serving each other. Close friends can achieve similar results by encouraging one another and finding that sweet spot of harmony and appreciation.

Happy paddling!

Dig deeper: *Ecclesiastes 4:9-12; 2 Corinthians 13:11; Galatians 3:28*

Brian Rupe

August 24

"...you don't know what your life will be like tomorrow. For what is your life? For you are a vapor that appears for a little time, and then vanishes away." James 4:14

Our family spends a lot of time camping on the Gunflint Trail in northeast Minnesota. August and September are my favorite times there for a couple reasons.

First, the bugs start to disappear!

Second, that time of year the nights are cooling off but the days stay warm. On calm, clear mornings if you're up early enough you'll see a layer of mist on the lakes. Sometimes it's just near the water's surface and other times it's like blankets of fog. I love to take a canoe out and paddle through the mist on mornings like that. It's magical.

Once the sun is high enough the mist burns off and it's gone, *"a vapor that appears for a little time, and then vanishes away."* Those who aren't up early enough miss it altogether.

Sometimes the Lord offers us opportunities that are temporary. It could be the chance to share His love with a harassed store employee, or your stressed-out server at a restaurant. It could be the chance to practice patience with your kids...or your parents... or a co-worker. It could be the chance to pray for someone on the spot.

In His mercy, He sometimes lets us revisit those opportunities when we miss it. But other times it's gone, like that mist on the lake that burns away in the sun. We had the opportunity but we didn't take hold of it.

There was a season in my life when my dad was in a memory care facility. One of the things I kept reminding myself was: "I don't want to have any regrets that I didn't spend time with him while I had the opportunity." I knew his life was like that vapor.

What short-term opportunities will God place before you today? How will you treat them before they vanish like the mist?

Dig deeper: *2 Kings 5:1-14; Galatians 6:10; 2 Timothy 4:2*

August 25

"This book of the law shall not depart from your mouth, but you shall meditate on it day and night, that you may observe to do according to all that is written in it; for then you shall make your way prosperous, and then you shall have good success." Joshua 1:8

What's the difference between a jungle and a desert?

A jungle is green, vibrantly green. It's packed with healthy, growing plants. It's loaded with animal life of all kinds. Life flourishes in jungles. In fact, they're the most biodiverse places on earth.

A desert? Brown. Dusty. Arid. There's a greenish plant here and there, and there's some animal life, too—but survival is a struggle. We think of sand dunes...the wind blowing tumbleweed and dust across a barren landscape.

What's the big difference between a jungle and a desert? Rain. Jungles are saturated with at least 80 inches of rain every year, and some of the world's jungles get several hundred inches of rain a year. On the other hand, deserts get just 10 inches a year, or less. Some areas get less than an inch of rain a year!

The more an environment is saturated with rain, the more life it can grow and be sustained.

This is true for our spiritual life, too. This verse for today is part of the Lord's instruction to Joshua, who's just been assigned as the new leader of the Hebrew people after Moses' death. *"This book of the law"* was what God had given to Moses to teach His people how to live.

Their way would be blessed and prosperous in this new land if they saturated in God's word to them—*"you shall meditate on it day and night..."*

Just like little rain brings little life, so short sprinkles of God's word in us here and there will bring little of God's life in us.

But when we saturate in God's word, the Bible, we'll be like a jungle. Life can't help growing in areas saturated with rain. Our spirits can't help growing when we saturate it with God's truth.

Dig deeper: Psalm 25:5; Matthew 4:4; 2 Timothy 3:16-17

August 26

"He said to them, 'You come apart into a deserted place, and rest awhile.' " Mark 6:31

Jesus' closest followers had just finished a ministry trip where they'd released healing and deliverance to all kinds of people. Because of that, they were being mobbed by those wanting help, so they didn't even have time to eat.

Jesus encouraged them to go away for a break. In this case it was across the Sea of Galilee to a secluded area of the shoreline away from the towns and people.

Times of rest from our work and ministry are vital. God established a pattern of work and rest way back at the beginning when He Himself rested after the six days of creation. When He gave Moses the law the Hebrews (or Israelites) would live by, it included every seventh day set aside as a *Sabbath*—a rest day to set work aside and be with Him.

The religious leaders eventually became so nit-picky about the Sabbath that in Jesus' day they took offense at Him healing people on the Sabbath. They were more devoted to their own rules than to the people who needed help. Modern Christianity went the other direction—most of us don't observe a Sabbath at all. Many even reject the idea because "that's the Law, and we're under grace."

But a Sabbath rest *is* grace! Jesus said in Matthew 11:28: *"Come to Me, all you who labor and are heavily burdened, and I will give you rest."* It's an invitation to come to Jesus.

This time of rest was never meant to be without God. Jesus did it Himself when He often went to the wilderness or a mountaintop to pray and be with His Father.

Will you *"come apart into a deserted place and rest awhile"?* For those of us who love nature, it could be a prayer cabin tucked away in the woods. Camping next to a lake or stream. Even half a day spent on a hike, paddling a kayak, or simply sitting next to a waterfall. These times of rest both restore us from work done, and prepare us for work to come.

Dig deeper: *Exodus 33:14; Psalm 127:2; Hebrews 4:9-11*

August 27

"God's temple that is in heaven was opened, and the ark of the Lord's covenant was seen in His temple. Lightnings, sounds, thunders, an earthquake, and great hail followed." Revelation 11:19

If you've ever been in the middle of a severe thunderstorm, hurricane, tornado or earthquake, you know their awe-inspiring and terrifying power. The best mankind's scientific advancements have been able to do is predict them. We've never been able to control them. They're too big for us.

But in one of humanity's biggest ironies, people—who can't control the weather—want to get rid of God, or control God, or set Him aside as an irrelevant myth. The One who created and controls not just our planet's weather systems and geographical events, but the movement of the planets, stars and galaxies.

The Bible often reminds us of God's relation to these natural events, maybe to remind us of His bigness, power and authority:

"There were thunders and lightnings, and a thick cloud on the mountain, and the sound of an exceedingly loud trumpet; and all the people who were in the camp trembled...All of Mount Sinai smoked, because Yahweh descended on it in fire; and its smoke ascended like the smoke of a furnace, and the whole mountain quaked greatly." (Exodus 19:16,18)

"Then Yahweh answered Job out of the whirlwind, 'Who is this who darkens counsel by words without knowledge?...Have you entered the treasuries of the snow?...By what way is the lightning distributed, or the east wind scattered on the earth?...Do you know the laws of the heavens? Can you establish its dominion over the earth?...Can you send out lightnings?'" (verses from Job 38)

When Jesus came to earth as a human, He also demonstrated His authority over weather events: *"Then he got up, rebuked the wind and the sea, and there was a great calm."* (Matthew 8:26)

That's a power no other human has. And yet this Creator who has authority over wind, waves, earthquakes and lightnings—He invites us into relationship with Him. Wow.

Dig deeper: *Nahum 1; Matthew 8:23-27; Mark 4:35-41*

August 28

"Lift up your eyes on high and see who created these, who brings out their army by number. He calls them all by name, by the greatness of His might. And because He is strong in power, not one is lacking." Isaiah 40:26

I usually sleep all through the night—except when we're camping and the night is cold.

Cold it was in the Rossport Islands of Ontario! I lay in my sleeping bag contemplating whether I really needed to unzip my bag, unzip the tent, unzip the fly, zip my jacket and go and wander in the cold to empty my bladder. What a dumb deliberation!

So, I asked God to give me thoughts of Him. But, even if God spoke to me in that moment, I knew I wouldn't hear because my over-filled bladder screamed and threatened nasty consequences.

Grumpy, I unzipped, unzipped and zipped another, unzipped a third, and zipped a fourth. I placed my warm feet into cold and sandy sandals and looked up. Oh, what a look up!

The view of the sky over the water was breathtaking. Stars in abundance. Along the horizon, the Northern Lights quietly and slowly danced, flinging white and green scarfs. There were streaks of red, too. Those gossamer scarfs went vertical, up to the North Star. They went horizontal and they floated on an invisible wind from every direction, and didn't stop.

I recalled that only moments before I had asked God to help me think of Him. It was God's handiwork—with a personal message attached. Like a banner in the sky: "God loves LeaAnn." Great, awe-inspiring, and unexpected.

He does these things because He loves it when we talk to Him.

In the quiet, in the noise, He is there, reading our inmost thoughts, speaking, though bladders be full and and zippers be many. But in our communication He wants us always to remember—He is God and He's bigger and more glorious than we can imagine. Yet, He finds joy in rewarding our conversations with Him by speaking a language we can understand.

Dig deeper: Isaiah 40:12-26

LeaAnn Schroeter

August 29

"Be patient therefore, brothers, until the coming of the Lord. Behold, the farmer waits for the precious fruit of the earth, being patient over it, until it receives the early and late rain. You also be patient. Establish your hearts, for the coming of the Lord is at hand." James 4:14

Patience is a rare commodity these days. We want what we want, and we want it now! Our culture is full of impatience, and even those of us who follow Jesus have trouble with this one.

It's such a good reminder that *"the farmer waits."* The farmer plants seeds in a certain season and knows those seeds take time to sprout, grow and produce their fruit. The type of fruit produced depends on the type of seed planted. And some seeds take longer to produce fruit than other seeds.

If you plant a blueberry bush, one of nature's fastest growing fruit plants, you'll still need to wait a year or two after planting before you'll be able to have that blueberry pie. Plant a pawpaw tree, on the other hand, and you'll have to wait five to seven years before you'll have fruit. Even our ordinary garden plants like peas and beans take several weeks to mature and produce their fruit.

Do you have promises from God that haven't produced fruit yet? Or have you been asking the Holy Spirit to grow His fruit in you, but haven't seen the results yet? Fruit takes time! And it takes a carefully cultivated environment to produce the healthiest fruit—plenty of water and sunshine, good soil.

And it takes patience. We don't like that! We like immediate results. But God is after good fruit in our life...and good fruit is never immediate.

Plant the seeds and patiently wait out the process.

While you wait do what all good farmers do: cultivate the ground, water it, provide nutrients, keep out the pests. And rely on God to do what only He can do—the actual growing and fruit-producing.

Dig deeper: *Jeremiah 17:7-8; John 15:5; John 15:16*

August 30

"By their fruits you will know them...every good tree produces good fruit..." Matthew 7:16-17

In this section of Matthew, Jesus is saying: Just like you can tell what kind of tree it is by the fruit it produces, so you can tell what kind of person he is by the fruit of his life. You can know which kingdom she's part of by seeing the fruit of her life.

Galatians 5:22 lists the good fruit that comes from good "trees"—from those who live by and walk with the Holy Spirit:

Love—God's kind of love, described in 1 Corinthians 13.
Joy—The kind that's rooted in the life of Jesus in us, that's not changed by our circumstances.
Peace—That wonderful *shalom* of God. Not just inner calm, but a whole-life settledness, prosperity of spirit and life, favor.
Patience—restfulness and trust in God's timing.
Kindness—the outward expression of God's love through us to others in words and actions.
Goodness—Godly actions and attitudes.
Gentleness—A sweet spirit, full of grace towards people, ready to serve and give.
Faithfulness—Consistently producing these godly fruits in our life by walking with Jesus daily.
Self-Control—Under the command of my spirit, not my flesh.

Sometimes we spend a ton of mental energy wondering what God's will is for our life. Well, let's begin here! What kind of fruit am I producing today?

Don't be discouraged if you're not seeing much evidence of these fruits in you. It's a life-long process, growing fruit! And just like trees go through seasons, so we go through seasons in life. Some of these seasons produce good fruit easily, and some are filled with storms and drought.

But unlike fruit trees, the fruits of your life don't have to be at the mercy of our external circumstances. They're wholly dependent on one thing: the Holy Spirit. That's good news!

Dig deeper: *Galatians 5:16-26; John 15:1-16*

August 31

"For Yahweh who created the heavens, the God who formed the earth and made it, who established it and didn't create it a waste, who formed it to be inhabited says: 'I am Yahweh. There is no other.' "
Isaiah 45:18

Of all the planets in our solar system, of all of what's known in our galaxy, why is Earth the only one with life? Why does Earth alone have water? Why is it the right distance from the sun to support life without scorching it? Why does it have the right mixture of gasses? The right gravitational pull? The right tilt to its axis for seasons, for days and for nights?

The Bible begins with this statement: *"In the beginning God created the heavens and the earth."* (Genesis 1:1) It's then echoed throughout the Bible, including here in Isaiah 45. And here it tells us of God's purpose for creating it: *to be inhabited.*

The Lord specifically formed the earth to be inhabited by living things, including people. In fact, according to Genesis 1, He created everything human beings would need to thrive here on earth before they entered the picture.

When the Lord formed Adam from the dust (Genesis 2:7), and later Eve from his rib (Genesis 2:22), He placed them in a finished world. And He charged them to care for and use the resources of that world (Genesis 1:28-30).

Our most valuable resources—metals, minerals, plant life, animals, energy, fuel—all were part of original creation. All were in place before people were. We call them natural resources.

Isn't God good? He didn't create our planet home as a waste, but to be inhabited. He filled it with these resources for us to learn about, use and develop. And He didn't stop at filling it with just utilitarian resources—things that are merely useful. He filled our planet with beauty, with color and fragrances and sounds of astounding variety.

What a gift! Thank You, Father, for Your goodness in creating this world of ours in such a way.

Dig deeper: Deuteronomy 31:8; Isaiah 43:2; 2 Peter 1:3-4

September

S. BRODIN

September 1

"But it is good for me to come close to God. I have made the Lord Yahweh my refuge, that I may tell of all Your works." Psalm 73:28

It's easy to look around at the world and sometimes wonder why we try so hard. I get discouraged when I fail, but also when it seems my pursuit of holiness goes not only unrewarded, but almost punished. I question God's goodness and love for me.

The temptation is to withdraw from Him and His Word. This kind of isolation isn't healthy. Instead, it's always better to go to Him and to His house and to His people (Psalm 73:17). Then I'm reminded there's a bigger picture I can't quite see yet.

No storm will last forever, and God is still in control. Not only is He aware of our storms, He alone has the power to redeem every hardship and hurt when we trust Him.

We're told of the ultimate demise of the unrighteous as a warning. God's love and grace provides a security found nowhere else. We can find comfort and satisfaction in knowing we will be on the winning side at the end.

But we're not saved for our own good and glory. Just like all of creation, we were made for worship. As the heavens declare His glory, the job given us is to tell of His works.

Make the Lord God your refuge and let the good you experience cause you to rejoice and praise Him. Tell Him how thankful you are and tell others who need to hear about Him. Those who don't know Him yet and those who do can always use a reminder and encouragement that He's faithful to His people and His promises.

Dig deeper: *Psalm 73*

Beth Poliquin

September 2

"...from whom all the body, being fitted and knit together through that which every joint supplies, according to the working in measure of each individual part, makes the body increase to the building up of itself in love." Ephesians 4:16

Paul often compares the Church to our human body, which is why he calls it "the Body of Christ."

There are things that define a human body: the various systems and organs, two legs and two arms, a reasoning mind, a feeling heart. Each part, even each cell, works together in a united, harmonious way. In a way that's been fitted and knit together—designed. When each of these parts does what it's designed to do, the body is healthy.

So it is with every living organism. From a one-celled bacterium to a giant redwood to a pelican to a shark to an elephant—each has a body fitted and knit together with complex systems that cause it to grow, function and reproduce.

That's how the Church—the Body of Christ—has been designed by Jesus to be, too. A myriad of different cells, systems, organs, structures that all work together for a common purpose. A healthy, functioning, growing and reproducing Body.

That's why the "Lone Ranger" Christian is really a contradiction in terms. By very definition, when someone repents and gives his or her life to Jesus, that person becomes part of Jesus' body—the Church. An eye can't say, "I'm tired of being part of this body. It's too much trouble. I'm on my own." An eye without the rest of the body is useless. And that body, without an eye, is now disabled.

We all struggle to be part of this imperfect and flawed Body of Christ (flawed because it's made up of flawed humans, like you and me). The ingredient that's most necessary for its ongoing work is *"the building up of itself in love."* Not feelings-based, gushy "love" but God's kind of love. You can read about it in 1 Corinthians 13.

Dig deeper: *Romans 12; 1 Corinthians 12-13*

September 3

"Early in the morning, while it was still dark, He rose up and went out, and departed into a deserted place, and prayed there."
Mark 1:35

The Greek word for *deserted place* here suggests an unpopulated place—a wilderness. This time it wasn't to be tempted by the devil, but to pray. To be with His Father alone for awhile without the people pressing Him with their needs.

As outdoor lovers, we're tempted to stay in the wilderness so we don't have to face the pressures of life. We can escape other people and our struggles with them for awhile. The wilderness often seems easier to deal with than people!

I'm sure it was that way for Jesus, too...but He never stayed in the wilderness with His Father. He knew His purpose took Him back to the people.

God is always about people. From the day He formed Adam as the pinnacle of creation, to setting aside the Hebrew people and the nation of Israel as a model for the other nations, to sending Jesus as the Sacrifice Lamb—He's always been about people.

Let's not use our love of wilderness and solitude as an excuse to escape the problems that come with conflict and pressure with people. People are God's mission! And because we're God's sons and daughters, people are our mission, too.

Mark 1:36, right after Jesus left for a deserted place to pray, *"Simon and those who were with Him searched for Him. They found Him and told Him, 'Everyone is looking for You.' "* Everyone is looking for You.

If you follow Jesus, everyone is looking for you, too, whether they realize it or not. People need what we have in Jesus. As His followers we don't have the choice to "opt out" of the people business.

That'll mean different things for different people. We have different skills, gifts and callings. But they'll all involve people at some level. So get into your *deserted place* to pray and be strengthened by the Lord...and then, as Jesus says, *"Let's go..."*

Dig deeper: *Mark 1*

September 4

"Early in the morning, while it was still dark, He rose up and went out, and departed into a deserted place, and prayed there."
Mark 1:35

Jesus drew His power, strength and wisdom from His times alone with His Father. He would go into these deserted places (the Greek word *erémos* means an unpopulated area, a wilderness) to connect with His Father.

Why did He go to deserted places? Wilderness places? To get away from the distractions so He could hear His Father's voice clearly. So He could be more sensitive to the Spirit's direction. Even Jesus never relied on His own strength and wisdom to carry out God's purposes for His life. And in order to know those purposes, He went to the wilderness to find out.

Here's a challenge for you...

Are you the kind of person who's always plugged-in to noise? It could be music. It could be audio books. Podcasts. The news. For us old timers, our car radio. It could be people around you. Do you ever cultivate silence in your life so you can hear the voice of God speaking to you? Ever?

Have you been praying for direction, and yet are so surrounded by noise that you wouldn't be able to hear the Lord even when He speaks to you?

There's a story in 1 Kings 19 where God shows the prophet Elijah that His voice wasn't heard in a windstorm, an earthquake or a fire...but in *"the sound of a gentle whisper."* (verse 12).

Has it been a long time since you've heard the Lord speak to you? Is it time to ditch the noise long enough to get into the wilderness (maybe not a literal wilderness—but maybe so) to hear that gentle whisper of God's voice?

One of the devil's strategies is to keep us in noise and distraction, in a frantic pace of life. Take Jesus' example and get away regularly with Him to a deserted place so you can hear His voice clearly and well.

Dig deeper: *Psalm 32:8; Jeremiah 29:13; John 16:13*

September 5

"But solid food is for those who are full grown, who by reason of use have their senses exercised to discern good and evil." Hebrews 4:12

I just watched a documentary about a man who's a glacier guide in northern Norway. In order to lead other people safely across, he's had to learn to discern the glacier. To be able to know the signs of both solid and unstable footing. To understand that the way the snow and ice looks and feels determines what's underneath, how it's melting and other factors.

Rock climbers learn the same kind of discernment—where to place their anchors, the best spots for their fingers and feet to bring them further up safely.

Good discernment, the ability to judge well, can be a matter of life or death. The higher the stakes, the more wise discernment is necessary.

Hikers hoping to summit a mountain need the ability to discern an incoming storm. Is it worth continuing with the risk of lightning coming on? Whitewater kayakers need discernment to judge whether the previous days' rainfall will raise the river levels too high for safety.

We learn to have our senses exercised to discern these kinds of conditions so we can proceed with safety, alter our course, or even turn back when the risk is simply too great.

We need to have our spiritual senses exercised for discernment, too, so we know what's good and what's evil. Part of following Jesus is knowing His teachings—what He calls good and evil. The New Testament writers warn us about false teachers. It also warns us about our enemy, the devil: *"Be watchful. Your adversary, the devil, walks around like a roaring lion, seeking whom he may devour."* (1 Peter 5:8)

God calls us to grow up in Him—to become mature. One big sign of maturity in Christ is having exercised and grown our ability to discern good and evil.

How is your "discernment muscle"? Does it need exercise?

Dig deeper: *2 Corinthians 11:13-15; 2 Timothy 4:1-5*

September 6

"I can do all things through Christ who strengthens me." Philippians 4:13

One of the great values of wilderness trips is that they often force us into situations that are much more physically, mentally and emotionally demanding than what most of us face in our daily lives.

Putting up with rush hour traffic twice a day may seem demanding when we're in it. But it's nothing like hauling a 65-pound 17-foot canoe up a switchback portage for half a mile, like my 5-foot-tall friend, Emilie, did (on her first canoe trip).

When you're faced with the elements, challenging terrain and the limits of daylight in the wilderness, you realize what it really means to need strength. When there's no other option than to keep going, you learn what it means to not quit.

And people throughout history have endured and accomplished without calling on God for His strength for help. He created people with an enormous ability to persevere in overwhelming odds.

But as children of our Heavenly Father, we have the privilege of walking with Him on this journey of life. As His children, we have access to *His* joy, *His* peace and *His* strength. We don't have to limit ourselves to our own.

Paul wrote these words *"I can do all things through Christ..."* while in prison. And He wrote them to the believers in Philippi, where he was once thrown in prison. After being beaten, he and his ministry partner, Silas, were placed in the inner dungeon (try to imagine the mental and emotional toll that would be).

Rather than letting despair, discouragement and defeat conquer them, they drew on God's strength. They sang hymns of praise out loud in that dirty, dark, stench-filled prison. Do you know what happened next? You can read about it in Acts 16.

We can do all things through Him, and be carried in His grace and strength whether in the wilderness, at work, at school, with hard people. All things.

Dig deeper: Acts 16:16-40; Philippians 4

September 7

"So the tongue is also a little member, and boasts great things. See how a small fire can spread to a large forest!" James 3:5

Have you ever had experience with a wildfire? If you've spent any time in the Rocky Mountains of the American West, you've probably seen the after-effects of one.

The beginning of a wildfire is always small. Maybe just a spark, a small flame or some smoldering material just waiting for the right conditions to burn. But by the time a fire is noticed by people, it's already burning rapidly. That small fire that could've been put out by a scoop or two of dirt or a bucket or two of water is now burning acres and acres of forest or grassland.

A few years ago my family was keeping a close eye on the Ham Lake Fire in the Boundary Waters because it was so close to a ministry we're involved with and our friends there. It burned areas we had been in many times. Smoldering ashes from one campfire ended up burning more than 75,000 acres in Minnesota and across the border into Ontario.

Then in the fall of 2020, my husband and I were in Colorado while the Cameron Peak Fire was burning. We could see its gigantic smoke plume for a couple hours as we drove toward the northern part of the state. We drove directly under the plume as it stretched from the western horizon to the east. That fire burned over 200,000 acres before it was contained.

So James' words: *"See how a small fire can spread to a large forest!"* gives me a vivid word picture. I've seen the devastation caused by wildfires. I've seen how the right conditions can cause uncontrollable growth in a very short amount of time.

What we say—our words—can cause similar devastation. You've probably experienced others' words causing that kind of harm to you. Words are powerful. They can be used for either great good or great evil—just like fire!

How will you use your words today?

Dig deeper: Psalm 34:13; Proverbs 18:21; James 3:4-5

September 8

"Innumerable evils have surrounded me...so that I am not able to look up..." Psalm 40:12

Hiking in the Boundary Waters Canoe Area (BWCA) of northern Minnesota is almost always a rocky experience. To maintain your footing it's absolutely critical that you look down.

At Camp du Nord I helped develop two trails connecting a new property acquisition called Pine Pointe. One of the trails is affectionately referred to as the *Goat Trail*. It's the shortest distance between the properties, crossing rocky outcrops and shaky footholds. The second trail was carefully plotted out for its level terrain. Though longer, this trail can be enjoyed walking side by side with your companion. This is called the *Pine Pointe Trail*.

The vision for the Pine Pointe Trail was to create a pleasant experience. It provides an ability to enjoy the scenery by *looking up* and not needing to be so concerned about tripping. But the more popular trail has become the Goat Trail. It seems that folks are more interested in taking the path that appears to get you to your destination more quickly, even though it's more dangerous and not conducive to looking up. To be clear, the scenery on the Goat Trail is more interesting—but most people don't stop to enjoy it!

After carefully measuring and timing my walk back and forth on both paths, I discovered that the longer Pine Pointe Trail was actually quicker than the shorter Goat Trail.

There are times when we walk on a smooth path and have the ability to enjoy the journey and see the way forward clearly. There are other times when we're on a narrow rocky path. We feel alone and we look down in our attempt to maintain a sure footing.

We must look down so we can be aware of our adversary and not trip and fall. But we must also stop along the rocky path and take time to look up. It's at these moments that the view is the best and the glory is the greatest.

Both paths have a purpose. Enjoy the journey!

Dig deeper: *Psalm 40; Psalm 23; Psalm 119:105*

Brian Rupe

September 9

"A man's steps are from Yahweh; how then can man understand his way?" Proverbs 20:24

I worked at a small discipleship camp in Minnesota's north woods many years ago. One of my most vivid memories are the "Quiet Walks" that were the main event on the first night of camp every session.

We would tell the kids to be sure to wear clothes they didn't mind getting dirty...possibly very dirty. But that's all they knew. In fact, at the first camp session of the summer, even us new counselors didn't know any more than that! The Camp Director didn't tell us what we were in for. We were told to walk single file, no talking, and just follow.

We started out walking the back road, then took a side trail. When we got to a creek we got in, knee-deep, and walked the creek for awhile, then back up on the shore. Not long after, we were back in the creek...but it was a little deeper there. Pretty soon we were slogging or swimming through muddy water up to our shoulders. Leeches and crawling through culverts may have been part of that adventure, too!

The point? Quiet Walks were an excellent way for the staff to see what kinds of attitudes to expect from the kids. An excellent way to get these mostly-city kids over being dirty, since the next two weeks would involve lots of wilderness activities involving grime with no showers—like a 7-day canoe trip.

For those of us who've chosen to follow Jesus in this life, He often seems a lot like this Camp Director! He leads us along paths we just don't understand sometimes. And you know what? That's how He works!

You know how many people in the Bible knew what God was really up to when they said "yes" to following Him?

Zero.

We get clues...hints...promises. But we have to be willing to follow His steps without understanding His ways.

It's called *trust*. Trust in a good and faithful Shepherd.

Dig Deeper: *Psalm 13; Proverbs 3:5-6; Luke 9:23*

September 10

"...so we, who are many, are one body in Christ, and individually members of one another..." Romans 12:5

A herd of elephants. A pack of wolves. A pod of orcas. A troop of chimpanzees. A colony of bats. A hive of bees. A band of gorillas. A mob of meerkats. What do these all have in common? They're animal species that live in social groups.

The funniest names are quite descriptive: A tower of giraffes. A romp of sea otters. A cackle of hyenas. And a pandemonium of parrots! (source: *worldatlas.com*)

In the New Testament, Paul calls Jesus' followers a *body*. The Body of Christ. Every Christian on the planet is part of the Body of Christ. His point is that followers of Jesus aren't just a social group that have things in common—they literally make a living organism. A body.

In verse 6 of Romans 12 through the rest of the chapter, Paul instructs the members of this body how to live. How to function as a whole body, with each member operating in the gift or function he or she is designed for. And how to treat each other in the the body: with love, not hypocrisy. In goodness, not evil. In humility...with respect...in forgiveness...with blessing.

As members of this Body, we can't live as if we're not part of that body. Not if we want to follow Jesus. We each have to make the individual decision to follow Him. But once that decision is made, it includes being part of His body.

The Bible gives other names for this body, too: the Church, or *ekklésia* in Greek. It means *called out from* (the world) and *into* (God's kingdom). The other New Testament word translated church is *kyriakos*—belonging to the Lord.

God's body or church is also described as a family, a bride, a flock, and even a city. All these words give us a different idea of what it's like to be part of this special body.

How will you live today as part of His body?

Dig deeper: *Romans 12; 1 Corinthians 12*

September 11

"In the day that I called, you answered me. You encouraged me with strength in my soul." Psalm 138:3

There are some things the human body needs, and nothing else can replace it. One of the best examples is oxygen. When you don't have oxygen, it doesn't really matter what else you have. Your body won't do what you think it should do. When something as critical as oxygen is missing, peak performance decreases significantly.

I learned this while hiking through Peru's Andes mountains at 15,000 feet. Every step was a challenge. I needed more water, more rest, more breaths. In my mind I wanted to go faster, but when I tried to push myself I paid for it with breathlessness, dizziness and a pounding pulse.

The same is true spiritually. When we don't have Christ working through us, everything is harder and things just don't work like they're supposed to. Even small daily thoughts and tasks are meant for us to complete with Christ, not alone. And it changes everything. Christ teaches us that His yoke is easy and His burden is light (Matthew 11:30). He also says, *"I will be with you, even until the end of the age."* (Matthew 28:20)

Seeing my weakness and Christ's strength working through me helps me accomplish more than I could imagine. It also keeps me humble. I remember that I truly can't do it on my own, and I want to give the glory to God rather than absorb it for myself.

The best thing is that God promises to never leave us or forsake us. Hebrews 13:21 says He'll *"make you complete in every good work to do His will."*

As much as we need physical resources to keep our physical body alive, it's truly God's power and sovereignty that have control over our lives—not anything we can do.

How does God want to equip you today to overcome in *His* strength rather than your own?

Dig Deeper: *Isaiah 61:1-2; 2 Corinthians 9:8; 2 Timothy 3:17*

Emilie O'Connor

September 12

"Worthy are You, our Lord and God, the Holy One, to receive the glory, the honor, and the power, for You created all things, and because of Your desire they existed, and were created." Revelation 4:11

I was raised in a Christian home. I don't remember a time when I didn't believe in God and want to serve Him...but there were plenty of times when doubts would creep in. How did I know this was really true? How did I know God is really there?

For me it always comes down to the world around us and how it got here. It always comes down to the question of origins. Was it random chance over billions of years? Or was it a Designer who created everything?

Whenever I go back to the mind-blowing complexity of how a human being is formed, starting with a single cell...or how a huge oak tree comes from a single acorn...or the fine-tuning of the universe to support life here on this planet...it always brings me back to God. And not just any god, but the God of the Bible.

Personally, I can't believe the complexity of human DNA happened over time by random chance anymore than I can believe the laptop and software I'm using to write this page could come about over time by random chance. I don't care how much time you throw at it! This laptop and the software that runs it is not just designed, it's designed by very smart people—people much smarter than me.

And it's not just the physical systems that exist. What about the human mind and emotions? The longing for purpose? Dreams? Desires? Where did those things come from?

Could it be that we, as humans, have these things because we were created in the image of an infinitely wise God who also has these things? That's what the Bible teaches. *"You created all things, and because of Your desire they existed, and were created."*

Not random chance, but purpose.

No wonder we worship Him! *Worthy are you, Lord, to receive the glory!*

Dig Deeper: *Revelation 4*

September 13

"...every good tree produces good fruit, but the corrupt tree produces evil fruit. A good tree can't produce evil fruit, neither can a corrupt tree produce good fruit." Matthew 7:17-18

What makes a tree or bush produce good fruit?

We love picking wild blueberries and raspberries in northern Minnesota where we spend a lot of time camping. We've also discovered serviceberries, also called Saskatoon berries, growing wild up there on tall bushes.

The things that make these bushes grow good fruit are sunshine (they're all sun lovers), rain, soil—although they must not mind rocky soil since that's about all they get up there. The best blueberries, we discovered, are in the areas that were swept by a forest fire back in 2006. The ashy soil combined with plenty of sunshine have made them super fruitful.

The health of the plant itself—the roots, branches and leaves—makes abundant fruit possible.

The context of this verse in Matthew is Jesus warning His followers about false teachers. He tells us to look at the fruit these teachers produce.

We can also apply this to our own lives. Ask yourself: "Am I producing good fruit in my life?"

What does good fruit look like? Well, Galatians 5:22 gives us a short list of the fruit the Holy Spirit produces in a life that's submitted to Him: Love. Joy. Peace. Patience. Kindness. Goodness. Faithfulness. Gentleness. Self-control or self-management.

What kind of tree produces that kind of fruit? One that belongs to Jesus (Galatians 5:24). One that walks by the Spirit (Galatians 5:25). One that lives in the sunshine of God's love, and is rooted firmly in His soil, and is watered with the words of His truth.

Do you want to be that tree?

Dig deeper: *Matthew 7:15-20; Galatians 5:13-26*

September 14

"Be still, and know that I am God. I will be exalted among the nations. I will be exalted in the earth." Psalm 46:10

"Immediately the Spirit drove Him out into the wilderness." Mark 1:12

Three days of silence. Three days walking, paragliding, praying, worshiping and seeking God in silence. I had only seriously sought God in silence once before, and only for one day. This time I sought Him with all my heart, soul, mind, and strength (Mark 12:30).

I began at the foot of Mt. Blanc in Chamonix, France. I launched my paraglider and flew out of the Chamonix valley to Sallenches. From there I climbed high and found a place to camp beside a chapel at the Refuge de Doran. I set up my tent there beneath a 20-foot cross. God met me at the foot of that cross.

The next day I flew and walked along the east side of the Aravis range of the Alps. I didn't fly very far that day. It was extremely hot. Thankfully I only had a short walk before coming upon a small mountain camping site with a beautiful view of the Aravis and Mt. Blanc in the distance. I sat in silence as I watched the sunset, marveling at the majesty of God's creation.

The third day I walked and flew the rest of the Aravis range. Soaring above those majestic peaks, I broke my silence with song and praise of God's greatness and glory. Overall, I had walked and flown a total of 60 miles in three days, which is not very far for a "hike and fly"—but that had not been my purpose.

I sought God in silence and was found by Him in His creation.

Have you ever gotten away to God's creation—if even for a short time—to seek Him?

Dig Deeper: *Deuteronomy 27:9; Psalm 62:5; Ecclesiastes 3:7*

Brian Doub

September 15

"Whatever Yahweh pleased, that He has done, in heaven and in earth, in the seas and in all deeps." Psalm 135:6

God is wild in the sense that He's untamed. You can't box Him in like a sheep in a pen, or harness Him like a team of Belgian horses. Our God is undomesticated and uncontrolled by us.

In a world where we humans make god in our image to suit our purposes, this wild and untamed God is important for believers to get to know. It's how we can discern what's of God and what's of a god we've created.

Meeting God in His wildness may well mean being in a state of wildness ourselves. Our spiritual senses are often most stimulated when we're immersed in a space physically, mentally and socially—in a state of wildness. What do I mean by wildness?

I spent time in Minnesota's north woods over several summers and several years. I cherished the tranquility, stunning beauty and stark contrast from city life, and I found a deep sense of humility in the face of God's majestic power. It profoundly impacted me.

Being outdoors is a tonic to the soul. Fresh air, time to think. Experiencing creation's wonders and freedom for the senses. Ahhh! Then one August a storm came through Lake Superior. I was abruptly reminded of the awesome power of nature as the wind, rain and waves angrily battered the lakeshore.

I learned a new truth: God is as present in the ferocious wind of a northern storm front as He is in the warm, sun-drenched vista of a calm lake. In one moment I'm heartened and comforted by His abiding love and faithfulness. And in another moment I'm in reverent awe of God's immense power and sovereignty over us, His people and His world.

Knowing God in both these extremes helps us connect with Him in a wider sense. It broadens our journey with Him outside the confines of our own thinking and experiences, and helps us discern what's of Him and what isn't.

Dig Deeper: *Psalm 135:1-14; Daniel 4:34-35; Revelation 19:11-16*

Paul Scoringe

September 16

"You are Yahweh, even You alone. You have made heaven, the heaven of heavens, with all their army, the earth and all things that are on it, the seas and all that is in them, and You preserve them all. The army of heaven worships You." Nehemiah 9:6

All of Nehemiah chapter 9 is a prayer by the children of Israel. It begins with worship (the end of verse 5)—*"Blessed be Your glorious name, which is exalted above all blessing and praise!"*—and continues with verse 6, above.

In Nehemiah's day, the mid-400s BC, people had no idea of the complexity of the natural systems of the heavens, the earth, and everything in it. But their faith in His creative power and greatness is well-founded. And it's interesting they not only recognize His creative works, but *"You preserve them all."* He cares for His created works.

Do you have any idea of what it takes to sustain life on this planet of ours? It's only been since the 20th Century that scientists have realized how fine-tuned the universe really is:

"There are four fundamental forces of nature: Strong Nuclear Force, Weak Nuclear Force, Electromagnetic Force, and Gravity. These forces interact with matter such as atoms at the quantum level and also at the macroscopic level such as planets and stars.

"These interactions are essential for molecules to come together to form larger forms of matter. They are also necessary for the formation of all the elements of nature, such as hydrogen, carbon, and oxygen. They are also required for the generation of heat and light. Gravity allows planets to orbit around stars.

"These forces are crucial for life to exist in the universe. But the story doesn't stop there. Physicists have discovered that the magnitude of these forces can only deviate from their current values by a small range or else the universe cannot exist in its current form."

Surely our God preserves all He's made, including us. Thank You, Father!

Dig Deeper: *1 Chronicles 16:23-31*

(quote from SecretsUnlocked.org. Do an online search of "fine-tuned universe" and tons of articles come up.)

September 17

"You are Yahweh, even You alone. You have made heaven, the heaven of heavens, with all their army, the earth and all things that are on it, the seas and all that is in them, and You preserve them all. The army of heaven worships You." Nehemiah 9:6

Forbes.com (a secular business website) ran an article in 2019 called "The Universe Really Is Fine-Tuned, and Our Existence is the Proof" (do an online search and you can read it). Here's an excerpt:

"A universe with too much matter-and-energy for its expansion rate will recollapse in short order; a universe with too little will expand into oblivion before it's possible to even form atoms. Yet not only has our universe neither recollapsed nor failed to yield atoms... those two sides of the equation appear to be perfectly in balance...

"The universe's initial expansion rate and the sum total of all the different forms of matter and energy in the universe not only need to balance, but they need to balance to more than 20 significant digits... The odds of that occurring naturally...are astronomically small."

Nehemiah and the Israelites of his day had no idea that this was the case. They just believed their God was responsible for creating all they saw. They also believed He was overseeing and working in their own lives—on both a personal level and on a national level.

That belief sustained them, grounded them, gave them direction and purpose and was reason for them to worship God as Lord and Creator of all. They also knew they were worshiping with the army of heaven—those angelic beings in God's service.

God has created and preserves—not just galaxies—but each one of us. You. You are fine-tuned for purpose. Have you gone to your Father, your Creator to find out what that is? Knowing purpose and going after it, as Nehemiah did in his time, is one of the most fulfilling goals we can know.

What a good God we have!

Dig Deeper: *Jeremiah 29:11; Ephesians 2:10; 1 Peter 2:9*

September 18

"You are Yahweh, even You alone. You have made heaven, the heaven of heavens, with all their army, the earth and all things that are on it, the seas and all that is in them, and You preserve them all. The army of heaven worships You." Nehemiah 9:6

Let's take one more day to look at how Yahweh, the Creator of heaven and earth, has fine-tuned this universe He's put us in. While this may seem an odd devotional topic, this kind of scientific evidence has been the #1 thing that's kept me firm in my belief of God's reality. See what you think:

Here are some formulas from physics, taken from *Evidenceto-Believe.net*:

"From galaxies to stars, down to atoms and subatomic particles, the very structure of our universe is determined by these numbers: speed of light: $c=299,792,458$ m s-1...gravitational constant: $G=6.673$ x $10-11$ m3 kg-1 s-2...ratio of electron to proton mass: $(1836.15)-1$...mass of electron, proton, neutron: 0.511; 983.3; 939.6 MeV..."

There are a seven more on the list, but you get the idea. These numbers mean nothing to me, and probably not to you either unless you're a physics geek. But here's the point:

"Scientists have come to the shocking realization that each of these numbers have been carefully dialed to an astonishingly precise value—a value that falls within an exceedingly narrow, life-permitting range. If any one of these numbers were altered by even a hair's breadth, no physical, interactive life of any kind could exist anywhere. There would be no stars, no planets, no chemistry, and no life."

The God who created *"heaven, the heaven of heavens"* and the rest with that kind of astronomical precision is certainly worthy of our honor and worship! Knowing this makes *"His ways are higher than our ways"* the biggest understatement of all time!

Yes, Father, surely we *"Enter into Your gates with thanksgiving, and into Your courts with praise. We give thanks to You, and bless Your name!"* (Psalm 100:4)

Dig Deeper: *Psalm 100; Romans 11:36*

September 19

"Keep me as the apple of Your eye." Psalm 17:8

The apple of someone's eye is the pupil or the black spot in the middle of your eye. It allows light and images to go into your cornea and your brain gives you information regarding what you're viewing.

If something is coming towards that part of our eye, our eyelids shut involuntarily in order to protect this precious thing.

Why is being the *apple of God's eye* such a big deal?

God refers to His people Israel as the apple of His eye receiving His protection: *"He surrounded him. He cared for him. He kept him as the apple of His eye."* (Deuteronomy 32:10)

Think about it. God protected them not because He had to, because He wanted to! You protect things that are precious to you. You protect these things because they have value.

And so this is one reason why we are called the apple of God's eye—because we have value. You have value to God!

In calling us the apple of His eye, God is calling us to a deeper understanding of His love for us and a deeper intimacy with Him. Because if you are the apple of His eye, you're close enough to God to see your own image in God's eyes reflecting back at you. God whispers to us that this is His desire, to go deeper and deeper into a relationship with us.

We see this even while we're in the wilderness. No other place seems to call to the very heart of us like the beauty of creation that surrounds us. And no other place seems to allow us to be still long enough to hear that intimate whisper from God revealing how precious we are to Him.

Dig deeper: *Deuteronomy 32:7-14; Psalm 17:8*

Laura Watson

September 20

"Confess your offenses to one another, and pray for one another, that you may be healed..." James 5:16

Isn't it a delight to see a fresh, pure mountain river? So cold, so clear. You can clearly see the rocks and vegetation on the bottom, the fish swimming around.

What happens if the streams that feed that pure mountain river lose their own pureness? Often after a heavy rain silt and dirt get washed into the streams and get taken down to the main river. It takes awhile for all of that to settle and for the river to become clear again.

It's much worse if toxins get into the streams from pollution and chemical run-off. Those toxins build up and flow from the streams into the river where it'll mean slow death for the plants and animals that live there.

When we confess our offenses and our sins to one another it's like cleaning up the toxins out of a stream. It's important to maintain a clean heart before the Lord, of course. But also before our brothers and sisters in the Body of Christ.

Each of us is like a stream that feeds into the main river—the Body. A bunch of polluted streams make a polluted river. But when the streams are pure again, the river is also pure. It's healed.

It's important to have other believers in our life we trust to talk to about our temptations, and who we can confess to when we mess things up. We can then pray for each other, as James reminds us.

1 John 5:7 is similar. It says, *"If we walk in the light, as He is in the light, we have fellowship with one another, and the blood of Jesus Christ, His Son, cleanses us from all sin."*

Walking in the light means to walk out in the open. With clearness and purity. It's there that we can be healed, forgiven, have fellowship with each other and be cleansed by Jesus' blood.

Is the Holy Spirit trying to pinpoint something in your stream today? Are you willing to let Him?

Dig deeper: *Psalm 24:3-5; Matthew 5:8; 1 John 3:3*

September 21

"Everyone therefore who hears these words of Mine and does them, I will liken him to a wise man who built his house on a rock." Matthew 7:24

Lake Superior, the world's largest freshwater lake, has three different types of coastline: sand, pebbles or cobblestones, and rock. The south shore is mostly sand and rock. The north shore is mostly pebbles, cobblestones and rock.

Because sand consists of teeny particles, the wind can blow it around easily, heavy rain can make canals in it, and waves toss it all over the place.

The pebble and cobblestone beaches are more durable. Wind and rain don't make much of a dent on them. But if you walk the same beach before and after a major storm you'll see the shape of the beach has changed. Superior's big waves can toss them around very easily—just as easily as the sand.

Lots of people have built homes along Superior's shores. But you'll notice this—not one of them is built on a sand or pebble beach. Why? The foundation is too unstable. The houses are all built on solid rock which wind, heavy rains and up to 30-foot waves can't shift.

Jesus is saying here that when we listen to His words and obey them it's like we've built our house on the solid rock. Jesus and His words give us a solid foundation that stands up to the elements.

Here's the rest of the passage: *"The rain came down, the floods came, and the winds blew and beat on that house; and it didn't fall, for it was founded on the rock. Everyone who hears these words of Mine and doesn't do them will be like a foolish man who built his house on the sand. The rain came down, the floods came, and the winds blew and beat on that house; and it fell—and its fall was great."* (Matthew 7:25-27)

What's the difference? Not the hearing of Jesus' words, but doing them. Obeying them. It's that obedience that gives the solid foundation.

Dig deeper: *Matthew 5-7*

September 22

"For the law of the Spirit of life in Christ Jesus made me free from the law of sin and of death." Romans 8:2

I've been contemplating the idea of authority lately and what that means for us as followers of Jesus.

Then a recent walk in a local park had me thinking about the Laws of Nature. Things like gravity. Animals' instincts. The seasons. The orbits of the planets around our sun.

We can choose to believe in or not believe in the laws of nature. But that doesn't change the reality of those laws.

No matter how much we deny that winter is coming, if we live in the north it's going to get cold. We'll be in trouble if we haven't prepared. No matter how much we deny that geese have an instinct to migrate south for the winter, that doesn't stop the geese from migrating. I can deny the law of gravity all I want, but if I step off the side of a cliff I'm still under gravity's law.

The same is true in the spiritual world. No matter how much people deny it, there's a real *law of sin and death*. If we sin, the result is death. Spiritual death, many times emotional death, sometimes physical death, and eventually eternal death.

Thank God, there's also a real law of *the Spirit of life in Christ Jesus*! And that law of the Spirit conquered the law of sin and death at the cross and through Jesus' resurrection.

Those who come under the law of the Spirit as followers of Jesus have been made free from the law of sin and death.

So just as we come under the law of gravity by being careful along cliff edges, so we need to come under the law of the Spirit.

We've come out from under the authority of sin and death, and we put ourselves under the authority of Jesus and the freedom He gives.

Dig deeper: *Romans 8:1-14*

September 23

"Be to me a rock of refuge to which I may always go." Psalm 71:3

My husband and I spent a week at a guest ranch in central Colorado one autumn. The dominant natural feature in that area is Sheeprock, a granite dome that sits at 8,877 feet.

We rode horses on many trail rides that week, a different route each day. Even though we'd never been there before, whenever I looked around me and could find Sheeprock I knew where everything else was. I could get my bearings.

From Sheeprock I could find all the other high places we learned about that week: Sawtooth Mountain, Government Ridge, Helen's Rock, Apache Rock, Table Rock.

And from Sheeprock I always knew where the ranch was, in the valley below it.

It was comforting in a way, even though we always had a wrangler with us who knew the trails backwards and forwards. If, by chance, we lost our way all we had to do was locate Sheeprock and we'd be good from there.

When I read Psalm 71 that week at the ranch, verse 3 stood out to me right away: *"Be to me a rock of refuge to which I may always go."* Sheeprock was that physical rock of refuge to me that week. Other Bible versions translate it as a rock of habitation...a sheltering rock.

No one would want to live on Sheeprock. It's just granite. There's no life on top. It's exposed to the elements. But the song writer here is saying to God: *"Be my rock of habitation. I want to dwell, to live with You."*

We're invited into the Father's presence. His strong, loving, peaceful, joyful presence. When we set Him up as our rock of refuge, we can always get our bearings no matter what life throws at us. When we respond to Jesus' invitation to *"Come to Me, all you who labor and are heavily burdened..."* (Matthew 11:28) we come to that rock of refuge.

The invitation is open—today!

Dig deeper: Psalm 71

September 24

"I have come as a light into the world, that whoever believes in Me may not remain in the darkness." John 12:46

Anyone who's been to the wilderness at night knows what it's like to be in darkness. No street lights, no light from cars, no light from homes or businesses. We can see the stars so well there because of the lack of artificial light.

But when it's clouded over—when the light from the moon and stars is blocked—the darkness can be so thick we can almost feel it. In that kind of darkness it's easy to stumble over anything in our path. We can't see anything around us. It's easy to get disoriented and lost in physical darkness. It can quickly become dangerous, even life threatening in some cases.

The Bible uses the word *darkness* to describe spiritual darkness, too. Spiritual darkness includes things like: lies, despair, hopelessness, hate, lust, idolatry, jealousy, envy, division, rage, pride, complaining, sexual sin, rebellion. There are lists of what the Bible calls "deeds of darkness" in Galatians 5, Ephesians 5 and Jude.

Jesus, though, came *as a light into the world*. He said those who believe in Him don't have to remain in spiritual darkness. Whether the darkness happens to us due to someone else's sinful choices or as a result of our own sinful choices—we don't have to stay there.

Spiritual light—the light Jesus is and brings—includes things like: clarity, purpose, confidence, trust, faith, peace, joy, goodness, self-control, kindness, faithfulness, patience, perseverance.

Just like we can hike down a trail with confidence and purpose with the sunlight, or even a headlamp...so with Jesus as the Light in us and for us, we can walk with Him with confidence and purpose in this journey of life.

We don't have to remain in darkness. We can choose it. Jesus won't stop us from choosing it. But He longs for us to walk in His light. He longs to be our Light. His invitation is for you—for all of us—to come into His Light.

Dig deeper: Romans 8

September 25

"Give diligence to present yourself approved by God...properly handling the Word of Truth." 2 Timothy 2:15

Those whose career is a professional wilderness guide or a canoe or kayak instructor will likely have certification in one or more training programs required for their job. The same is true for those in wilderness ministry anytime they take students on backcountry trips, or those who work at summer camps for kids.

It could be certification in *Leave No Trace*. It could be American Canoe Association certification for any level of canoe, sea kayak or whitewater paddle skills. It could be Wilderness First Aid.

These certifications are so those responsible for others in the wilderness or in outdoor activities "present themselves approved" to people, to "handle accurately the word of truth" for their field.

That's also the point behind seminary and Bible college for believers who are called into ministry in some form or other. But it's not just those in full-time church, ministry or missions careers who need to take note of this verse. Paul's words to Timothy are for *all of us* who call ourselves followers of Jesus.

One of my favorite quotes I've read recently is this: "If you're a full-time Christian, you're in full-time ministry."

Each of us is to *give diligence to present ourself approved to God*. To know what He asks of us and obey it. Each of us is to *handle accurately the word of truth*. And if we are to handle His word accurately, we need to *know* His word—all of it, not just a few of our favorite verses.

Have you said "yes" to Jesus when He invited you to follow Him? If you have, this is for you! It's for me, too. It's for all those who are on this journey with Him through life.

Dig deeper: Psalm 119 *(it's long, but worth it!)*

September 26

"Our soul has waited for Yahweh. He is our help and our shield. For our heart rejoices in Him, because we have trusted in His holy name." Psalm 33:20-21

When you're rock climbing or bouldering, it's good to keep moving. Getting stuck on the wall is so hard because every second you're there trying to determine your next move, your muscles become more fatigued.

It can feel like this in life, too. We can feel stuck in one spot and then feel like what's required of us to stay there takes away the energy needed to move forward.

Dreaming and reaching for something in life can feel like reaching for the next hold on the rock wall—just out of reach.

Thankfully, our Heavenly Father says that He's prepared a path for us to walk. He cares about our hopes and dreams even more than we do. When we dream, God wants us to put our hope in Him. In Matthew 6:33, Jesus talks about how to orient our hearts so we reach for God, and trust that God holds our dreams.

He says, *"Seek first God's Kingdom and His righteousness; and all these things will be given to you as well."* (Matthew 6:33) When we put God first, He's faithful to meet all our needs and fulfill our dreams as well. And when we know God relationally, our heart and mind are aligned with His. We begin to have dreams for our life that align with our calling and what God wants to give us.

I've learned that when I put my hopes and dreams in God, I don't feel stuck and weary with no place to go. It's no longer about my perspective, rather it's about God's perspective.

He sees so much more. God promises that when we seek Him, we will find Him. Our dreams can never be stagnant when we seek God, because God is always willing to show us more of Himself.

Dig Deeper: *Proverbs 16:3; Matthew 7:7; Philippians 1:6*

Emilie O'Connor

September 27

"He said with a loud voice, 'Fear the Lord, and give Him glory... Worship Him who made the heaven, the earth, the sea and the springs of waters!' " Revelation 14:7

Have you stood at the brink of Niagara Falls and witnessed the volume and power of the water flowing down? Have you stood on a mountain top, awestruck by the majesty all around you? Have you wondered at a crystal-clear river running over rocks or the exquisite petals of a wildflower?

When you have, where did your thoughts turn?

What does your belief system tell you about how all these things came to be?

The Bible tells us from Genesis to Revelation that God is the one *"who made the heaven, the earth, the sea and the springs of water"*—everything in heaven and earth. And then, as the angel in Revelation says with a loud voice: Fear Him and worship Him. Give Him the reverence and honor He deserves. He is Lord.

Christianity in our culture has tended to make moral issues the main thing. But morality isn't the main thing—*authority* is. Who's in charge? Who has the right to tell us what to do and how to live?

Who or what is the authority in *your* life? Who gets to call the shots? Who decides? If you're an American like me, rebellion and independence run deep in our culture. If we're not careful, even as followers of Jesus we allow that independence and self-rule to be our authority. We can easily give in to: "You can't tell me what to do or how to think!"

There's a reason we call Him: *Lord Jesus.* There's a reason the Bible emphasizes the fear of God. It's not an afraid fear, it's a reverent, honoring fear. He is God and I am not.

When we receive Jesus as our Savior we also say to Him: "You're my Lord...my King...my authority. I will obey You."

Worshiping Him without bowing the knee to His authority in our everyday life is just emotionalism.

Dig deeper: *Exodus 19:5; John 15; Romans 6:16-18*

September 28

"Your way was through the sea; Your paths through the great waters. Your footsteps were not known." Psalm 77:19

Has it ever occurred to you that God's way might be through the sea?

The psalmist here is recounting the story of the Hebrews' triumphant Exodus out of Egypt, the land of their slavery. They left loaded with riches—the plunder of the Egyptians—rejoicing, confident, free.

But very soon they experienced "the death of the vision." They were trapped with the Red Sea in front of them and the entire Egyptian army closing in behind them.

The Hebrews had already witnessed ten miraculous plagues or judgments God had used to humble Pharaoh and his mighty empire (told in Exodus 7-12). Yet faced with this impossible situation, they immediately fell into fear and unbelief. They couldn't see a way out so they assumed there wasn't one.

They didn't know God's way was through the sea—without a boat!

Maybe you're faced with an impossible situation, too. You have a sea in front of you, no boat, and a threatening army behind you. Where's God in this?

Maybe you were following God's instructions when you ended up here. The Hebrews were! God told Moses exactly where they were to camp that night. And they ended up sitting ducks for Pharaoh and his soldiers.

But God had an idea no one had thought of. His path was through the sea. Through the impossible. He wasn't limited by *normal*. He still isn't limited by normal.

Some of our life situations are more impossible than others. But in all of them, we can pull down the panic and fear that naturally rises up, and choose to listen to the Lord's voice. What's He saying here at the edge of the sea?

The way we find out is to be still before Him, listen to His voice and then do what He says.

Dig deeper: Jeremiah 32:27; Matthew 19:26; Luke 18:27

September 29

"For the body is not one member, but many." 1 Corinthians 12:14

Read through 1 Corinthians 12:14-27. Then read it again.

Think of a large human body laying flat on the ground on his or her back. Where's the head? Where are the feet and hands? Where's the heart and the bones?

What body part do you consider yourself to be in the Kingdom of God? In your mind, move to that part of the body on the grass and stand there. What about your friends and others in your life. Where would they stand in that imaginary body?

Why did you put yourself where you did? For example, if you see yourself as a hand, what reasons do you have for that? Is that where you'd like to be? If not, what might need to happen for you to "become" that new body part? And if you are where you want to be, what makes that a good fit for you?

In this passage, Paul tries to get us to see our value to God and God's Kingdom. It gets us to see our role in relation to others. Realize that you can shift roles—no one is forcing you to be the body part you first identified in yourself. You might even ask your friends or family members in the "body" to tell you which body part they see you as.

Now, read the passage one more time. Thank the Lord for placing you in His body in just the way He did. Ask Him to show you new ways you can serve His body in that role. Or ask Him to help you become the "body part" He designed for you.

Dig Deeper: *Romans 12*

Tom Smith

September 30

"For the invisible things of Him since the creation of the world are clearly seen, being perceived through the things that are made, even His everlasting power and divinity..." Romans 1:20

This is an incredible truth: we can know who God is, in part, through Creation. He's put glimpses of Himself in what He's made.

We know God is creative because our world is full of variety. Not just one kind of bird, but thousands of bird species. Not just one kind of bee, but thousands of bee species. Not just one kind of flower, but thousands of flower species.

We know God is strong because of the immovability of mountains. The power of ocean waves. The immense energy released through volcanoes.

We know God loves beauty because of the vast arrays of colors, textures and sounds in the natural world. (That's one of the reasons wilderness is so special—we get to see beauty there that few others make the effort to see!)

We know God gives great attention to detail because of the staggering details in nature—some of which scientists are still discovering. The tiny organisms that color the hot springs of Yellowstone...the mind-blowing DNA coding in the cells of every living organism...the construction of every bird feature.

We know God is tenacious. We can get a glimpse of it by seeing trees growing out of mountainsides. By watching a mother defend its young.

We know God is orderly by looking into the heavens. The billions of stars out there seem random, but they're not! If we can find the Big Dipper, we know which way north is.

We know God loves redemption. Just go back to a forest the year after a wildfire—even later in the same season. New growth starts coming up surprisingly soon.

Next time you're out in nature, ask God to show you Himself in what He's created!

Dig deeper: *Isaiah 40:28; Hebrews 1:3; James 1:17*

October

October 1

"If anyone is thirsty, let him come to me and drink!" John 7:37

In John 4 we read about how Jesus meets a Samaritan woman who was drawing water at Jacob's well. Jesus asked the woman for a drink of water, thus beginning a conversation about a different kind of water—one spiritual in nature, of which she knew nothing about.

We know water is naturally beneficial to us, and Jesus offers water that is spiritually beneficial.

For those of us who love to enjoy the great outdoors, we know that water is therapeutically beneficial as well. As a kayaker, I know being on the water is both calming and healing.

My family has the privilege of hosting a few thousand people on the water, via kayak, each year. While some want to see birds and animals, others just want to enjoy a quiet, relaxing experience.

Regardless of the motive, experiencing water brings a peaceful and calming effect to our souls. The busyness of our society can create a stressful environment, and kayaking is one way to counter stress by creating an avenue for physical and spiritual health.

Drinking water is necessary for the survival of our bodies, and its therapeutic value is not to be overlooked either.

But the most important benefit to us is the spiritual water Christ offers: *"Now on the last and greatest day of the feast, Jesus stood and cried out, 'If anyone is thirsty, let him come to Me and drink! He who believes in Me, as the Scripture has said, from within him will flow rivers of living water.' "* (John 7:37-38)

Dig deeper: John 4:1-42

Mark Bullington

October 2

"...But we have Christ's mind." 1 Corinthians 2:16

Let's back up a little bit in this chapter: *"...no one knows the things of God, except God's Spirit. But we received not the spirit of the world, but the Spirit which is from God, that we might know the things that were freely given to us by God."* (1 Corinthians 2:11-12)

That's what is means to have Christ's mind. Those who've been born again into the life of God received the Spirit of God—the Holy Spirit. He teaches us Christ's mind, according to this passage.

In the past few years I've been very aware of a specific part of Christ's mind: His creativity. Just look around you at the world He made. Look at the variety of trees, grasses, flowers and edible plants. He thought up all the different mammals, insects, fish, reptiles. The variety of rocks, gemstones and minerals came out of His mind. The planets, stars and galaxies, too. It's astounding!

This three-in-one God—Father, Son and Holy Spirit—is the most creative Person in the universe!

Because all people are made in God's image, everyone has God-given creativity, too. But here in 1 Corinthians it says we can have Christ's mind. That's creativity on a whole other level. One author calls it "our unfair advantage"!

So I've been on a journey the past few years of asking Him for His creativity. I say, "Lord, You're the most creative Person in the universe. I need Your creativity here. Please give me Your idea for this!"

Sometimes it's a problem that needs to be solved. Sometimes I need a creative idea for a writing or a design project. Sometimes it's how to answer someone's question. It's definitely not limited to what we usually think of as "spiritual." Rather, we want Jesus' creative mind for every part of life.

Have you thought of this before? The incredibly creative mind of God? If you're His son or daughter, you have access to His thoughts through your relationship with Him. Ask Him!

Dig deeper: *1 Corinthians 2*

October 3

"...that you may walk worthily of the Lord, to please Him in all respects, bearing fruit in every good work and increasing in the knowledge of God..." Colossians 1:10

The Bible uses this metaphor of bearing fruit often. We see fruit-bearing plants and trees all around us in nature. What we see in the physical world, God wants to be true of us, too—*"bearing fruit in every good work..."*

Strawberry plants, banana trees, grape vines—these plants bear a specific kind of fruit because it's in their DNA. The genetic code in each of the fruit-bearing plants tells it how and what sort of fruit to grow. Wild or cultivated, plants designed to bear fruit will bear fruit.

When we join God's family by repenting of our sins and accepting Jesus' work of salvation, He puts His DNA in us to bear fruit for His Kingdom. Fruit-bearing becomes part of who we are as we *"walk worthily"* of Him and *"please Him in all respects."*

It's like blueberry bushes. All are designed to bear fruit...but the ones with the biggest, tastiest fruit are the ones in the best conditions—plenty of sun, ashy soil, enough rain. We're like that, too. When our spirit and mind are growing in the right conditions, healthy fruit comes naturally.

Are you seeing God's good fruit in your life? Examples can be:
- Healthy relationships with others
- The Fruit of the Spirit: love, joy, peace, patience and the rest
- An emotional life that's not ruled by things like anxiety, fear and anger
- A growing desire to know more of God and His word, for prayer and worship
- A growing desire to share the Lord with others, and to disciple or mentor others

If these fruits aren't developing in your life the way you'd like them to be, check your conditions. Ask the Holy Spirit to help you walk worthily, please Him and increase in His knowledge. Look for good works you can get involved in. And then trust Him to do the fruit bearing through you!

Dig deeper: *Ezekiel 17:23; Matthew 3:7-10; Galatians 5:22-23*

October 4

"By faith, we understand that the universe has been framed by the word of God, so that what is seen has not been made out of things which are visible." Hebrews 11:3

The mystery of the ages: how did all that we see around us get here? Including us.

Science thinks it's answered that question: random chance + natural processes + eons of time = all that we see around us.

But when it comes down to it, science can't explain it either. How did the natural processes begin? Where did all the matter come from? How can billions of pieces of genetic code come from nothing?

Scientists have to take it by faith and ask *us* to take it by faith, too. But faith in what? They also have to believe that what is seen has not been made out of things which are visible because at some point in the past, there was nothing visible. And yet, if they reject God as a fable, what option do they have?

Oh, they keep coming up with theories. But the more science discovers about the unbelievable complexity and interrelation of everything around us, the more these theories seem crazier than the idea of God!

The Bible assumes it was His idea and His action. It's a theme throughout the whole Bible—God is the Creator. This world was made—not by chance—but by a Mind so wise, so creative, so over-the-top above us that we can't hope to understand it.

"For as the heavens are higher than the earth, so are my ways higher than your ways, and my thoughts than your thoughts." Isaiah 55:9

It's a mystery! We can't explain it—but we can believe it and wonder at it and thank Him for it.

Dig deeper: *I encourage you to read books by Christian PHDs on their findings in their arenas of science. A great one to start with is "Undeniable: How Biology Confirms our Intuition that Life is Designed" by Dr. Douglas Axe. It's written for the everyday reader.*

October 5

"...but we also rejoice in our sufferings, knowing that suffering produces perseverance..." Romans 5:3

In the summer of 1999 there was a tremendous straight-line wind that swept across the Boundary Waters Canoe Area that toppled nearly 500,000 acres of trees. The damage was beyond belief. Though it was a sad day, it was also part of the way God works in establishing a new beginning and renewing the forest.

Some trees in the path of the wind survived. It would be these trees that would help in the process of healing and creating the next generation of forests.

Perhaps the greatest attributes of the surviving trees were a deep root system and a stronger trunk. There's an amazing process within a tree that teaches us a critical spiritual truth. As the wind blows, chemicals are released within the tree, causing the trunk to grow larger in diameter—not just larger overall, but larger in relationship to the wind direction.

In other words, the tree has an understanding of the direction adversity is coming from and prepares itself for future challenges. Stronger winds equal healthier trees!

The winds of adversity are no stranger to any human soul and no one gleefully signs up for hard times. But ultimately it's the storms of life that cause our spirits to grow stronger and our roots to go deeper.

The storms are part of the equation—the other part is our response. In difficult times, will we bend to His love and purpose for our lives? Will we remind ourselves that God is doing a work inside of us even if we don't yet understand what it is?

In Romans 5:3-5 Paul explains the process: *"...we also rejoice in our sufferings, knowing that suffering produces perseverance; and perseverance, proven character; and proven character, hope: and hope doesn't disappoint us, because God's love has been poured into our hearts through the Holy Spirit..."*

Let's press on to know the Lord in the good times and in the hard times.

Dig deeper: *Psalm 107:28-31; Nahum 1:7; James 1:2-5*

Brian Rupe

October 6

"The heavens are Yours. The earth also is Yours, the world and its fullness. You have founded them." Psalm 89:11

We recognize that, while the Lord has given us stewardship of the earth, it's *His* because He founded or established it.

So what does that mean for us as people? As *His* people? As soon as God created Adam *"Yahweh God took the man, and put him into the garden of Eden to cultivate and keep it."* (Genesis 2:15)

While, as Christians, people are first in priority, part of our assignment from the Lord is care for the environment He's placed us in. This can include our home, if we have one. Our yard and neighborhood. Local parks and natural areas. And also wilderness, natural resources, animal and plant life in all different ecosystems.

The world and its fullness are God's, but He's placed them under our care. It's an act of worship back to Him when we cultivate and care for the things He's created.

That can be worked out practically in so many different ways!

It can mean growing beautiful flower gardens in your yard. It could be planting a community garden for you and your neighbors. If you're an animal lover it can mean volunteering at a local rescue or rehab center.

It can mean getting on trail clean-up crews to help others enjoy the trails. It can mean recycling, conserving energy, cleaning up your local waterways when you see garbage. It can mean being a careful consumer, only replacing items when you need them instead of when the newest model comes out.

Ask the Lord today if you need a change of heart and mind about this. If the earth and heavens are His, does that change how you view them? Is there something He's calling you to do, or do differently?

How can you partner with God to care for His world?

Dig deeper: *Genesis 2; Psalm 8*

October 7

"...walk just like He walked." 1 John 2:6

There's a John Muir quote I like: "People ought to saunter in the mountains, not hike!"

"Are you sauntering or hiking?" one of my students asked me as he walked behind me on the trail. "I'm living in the tension," I replied.

We were on our fall backpacking trip in Michigan's Pictured Rocks, hiking the cliff tops and beaches of Lake Superior. It had been an amazing day, full of the beauty of peak fall colors and miles-wide views of the world's largest lake.

That morning we had read a story together about the naturalist, John Muir, who exhorted those he met to saunter down the trail and not hike too quickly and miss what the trail had to offer. I had encouraged our group to take their time, revel in the wonder, and soak up everything we were seeing.

As we kept walking, I realized that, while I wanted the group to enjoy the walk, I also knew that we had to hike a certain distance before dark to make it to our campsite. So I was living in the tension of wanting to saunter slowly, yet needing to move the group along and make it to our destination.

That night around the campfire, I shared our conversation with the whole group and explained we had been living a metaphor that day of what it's like to keep God present in our everyday lives. On our backpacking trips students are offered space to slow down and spend focused, intimate time with God—to saunter. But at the end of the trip we all have to return to our daily lives and continue the hike.

I encouraged them to keep living in the tension of slowing down to be with God while moving through the busyness of their college lives. And ultimately, not to divide the two experiences, but to allow our hiking to be infused with sauntering. To allow God's presence and our attention to Him to infuse all of our living.

Dig deeper: *Matthew 14:23; Ephesians 2:10; 1 John 2:6*

William Hayes

October 8

"Whoever dwells in the shelter of the Most High will rest in the shadow of the Almighty." Psalm 91:1

Other versions translate it *secret place* or *hiding place* instead of *shelter*. But here's the point: Whoever dwells there will rest in the shadow of the Almighty. Will be covered and protected by the Lord.

If you're an outdoor lover you may love to go camping. It could be 10 miles from home, in a nearby state park or off the grid in the backcountry somewhere. One of the things that defines camping: it's temporary.

You find a campsite or backcountry spot you like and you set up camp there. It might be overnight...it might be for the weekend...it might be for a week or two. But you know it's temporary. That's why tents are designed to be put up and taken down easily and quickly.

We bring things along we'll need in our car or backpack—or canoe or kayak, if it's a paddle trip. But usually we pack pretty light because we know it's just for a little while. And, especially with wilderness camping, you want to leave the campsite as if no one had been there.

This isn't what the psalmist is talking about. It doesn't say "Whoever *camps* in the shelter of the Most High..." It says "Whoever *dwells*..." Whoever lives there.

It's not just setting up camp for a few days—a weekend conference or a year in Bible school. It's building a house there. Moving in with all your stuff. Changing your address. Planting a garden. Those are the ones who are sheltered and protected by the shadow of the Almighty.

What does it look like to live in the *shelter*, in the *secret place* of God? What is the secret place? It's God's presence. It's in His word. Jesus talks about going to our inner closet to pray—it's that inner closet with the door shut, to be with Him, away from distraction and attention (Matthew 6:6).

Are you camping or living in God's shelter? His secret place?

Dig deeper: Psalm 91

October 9

"Walk in love, even as Christ also loved us and gave Himself up for us, an offering and a sacrifice to God for a sweet-smelling fragrance." Ephesians 5:2

Wouldn't the world be a much less beautiful place without the sweet-smelling fragrances of flowers? The ability to smell—limited as it is for us humans, compared to other members of creation—makes life so rich.

Here in Minnesota the lilacs bloom in late May or early June every year. You can smell the sweet fragrance of these flowers from several feet away. It always makes me close my eyes, breathe in deeply and be thankful for something so wonderful!

Whether in the fields and woods, in our gardens at home, or cut in a vase inside, flowers bless us with their fragrance.

Did you know we can bless our Heavenly Father with a sweet-smelling fragrance, too? We do that when we *walk in love*. Imagine the Father closing His eyes, breathing in deeply and being blessed by the sweet-smelling fragrance that rises up when you walk in love toward others around you.

Keep in mind this love isn't what our culture means—feelings of emotion towards other people. This is God's kind of love that was lived out by Jesus when He took our punishment on the cross. It's the kind of love described in 1 Corinthians 13 (have you read that lately?).

To walk in love, even as Christ also loved us, is simple—but it's not always easy. In fact, sometimes it seems impossible! But it's part of God's purpose for us as long as we're living on this earth. It's part of what defines His people.

And even if the people around us—especially the impossible people in our life—don't appreciate it when we love them by our actions, to God it's a sweet-smelling fragrance! That's reason enough to obey this command to *walk in love*.

How can you walk in love with those around you today?

Dig deeper: Ephesians 5

October 10

"He sent from on high. He took me. He drew me out of many waters." Psalm 18:16

I hated my middle name—Douglas. Yech. My parents told me Douglas means *seeker of light*. Whatever. My outlook was not improved when I learned the name in ancient Scottish meant *of dark or muddy water*.

My quest for a clear self-image led to the conclusion that some people are made to be capable, successful and close to God in their divinely-given mission. Others, like me, are meant to be used, quiet, doing the dirty work for others' benefit.

By my twenties the irritation with my name faded, but the feeling of neglect and low station in life persisted.

As my camping career advanced, I found I had a passion for wilderness guiding. I found shepherding others to a new way of seeing themselves so they could experience God to be very promising...for them. I still feared facing my true beliefs about God's heart.

One day I opened my Bible and read these words: *"He reached down from on high and took hold of me; He drew me up out of muddy waters...He brought me out into a spacious space; He rescued me because He delighted in me."* (Psalm 18:16, 19 NIV)

My name came to life with breath from the Creator! God had saved these words just for me for almost 3,000 years. I felt simultaneously loved and corrected.

Purpose and kindness combined with the knowledge that I had lost many years to the fear that God could not overcome my worthlessness. I was being invited into a space in front of the throne that Jesus had saved for me. But I had to be willing to move into that space.

What about you? Is your picture of yourself standing in the way of seeing yourself as Jesus does? Are you losing time that could be spent with Him and spending it instead on living out your fear of Him because you think He has the same thoughts about you that you do?

Dig deeper: Psalm 18

Matt White

October 11

"Oh give thanks to Yahweh, for He is good. His love endures for-ever." 1 Chronicles 16:34

When we focus on gratitude there's a literal change in our brains! Like a switch that gets flipped from being in the *off* to the *on* position.

Why does it matter if our switch is off or on?

Well, that "switch" in our brains is what helps us connect, engage and develop healthy relationships. God wants a relationship with us, and He wants us to build healthy relationships with others—family, friends, co-workers, other students.

How do you know if your switch is on or off? An organization called *LifeModelWork.org* developed these indicators to ask yourself whether your relationship switch is turned off:

- I just want to make a problem, person or feeling go away
- I don't want to listen to what others feel or say
- I'm dwelling on a situation that's upsetting
- I'm not willing to hear what others feel or say
- I can't feel gratitude or appreciation

If any of these sound like you, your relational switch is likely off. Hey, it's ok. We all end up there from time to time. But if you're stuck in that place, you're missing out on so much. An *off* switch means you're in survival mode. But instead of just surviving, God wants us to thrive! And it starts with a flip of a switch.

Engaging in an attitude of gratitude is one of the things you can do to turn the switch *on*. A gratitude moment will help you reconnect to many of the fruits of the Spirit: joy, peace, kindness and others.

I know, it's hard in moments of stress to stop and have a gratitude moment. But I'm putting it to you: Try this in your own life. Just find one thing to be grateful for today. Just one. See the difference it'll make in your relationship with God and other people. Because why wouldn't you want more peace and joy in your life?

Dig deeper: *Psalm 118:29; Psalm 126:2; 1 Corinthians 15:57*

Laura Watson

October 12

"For every kind of animal, bird, creeping thing, and sea creature is tamed, and has been tamed by mankind; but nobody can tame the tongue. It is a restless evil, full of deadly poison." James 3:7-8

By James' day, about two thousand years ago, people had successfully tamed all kinds of animals. But the tongue had been untamable. Our words, James says, have the potential to be deadly poison.

In our day people have "tamed" even more—germs and disease, weather, gravity (through air and space travel) and other things James and his contemporaries never dreamed of. And yet the tongue is still untamed.

Why is that? The Bible tells us it's because *"out of the abundance of the heart, his mouth speaks."* (Luke 6:45) And *"The heart is deceitful above all things and it is exceedingly corrupt."* (Jeremiah 17:9)

The tongue speaks out of what's in our heart. If our heart isn't cleaned up through Jesus' blood—if we haven't repented and invited Him in as our Savior and as our King—it's at the mercy of the sin we were born with.

You only have to look as far as online forums and social media to see the *restless evil and deadly poison* of peoples' words. Kids are killing themselves to escape the online bullying of their peers. Adults rant at each other like toddlers. And offline, families tear each other apart with their words.

James says, *"We put bits into the horses' mouths so that they may obey us, and we guide their whole body"* (verse 3) but we have yet to put a bit into our own mouth to guide our words.

Even as followers of Jesus we struggle with this. We truly need the Holy Spirit to fill us up and give us His power in this area!

The good news is that He'll help us! One of the fruits of the Spirit listed in Galatians 5 is *self-control*, or self-government.

We, with the Spirit's help, can control what comes out of our mouth, whether it's spoken or written. Help us, Holy Spirit!

Dig deeper: *Proverbs 15:4; Proverbs 16:24; James 5:17-18*

October 13

"The righteous shall flourish like the palm tree. He will grow like a cedar in Lebanon...They will still produce fruit in old age. They will be full of sap and green..." Psalm 92:12, 14

At this time of my life, what I call "on the slippery side of my 50s," verses like this are so encouraging! (If you're young, you'll understand someday.) There's a promise for God's people that as we walk in His ways, according to His righteousness we'll *still produce fruit* into old age.

There's no retirement in God's kingdom! Yes, we have to slow down eventually. We won't have the same physical energy and stamina as in our younger days. But—like the date palm and cedar of Lebanon—we can keep being fruitful, keep full of sap and green...at least on the inside, in our spirit and soul.

If you do an online search for "2,000 year old palm seed" you'll find a bunch of articles about some date palm seeds that had been hidden away in an ancient jar. The jar, thought to be about 2,000 years old, was discovered in an archeological dig in Israel in the 1960s.

About 40 years later, someone thought to plant one of these seeds. That 2,000 year old seed not only sprouted, it matured and pollinated a female date palm, which produced dates! That's what you call being fruitful in old age!

The key to that fruitfulness is found in verse 13 of Psalm 92: *"They are planted in Yahweh's house. They will flourish in our God's courts."*

We're kept in God house. In Christ. We live there. We abide there. We stay full of the Holy Spirit and His life. We stay in God's word. We stay in God's presence. We don't get cantankerous and crotchety.

The DNA as a fruit-bearer is there in all of us, no matter our age. Will we provide an atmosphere of life within us? Or let our inner life dry up and be fruitless, thinking our time is over?

It's really our choice.

Dig deeper: *Matthew 5:16; Philippians 1:6; 2 Timothy 4:6-8*

October 14

"The construction of its wall was jasper. The city was pure gold, like pure glass. The foundations of the city's wall were adorned with all kinds of precious stones. The first foundation was jasper; the second, sapphire; the third, chalcedony; the fourth, emerald; the fifth, sardonyx; the sixth, sardius; the seventh, chrysolite; the eighth, beryl; the ninth, topaz; the tenth, chrysoprase; the eleventh, jacinth; and the twelfth, amethyst. The twelve gates were twelve pearls. Each one of the gates was made of one pearl. The street of the city was pure gold, like transparent glass." Revelation 21:18-21

These verses in Revelation are describing the heavenly city: *"...the holy city, Jerusalem, coming down out of heaven from God, having the glory of God..."* (verses 10-11)

How is the glory of God described here? As gemstones, precious stones. Jasper, sapphire, emerald, amethyst...and the precious metal gold...and as pearls. Not just bits and pieces of these sought-after and valuable minerals, but huge reserves of them. Enough to be the foundation of a city or the gate in a wall.

What does this tell us? Well, for one, that God loves beauty! These stones are all exquisite in their own colors and translucence. Blues, greens, reds, yellows and purples. God created all of them, hid them in the earth and waited for people to discover them. To also find them delightful, worth looking for and crafting into beautiful objects.

God gave Moses specific instructions about how to build His tabernacle. Later, He did the same with Solomon, who built His temple. These descriptions are found in Exodus chapters 25-31 and in 1 Kings 6. The overriding themes in all three of these constructions—the tabernacle, the temple and the heavenly city—are beauty, color and magnificence.

And since people are made in God's image, we instinctively yearn for those things, too. We respond to them. Sometimes we can get too utilitarian with our thinking as Christians: "What use it it?" "Will it solve a problem?"

God loves and created beauty for its own sake—for His delight, and ours!

Dig deeper: *Revelation 21*

October 15

"For everything there is a season, and a time for every purpose under heaven: a time to be born, and a time to die..." Ecclesiastes 3:1-2

The multitude of autumn colours is so beautiful in the mountains. It inspires pictures, paintings, poems and stories. Sitting on the hill below Alpinis, surrounded by the bright orange birch trees, I wondered what would it inspire in me—not a poet, nor a painter.

A scene so common every autumn, after the first frost, leaves turn from the full bright green to the rich variety of yellow–orange–gold. Soon they fall, leaving the white trees barren for the winter. When spring buds turn to green again, all is beautiful, but we are not as taken by it as we are in the autumn.

The change of colours is a sign of aging and death, of passing and loss of vitality. In a world that worships youth, beauty and health nature has no problem with aging and changing. The Teacher in Ecclesiastes says, *"For everything there is a season."* We struggle to embrace the passing, the aging. Some seek to compensate with esthetics, trying to remain, or at least look, young. Esthetic surgery and cosmetics are good business.

The bright change of colours are also a sign of falling asleep. Nature goes to bed over the winter, resting and preparing for new life in the spring. Sleeping peacefully is a blessing, David counts it a sign of feeling safe: *"In peace I will both lay myself down and sleep, for you, Yahweh alone, make me live in safety."* (Psalm 4:8). Safety and peace are found in the Lord. In Him we rest well.

Leaves don't just turn bright and die—the richest soil is enriched by leaves. They become the fertiliser for life to continue. The bright faith we model and show by aging beautifully leaves a legacy of faith. It nourishes and enriches the faith of those who come after us.

Dig deeper: *Genesis 8:22; Ezekiel 34:26; Acts 1:7*

Emil Toader

October 16

"For everything there is a season, and a time for every purpose under heaven: a time to be born, and a time to die..." Ecclesiastes 3:1-2

Can aging be beautiful? Birch trees in the autumn say "Yes!" I am sure we all know people who age(d) in a way that made us admire their bright orange leaves. Next to me as I write there are the memories of four dear friends who taught us this lesson: Bonnie, Bill, Alec and Pati. Beautiful, bright lives full of colour to the last moment!

Aging is not giving up or giving in, but embracing the meaning of the new season. I once asked a friend how I could pray for him. His words were very simple: "Pray that I finish well."

"For everything there is a season, and a time for every purpose under heaven..."

Leaves bring healing and hope. Ezekiel 47 paints a beautiful image of the healing river springing from the altar in the Temple and bringing healing to the nations. *"By the river on its bank, on this side and on that side, will grow every tree for food, whose leaf won't wither, neither will its fruit fail. It will produce new fruit every month, because its waters issue out of the sanctuary. Its fruit will be for food, and its leaf for healing."* (verse 12)

That healing comes to us through another tree and its fruit: the cross. The bright orange birch is also an image of the cross where the Man of Sorrow accustomed to pain gave up life, experienced the frostbite of death. He embraced pain, suffering, shame and disease. By His wounds we are healed.

Jesus embraced our experience so we might be healed, restored and receive the fullest life. His tree became the symbol of our new life, the true way of life: *"If anyone desires to come after Me, let him deny himself, take up his cross, and follow Me. For whoever desires to save his life will lose it, and whoever will lose his life for My sake will find it."* (Matthew 16:24-25)

Dig deeper: *Psalm 31:14; Jeremiah 5:24; James 5:7*

Emil Toader

October 17

"Oh the depth of the riches both of the wisdom and the knowledge of God! How unsearchable are His judgments, and His ways past tracing out!" Romans 11:33

Nature has shown, even in our advanced scientific age, that there are many things we don't understand about it. An online search for "when nature stumps scientists" shows headlines like:

"Why Quantum Mechanics Still Stumps Physicists"

"Mysterious Seismic Event Stumps Scientists"

"Strange, Super-Sized Pulsar Stumps Scientists"

"Mystery Childhood Paralysis Stumps Researchers"

And even "Left-Handedness Stumps Science"

If we believe God created all of nature—which is what the Bible clearly teaches—and we still don't understand many things about the whys and whens...how do we think we can understand God's thoughts, ways and judgments?

We can understand what He shows us, what He reveals. But to think we have Him figured out is amazingly arrogant. Further, to judge Him, thinking we know better about a situation than He does, is setting ourselves above Him in wisdom and knowledge.

Directly after writing verse 33, Paul quotes from Isaiah 40:13: *"For who has known the mind of the Lord? Or who has been His counselor?"* (Romans 11:34)

The answer is *no one!* Just as so many of the things in our natural world are still a mystery, so God's ways in our lives, in the timeline of history, in nations—some of those things are simply a mystery.

It's easy to try to narrow Him down to how He's working in our own life, and then project that onto other people in their situations. But we can't know God's mind about what He hasn't told us. This should be humbling. And it should turn us to praise and gratitude, that this unsearchable God has gone so far to "graft us in" to His olive tree, the picture Paul uses in Romans 11.

"For of Him, and through Him, and to Him are all things. To Him be the glory for ever! Amen." (Romans 11:36)

Dig deeper: *Romans 11*

October 18

"Yahweh is a great God, a great King above all gods. In His hand are the deep places of the earth. The heights of the mountains are also His. The sea is His, and He made it. His hands formed the dry land. Oh come, let's worship and bow down. Let's kneel before Yahweh, our Maker, for He is our God." Psalm 95:3-7

In troubling times, it's so encouraging to realize and believe that God holds us. He holds the deep places. He holds the high places. He holds the seas and the dry land. He designed every "law of nature." He's the one who connected all of this.

That's why we can worship Him even when things in our own lives seem chaotic. We may be struggling with health, with hard relationships, with a job or school, with finances, with the future or the past. But He holds it all.

You may be asking, "Then why do I have to go through this? Where's God in all this?"

Many times we need to stop looking around at all the hard things and instead, look up. Or look out. Look at the deep places of the earth. Look at the heights of the mountains. The sea and dry land.

Remember Jesus' words to the people: *"See the birds of the sky... consider the lilies of the field...Don't be anxious, saying, 'What will we eat?', 'What will we drink?' or, 'With what will we be clothed?' But seek first God's Kingdom and his righteousness; and all these things will be given to you as well."* (Matthew 6:26-33)

If God holds all this, He holds you and me, too.

Seek first God's kingdom is what this Psalm writer did when he starts with worship and ends with worship: *"Yahweh is a great God, a great King above all gods...Let's kneel before Yahweh, our Maker..."*

Dig deeper: *Psalm 95; Matthew 6*

October 19

"Then Jesus was led by the Spirit into the wilderness to be tempted by the devil." Matthew 4:1

What sends you into the wilderness? What's the attraction, the pull? Is it your desire to get away from the city, from your work, routine at home? Is it just a change of scenery, a break from your relationships, a chance to be alone? Do you enjoy backpacking, canoe or kayak camping, car camping, biking or day hiking, or running trails? Maybe for you it's just driving to see the mountains, fall colors, waterfalls or wildlife.

Do you ever think that maybe it's the Holy Spirit leading you? I suspect the Spirit is a significant wind in our sails driving us to the wilderness!

Why would the Spirit want you in the wilderness? There are likely a lot of different answers, but let me suggest a few.

First, the Lord knows we need rest. Call it a vacation or call it a sabbath. We benefit from a break, a recharge of our energy.

Second, in special ways, creation brings us close to God: *"The heavens declare the glory of God..."* (Psalm 19:1)

Third, as with Jesus, the challenges of wilderness cause us to rely heavily on the Lord. The further into wilderness we go, the more vulnerable we grow. With vulnerability comes a deeper reliance on the Spirit. It's you and the Lord!

Fourth, wilderness has a way of bringing a special quietness to life. The usual sounds of work, sports, family, church, news, social media, personal conflicts and politics are quieted. In this quietness there's no other sound than the sweet soft voice of God. During these special times the Spirit has a way of talking to us! We may learn, perhaps, that God even has a new direction for our lives!

Jesus was led by the Spirit into the wilderness. There He was challenged. There He had close fellowship with His Father, and was strengthened by the Spirit. May we sense the Spirit's work in our lives as we pursue our wilderness experiences!

Dig deeper: *1 Kings 19:1-18*

Neal Schroeter

October 20

"When He had fasted forty days and forty nights, He was hungry afterward. The tempter came and said to Him, 'If You are the Son of God, command that these stones become bread.' " Matthew 4:2

Forty days in the wilderness is a long time! We would likely call that an *expedition*. The further out into the wilderness you go, the longer you stay, the more alone you are, the more it's just God and you. God will likely talk to you in unique ways.

Add to the remoteness, isolation and length of time an absence of food. Wow! For 40 days, Jesus had no food. Here the Bible states the obvious: *"He was hungry."*

I bet you like to eat when you're camping. We all do. Food has a way of tasting better. Some camping foods I'm not sure I'd care to eat at home, but are great for camping. Jesus didn't have anything. Starvation added to the adversity of His experience.

Wilderness has a way of challenging us with adversity. It creates vulnerability, which in turn clarifies the presence of and strengthens our relationship with the Lord.

Jesus went through sort of a "boot camp" preparation for His public ministry. He dealt directly with temptations and won. He was hungry...He was starving. Wouldn't it be wonderful to have some fresh bread? Jesus was the Creator—He could make some on the spot. But it was the devil's idea.

Jesus teaches us a most important lesson– spiritual food is more important than physical food: *"But He answered, 'It is written: 'Man shall not live by bread alone, but by every word that proceeds out of God's mouth.' " (Matthew 4:4)*

As important as food is to us, spiritual food is even more important. We need to feed off God's Word, the Bible regularly. Find time to read, study, contemplate and apply it.

Go to the wilderness! The Spirit is leading you. Be alone with God. Let Him talk to you. The usual sounds and pressures of life are gone. Read His Word. Listen to God!

Dig deeper: *Mark 1:35-39; John 4:28-38*

Neal Schroeter

307

October 21

"Then the devil...set Him on the pinnacle of the temple. 'If You are the Son of God,' he said, 'throw Yourself down, for it is written, 'He will command his angels concerning you...' " Matthew 4:5-6

Risk management is an important part of wilderness experience, both personally and if we're leading groups. It's not that we don't take risks. Risks are a necessary aspect of all wilderness journeys. Without risk, our jaunts to the wilderness would be bland and, likely, purposeless. It's not that we don't take risks—we manage risks.

A huge aspect of risk management is awareness of risks and avoidance of unwanted risk. We need a good understanding of the limits of our abilities, equipment and support. This can be distorted by peer pressure, over-achieving goals and schedules ("summit fever"), performance for video, over-confidence, etc.

Jesus had gone into the wilderness. This was a very special time where God the Son followed the direction of God the Spirit to spend intimate time with God the Father. It was a time of vulnerability. It was physically demanding. Then the devil showed up to interfere with this special fellowship of the Trinity.

One of the three temptations thrown at Jesus was this foolish risk of jumping off a high place and trusting angels to protect Him. Jesus answers: *"It is also written: 'Do not put the Lord your God to the test.' "*

There are a number of ways to understand and apply this, but one thing is obvious—be careful taking foolish risks. Risks that can harm or end our lives.

God has plans for you! He wants to use your life in a very meaningful way in service for His kingdom! Don't throw your life away. Praise the Lord for the joy of thrill seeking and adventure. But let's be careful. Use good risk management. Minimize risk of harm, while maximizing experience.

Let your time in the wilderness be a time where God shows you where and how He wants you to fit into His plan. God will give you purpose, value and fulfillment!

Dig deeper: *Romans 12:1-8*

Neal Schroeter

October 22

"Again, the devil took Him to an exceedingly high mountain, and showed Him all the kingdoms of the world and their glory. He said to Him, 'I will give you all of these things, if You will fall down and worship me.'" Matthew 4:8-9

If you're like me, when you've been in the wilderness you begin to look forward to certain things of civilization—running water, a soft bed, a good movie, potato chips, pizza, ice cream...and the list goes on!

Jesus was in the wilderness for a long time—40 days. He had nothing, and yet, He had everything: intimate fellowship with God the Spirit and God the Father. Enter the devil. He tried to tempt Him into thinking there was something better. The world could be His.

How foolish! The world *was* His. He created it all to begin with, and holds it all together. The devil comes up with some real dumb ideas, yet we're tempted. Temptations are really foolish when you get the right perspective.

Jesus later said, *"What does it profit a man if he gains the whole world, and loses or forfeits his own self?"* (Luke 9:25). God has already given us the best there is in all of life and eternity. Why would we sell our soul to the devil to get junk and heartache? Yet, we do, don't we? Foolish!

As always, Jesus serves as the perfect example. After being in the wilderness for 40 days without food, the world was looking good. But keep your perspective. Keep your relationship and commitment to God your utmost priority. Worship God, and God alone.

Spend time alone with God like Jesus did. The wilderness is a great place for that. But most of the time it's just a room in your home, or a bench in the park, a long bike ride or run, a cabin. Communicate with your heavenly Father. Be filled with the Spirit through your faith in Jesus. Wholeheartedly commit your life to the Lord in worship. Don't get fooled into thinking the world apart from God has more to offer!

Dig deeper: *1 John 2:15-17; James 1:17; Romans 8:32*

Neal Schroeter

October 23

"Praise Yahweh, all you works of His, in all places of His dominion..." Psalm 103:22

Let's do a little Hebrew study with this short phrase:

Praise is translated here from the Hebrew word *barak*, which means to kneel or bless. It's used over 300 times in the Bible. We're being called to kneel before God, bless Him, worship Him.

Yahweh is the name God calls Himself in Exodus 3:15. It's an actual proper name, not just the generic *god*. As followers of Jesus, it's not just some god we praise, it's Yahweh—a specific Person. Jesus called this Person His Father.

All you works of His. The Hebrew word for works is *maaseh*: workmanship, accomplishments, works. What are God's works? What and who should praise Him? Everything we see! The earth... plant and animal life...the seas, lakes and rivers...the mountains, deserts and valleys. It also includes everything we can't see—the microscopic world and the far stretches of the universe.

All His works praise Him by being what He created them to be and doing what He created them to do. That includes us, by the way! *"We are His workmanship, created in Christ Jesus for good works..."* (Ephesians 2:10)

In all places of His dominion. The word translated dominion is *memshalah*—rule, dominion, realm. A realm that's controlled by a king or government.

Is there anything outside of God's dominion? 2 Chronicles 29:11 says: *"Yours, Yahweh, is the greatness, the power, the glory, the victory, and the majesty! For all that is in the heavens and in the earth is yours. Yours is the kingdom, Yahweh, and you are exalted as head above all."*

Part of His kingdom—the earth—has been under assault by the devil and his angels for many thousands of years. But even they are under Yahweh's dominion, which they'll finally taste at the end of the age.

Praise God today and join the rest of creation as it praises Him, too!

Dig deeper: Psalm 103

October 24

"I am the true vine, and My Father is the farmer. Every branch in Me that doesn't bear fruit, He takes away. Every branch that bears fruit, He prunes, that it may bear more fruit." John 15:1-2

How does a farmer take away a branch that doesn't bear fruit? He cuts it off. How does a farmer prune a branch to bear more fruit? She cuts it off.

Either way, it's cut off! How do we know if it's a cutting off because of unfruitfulness...or if it's pruning? We don't know—at first. It can look the same. It can hurt the same. It's cutting, after all. It can be discouraging to experience the cutting away and think, "Where are You, God? Why is this happening?"

But remember—He's the Divine Farmer. He's an expert at cutting and pruning. Trust in His wisdom to cut away the unfruitful parts of your life, no matter how good they look or feel to you. And trust Him to know the best way to prune you so you can bear the most fruit possible.

How do we know if it's a cutting off because of unfruitfulness or if it's pruning? If it's pruning, you'll see fruit again eventually. And more fruit than ever.

A farmer prunes for one reason: to produce a healthier, more vibrant and more fruitful plant. It can look like death at first... but it's for more life. More abundance.

How can we be sure we're not that branch that's cut off for unfruitfulness? Jesus goes on to say in John 15:6: *"If a man doesn't remain in Me, he is thrown out as a branch and is withered..."* It's the remaining in Jesus. And what does remaining in Jesus look like? *"He who keeps His commandments remains in Him, and He in him."* (1 John 3:24). It looks like obedience.

So as you obey, as you remain in the Vine, in Jesus, you'll feel painful "cuts" in your life occasionally. That's the Father pruning you. Trust in His wisdom for your fruitfulness.

Dig deeper: John 15

October 25

"My soul, wait in silence for God alone, for my expectation is from Him." Psalm 62:5

One piece of nature I'm thankful for is stillness. Silence.

When I'm in the woods, it feels like my brain slows down and I can hear God's voice more clearly. Do you relate to this?

The opportunity to be truly alone is rare in most areas of life. This solitude is part of what draws many to nature and deepens our appreciation for it.

In His ministry, Jesus sought time to be alone in the land where He lived and ministered. He needed times of stillness and intimacy with His Heavenly Father in order to complete His calling on the earth. We also need connection and times of refreshing with God.

In the Gospels we often see Jesus turning to solitude in nature as a place to pray. Often it was before long days of connecting with the people around him, or after long days of ministering. We're called to connect to the world around us, but not be overtaken by it. Jesus modeled a life of stepping into pain and brokenness, but also stepping back into a place of direct relationship with God.

As I have grown in my love and appreciation of the outdoors, God has spoken to me about not using the solitude of nature to run from the world around me or the problems I don't want to face. Instead, I can be filled up in times of stillness and relationship, and then sent out into the world to represent Christ to those around me.

Where can you find stillness to connect with God today? Where do you find you relate to God the most? How does God speak to you in those places?

I pray today you would feel an intimate relational connection with God that would fill you and fuel you for your day.

Dig Deeper: *Matthew 14; Mark 1:35; Luke 5:16*

Emilie O'Connor

October 26

"The Spirit of God has made me, and the breath of the Almighty gives me life." Job 33:4

Do you believe that? That you were made, fashioned, given life by Almighty God? The alternative is the prevailing idea that you evolved through random chance in a purely naturalistic system. Does it make a difference what you believe?

It makes a life-and-death difference!

Are you simply the by-product of a meaningless, purposeless system that somehow managed to produce everything we see? If so, then "we're ultimately as purposeless as the very process which brought us into existence" as *allaboutphilosophy.org* comments.

That's what kids are being taught in every public school and university in America today.

Isn't it amazing—though so many people believe that, they're still grasping for meaning and purpose in life? Still intent on finding moral truth, even while they maintain there's no moral absolute?

The Bible is crystal clear about how you and I came about. Not through random, meaningless chance—but by the Spirit of God. Our breath is given to us by God Himself.

If that's true—if we've been handcrafted by this God powerful enough and wise enough to have created everything we see—that changes everything! That means there's both purpose and meaning.

Admittedly, it's often hard to understand what it is. Life is difficult...things happen...a lot of things seem meaningless. Even in the Bible there are so many stories of failure, harshness, error.

But the God of the Bible has been working His plan through human history. His plan of redemption, of reconciling people back to Himself.

If you're a follower of Jesus and you believe it's the breath of the Almighty that gives you life, then you're part of that plan. What an amazing, meaningful purpose that is!

Dig deeper: *Psalm 33:11; Jeremiah 29:11; Romans 8:28-39*

October 27

"The rain came down, the floods came, and the winds blew and beat on that house; and it didn't fall, for it was founded on the rock."
Matthew 7:25

There's one thing that's certain to happen in all our lives—the rain and floods will come and the winds will blow. None of us is exempt from the storms of life.

Somehow many of us have the idea that when we give our lives to Jesus, we'll get this trouble-free life. I'm not sure where we get that from, but it certainly isn't from the Bible!

While there are verses, even whole chapters, that talk about joy and peace in our lives—which is absolutely real fruit of following Jesus—we want to be careful not to cherry pick them as separate from the rest of God's word.

For example, as Psalm 23 says, He makes us lie down in green pastures and by still waters (verse 2). Hallelujah! But we also experience the valley of the shadow of death (verse 4) and the presence of our enemies (verse 5).

Jesus' teaching isn't that the storms won't come into the lives of His people. In fact, He says *"In the world you have trouble; but cheer up! I have overcome the world."* (John 16:33)

His teaching is that He's with us in the storms. His teaching in the passage in Matthew 7 is that when the storms come, they won't destroy the house (the person) built on the firm foundation of obedience to His teachings. Of walking with Him through life of ups and downs.

In this passage, Jesus is wrapping up His Sermon on the Mount with this illustration of how the same storm affects two different kinds of people. Both of them have heard Jesus' words. That's really important to see!

Both of them hear His words, but only one of them acts on His words (Matthew 7:24). That's obedience. Acting on Jesus' words means we'll stand firm through the storms. Not acting on His words? *"...and great was its fall."* It's pretty straightforward.

Dig deeper: *Proverbs 10:25; Matthew 7:21-29; 2 Corinthians 4:8-9*

October 28

"Yahweh, how many are your works! In wisdom, you have made them all. The earth is full of your riches." Psalm 104:24

The complexity and inter-connectedness of all that's in our natural world is simply amazing! Even one-celled organisms are incredibly complex. The more we learn and know, the more we realize how amazing it is.

Within the human body are many systems that, when working properly, all work together intricately. Our brain and nervous system, our heart and circulatory system, skin, bones, digestive system, reproductive system, lungs and pulmonary system, immune system—all have to work together in order, in perfection. And all of it begins as just one cell, produced by a male sperm and a female egg.

Truly it took wisdom beyond our comprehension to design the human body! People have never been able to come close to producing anything like it. Scientists have not been able to produce even a single-celled organism.

And yet, how many are these works of His! The earth is full of them—every plant, every mineral, every animal. Water and the seas. The laws of nature itself—gravity, the seasons, our relationship with our sun, the planets, our galaxy and the rest of the universe.

No wonder the psalmist moves into worship and praise: *"I will sing to Yahweh as long as I live. I will sing praise to my God while I have my being."* (verse 33)

If we stop to see and recognize the hand of God in this wonderful earth, that's our response, too..."Wow, God! We don't know how You did it, but we're sure glad you did!"

Thank Him today. Thank Him for His many works, His riches around you, in you, for you.

Surely in wisdom He's made them all!

Dig deeper: *Psalm 104; Psalm 148*

"Jesus, full of the Holy Spirit, returned from the Jordan, and was led by the Spirit into the wilderness for forty days, being tempted by the devil." Luke 4:1-2

Jesus spent 40 days in the wilderness where He was tempted by the devil. Instead of avoiding these trials, Jesus walked into them head on. He knew that facing trials would only strengthen His faith. No growth can be achieved through avoiding challenges. We can only strengthen our faith if we're willing to face trials.

If trials of temptation are a means for spiritual growth, why does Jesus tell us to pray: *"...lead us not into temptation"*? Jesus isn't asking us to pray to avoid temptation. In fact, this prayer implies that we certainly *will* be tempted. Jesus is asking us to pray that we will not *give in* to temptation. By teaching us how to pray He's helping us be better equipped to overcome these trials and grow stronger through them.

At Gethsemane, Jesus asks His disciples three times to *"watch and pray so that you will not fall into temptation,"* but each time they failed Him and fell asleep. This is perhaps the most danger-ous of temptations for us as Christians: to fall asleep in our faith and choose the easy road to avoid trials.

This is why it's important to go into the wilderness like Jesus and so many other significant Bible figures did. By spending time in the wilderness, we can break free from distractions and inten-tionally step into trials of temptation.

For example, on a long hike the temptation might be to stop and turn back short of the summit. Or if we choose to fast in the wilderness, we might learn that God provides when we need it and trust Him more deeply through a time of financial struggle.

By going into the wilderness to practice doing the hard things, we can set ourselves up for success in the real world when it comes to facing trials of temptation we don't choose.

Dig deeper: *Matthew 6:9-13; Matthew 26:36-46*

Alex Witmer

October 30

"In all your ways acknowledge Him, and He will make your paths straight." Proverbs 3:5

God, I just want to see a moose today. Those were my thoughts that late October morning. When this city girl breaks away from the city for a wilderness get-away, my normal routine is to spend an extended time in the word of God in the morning. On this particular morning I really just wanted to see a moose.

It had been a week. *Lord, am I really hearing You? Have I acknowledged You in all my ways? Are You directing my path?*

I felt like I was supposed to take a drive down the back road. *God, I acknowledge You. I'm letting You know that I would just like to see a moose, but truly the whole earth is full of Your glory and I thank You that You are right here with me.*

I came to a T in the road: Go right? Go left? I felt like I was supposed to go left. No audible voice, just a thought.

Twenty minutes into my drive, still no moose. Should I turn around? Should I stop? Keep going? I can't explain how I hear God, but there are moments when I know I hear Him. When we intentionally acknowledge Him, He directs our path. I heard His direction, "Get your camera ready, now." I did.

Literally, the second my finger was ready to take a picture a moose stepped out of the woods and onto the road in front of me. I was giddy, just like a kid who had seen a moose for the first time. I snapped a few pictures and took a video, and giggled.

I thanked God that I heard Him, and He reminded me that before I heard Him, He heard me. He hears our prayers. He hears the longings of our heart. He hears every word we speak and even the unspoken thoughts. He longs to show us how deeply He loves us and cares for us. Sometimes He uses a moose to do it.

God is always speaking, but He is easier to hear in some places. Do you have a place like that? Somewhere you go to intentionally speak and listen to God? Share your heart with Him and let Him share His heart with you.

Dig deeper: *Genesis 16:13; Proverbs 3*

Kirsten Voorhees

October 31

"Sing to Him, sing praises to Him! Tell of all His marvelous works." Psalm 105:2

When we tell of the marvelous works of God, we usually think of our personal testimony, or a recent answer to prayer, or someone surrendering to Him.

And those are all marvelous, yes!

But these marvelous works also include those He did at the beginning when *"God created the heavens and the earth."* (Genesis 1:1)

The Bible just skims over these works lightly: *"God said, 'Let there be light,' and there was light."* It doesn't go into the mystery of how light works and how our eyes are designed to interpret that light. How light is necessary for life, and how it affects days, nights and seasons.

He's left that for us to discover and learn about. As Proverbs 25:2 says: *"It is the glory of God to conceal a thing, but the glory of kings is to search out a matter."*

To tell about His marvelous works includes appreciating the inter-relationships between created things. It includes beauty, strength, tenacity, rest, activity and other characteristics we see in nature that we can apply to our own lives.

The more we learn about God's marvelous works, the more miraculous they seem. The more scientists dig into the complexities of cell structure and DNA at the subatomic level, and the incomprehensible size of galaxies and space—the more we marvel at it all.

Nature and wilderness isn't just a place we love to go to, to be in. It's a world overflowing with marvels, both living and nonliving. Just like we love it when other people learn about and enjoy something we've made or done—so Jesus loves it when we marvel at His works, when we learn about them, appreciate them.

When we approach creation like that, it's easy to *"Sing praises to Him!"*

Dig Deeper: *Genesis 1-2; Job 38-39*

November

November 1

"He Himself was in the stern, asleep..." Mark 4:38

Jesus was in the back of the boat sleeping while there was a storm raging around them.

I haven't experienced being in a small boat in big waves like this, but I can tell you, even being in a canoe in wind and 2-3 foot waves is scary! The Sea of Galilee, where Jesus and His disciples were, is known for its sudden squalls. There are plenty of boats sitting on the sea floor there to prove these storms can be violent.

Water is powerful! Waves, waterfalls, currents—they're powerful. They can destroy property, sink ships, erode shorelines, cause drownings.

And here was Jesus sleeping, completely unconcerned. Completely at peace. How could He do that? His disciples were frantic!

After Jesus calmed the storm with a word or two (*"Peace! Be still"* verse 39), He said to his fellow shipmates, *"Why are you so afraid? How is it that you have no faith?"* (verse 40)

Jesus could be at peace in the middle of this storm because He was full of faith. Faith in His Father, faith in His own purpose and calling, faith in His authority over nature (after all, He *created* nature!).

And we say, "Yeah, but He's *Jesus*!" Tomorrow we'll look at how someone else went through a raging storm. But for now, what about this—"Yeah, but *Jesus* is in you!"

The Bible is full of this command: *"Fear not!"* It's in there several hundred times. Fear is one of the devil's prime strategies—but fear is under Jesus' authority. Which means it's under our authority if we're following Jesus and under His authority.

We can't beat fear on our own any more than the disciples could that night in the boat. But as we keep building our foundation on the Rock—on Jesus and the Word of God, the Bible—He promises that even when the storms come, our foundation is sure. We can be at peace in the middle of them, too.

Dig deeper: Psalm 34:4; 2 Timothy 1:7; 1 John 4:18

November 2

"...the fourteenth night had come, as we were driven back and forth in the Adriatic Sea..." Acts 27:27

This is the story of another storm at sea—this time it's Paul, an apostle and missionary, who brings calm and peace...not to the sea, but to the other 275 passengers on the ship with him.

This chapter tells how amazingly God can use His people when we choose to keep our eyes on Him instead of the storm around us. Paul was in a real storm in the Mediterranean Sea. They'd been tossed around for two weeks already. Can you imagine how frightening that would be?

And yet he was so assured of God's call for him, so assured of God's presence with him that he was able to encourage, to give sound wisdom to the crew and bring calm to the other passengers in the middle of this nightmarish situation.

Finally they were shipwrecked on an island with not one person losing his life in the waves. It was miraculous! But there's more.

Paul didn't stop serving and ministering after swimming to shore. I'm sure he was relieved to be on dry ground again, but when he joined others in gathering fuel for a fire he was bitten by a poisonous snake, of all things. Did that stop him? Nope. He shook it off and trusted His Lord's protection over that, too. Then he began to minister to the residents of this island, healing all those who came to him with their sicknesses.

What does it take to live like that?

It takes a serious, committed dedication to a living God. To living in His presence. In His Word. Paul didn't get to this place with God on the ship. He'd been building his foundation in the Lord for many years already by this time.

Jesus doesn't call us to a safe, protected life. The only way we'll make it through the adventures He wants to take us on is by having that rock-solid foundation in Him.

Dig deeper: *Acts 27-28*

November 3

"You are the salt of the earth, but if the salt has lost its flavor, with what will it be salted? It is then good for nothing, but to be cast out and trodden under the feet of men." Matthew 5:13

One of my favorite parts of engaging in outdoor pursuits is the opportunity it affords to make new friends, get to know existing friends at a deeper level and build community.

On the eve of a 17-day mountaineering expedition with a group of 12 people I had met just a few hours earlier, a friend of mine dropped me a quick text to encourage me and challenge me.

The context of my expedition wasn't ministry related, per se. But my friend, knowing my heart, knew that my greatest desire in life is to testify to Christ's amazing invitation into life and life abundant. With that, he encouraged me to reflect on Matthew 5:13 and to specifically think on, and initiate action on, this question: "How can I add flavor and prevent rot as the salt of the earth on the ensuing expedition?"

On day 14 of the expedition, after having summited our objective the day before, I sat content, feasting on carbs and overlooking the valley below. I reflected on the opportunities I had to "add salt and prevent rot" on this expedition. My particular flavors included:

- Be vulnerable and honest
- Live out "Christ in me as me" and share my gifts
- Live out my firm identity as a child of God
- Reflect light and His glory, don't absorb it
- Live holy, different and set apart
- Be kind and serve
- Celebrate marriage, family and children

So for your next expedition—whether you're leading it, are a member of the team or just out for a walk with a friend—I encourage you to think on how you can add flavor to another person's life and prevent rot in your community.

Dig deeper: *Mark 9:50; Luke 14:34-35; Colossians 4:6*

Nathan Russell

November 4

"For as the rain comes down and the snow from the sky, and doesn't return there, but waters the earth, and makes it grow and bud, and gives seed to the sower and bread to the eater; so is My word that goes out of My mouth: it will not return to Me void, but it will accomplish that which I please, and it will prosper in the thing I sent it to do." Isaiah 55:10-11

As children we all learned how plants grow: they need sunlight, soil and water. We've done our experiments in science class, some of us have had gardens in our yard, and we witness it all the time in the world around us.

We study it to know that it works: *"as the rain comes down and the snow from the sky, and doesn't return there, but waters the earth, and makes it grow and bud..."* But we don't really know the *how*, and scientists have never been able to create life in the lab, brand new life that grows and reproduces.

It's a mystery the way a seed can be packed with the genetic material needed to bud and grow into what it's been designed to grow into. Maybe a rose bush...maybe a giant sequoia...maybe wheat or oats.

Here in this passage in Isaiah, God compares His word to the plant life on earth. Just as He designed rain and snow to water the earth and cause the plant life to bud and grow, so His word *"will accomplish that which I please, and it will prosper in the thing I sent it to do."*

We don't know how—it's a mystery. We just know that it does! Hundreds of prophecies recorded in the Bible's Old Testament have already come to pass (do an online search to find them). That's God's word accomplishing that which He pleased.

There are more prophecies that haven't yet been fulfilled, but we can trust they will be sometime in the future, because His word *"will not return to Me void."*

His word never comes to nothing.

Dig deeper: *Isaiah 55*

November 5

"Yahweh's works are great, pondered by all those who delight in them." Psalm 111:2

The works of God—or *Yahweh*, in Hebrew—can be circumstances in our lives or it can be world events. We certainly love to ponder the things He's done in our lives and in the lives of those we love.

The works of God also include His creation. All we see, hear, taste, smell and touch are His works. And pondering them, thinking about them, studying them, learning about them is a godly way to respond to them!

Those who love nature delight in the things of nature. And that's a God-given love. It's not "secular" or somehow worldly to be caught up in the beauty of a mountain or waterfall. To be blown away by the rich colors of spring wildflowers. To love to watch a horse gallop...or a dolphin leap above the waves...or to snuggle with your dog.

Our modern culture takes those works for granted. It reduces down their mystery and wonder by telling us they're just the result of eons of random chance—as if random chance could produce a DNA molecule that has billions of letters of code in precise order.

In fact, the more we ponder God's works, the more wonderful they become!

When you're doing your favorite outdoor activity, do you take time to ponder your surroundings? If you're reading this devotional, you probably do! You're the kind of person who stops and just looks around you in appreciation. You breathe in the fresh air. You soak in the beauty. You marvel at the power.

It glorifies the Lord when we delight in His works. That can include our personal testimony, or what He's done in the life of someone else. It can be His work in our city, in our region or in the nations. And it can certainly include our delight in the natural world He's made and placed us in.

So drink it in, rejoice in it! And be thankful that He created us to be able to appreciate it.

Dig deeper: *Job 38-41; Psalm 139:1-18*

November 6

"...then the waters would have overwhelmed us, the stream would have gone over our soul; then the proud waters would have gone over our soul...Our help is in Yahweh's name, who made heaven and earth." Psalm 124:4-5, 8

Have you ever been in floodwaters? Or in a river and gotten caught in the current? Or been taken out by an ocean wave? Water can be so powerful. It's not hard to think of a scenario where *"the waters would have overwhelmed us."*

In this Psalm the waters are figurative. David, the song writer, isn't worried about being caught in a flood—he's saying his enemies are like proud waters, wanting to overwhelm him. But, he says, *"Our help is in Yahweh's name, who made heaven and earth."*

Earlier, in verse 1, he writes: *"If it had not been Yahweh who was on our side..."* If the One who made heaven and earth—including the waters—wasn't on our side they would've been overwhelmed.

That's how the disciples must've felt when they were in the boat in the Sea of Galilee that night of the storm. (Matthew 8). If it hadn't been for Jesus they would've been overwhelmed by literal waves...not just figurative ones.

What they didn't realize at the time was that they had the Creator of heaven and earth in their boat with them. Jesus wasn't anxious at all, in fact, He was asleep! When His friends woke Him up and tried to get Him to panic as much as they were panicking, He simply spoke to the storm.

David and his men had real enemies who were really trying to kill them. The Lord didn't say "Be still" to his enemies. But because David trusted in Him for help, he wasn't overtaken by them.

So whether or not He calms the waves and floodwaters, the Lord is with us in those times. As the song says: "Sometimes He calms the storm, and other times He calms His child." (Scott Krippayne, *Sometimes He Calms the Storm*)

Dig deeper: *Psalm 124; Matthew 8:23-27*

November 7

"Out of the same mouth comes blessing and cursing. My brothers, these things ought not to be so. Does a spring send out from the same opening fresh and bitter water? Can a fig tree, my brothers, yield olives, or a vine figs? Thus no spring yields both salt water and fresh water." James 3:10-12

One of the hardest things to bring under Jesus' authority is what comes out of our mouth—our words. It can be our words to other people. It can be our words to ourselves (self-talk). It can be our words to God.

James makes a great point here: How can a spring send out both fresh and bitter water? The answer? It can't! How can a fig tree produce olives? Or a vine produce figs? The answer: they can't! It's impossible.

Our mouth is the fountain or spring of our inside person—our heart, emotions, thoughts, attitudes and choices. We regularly speak out what's inside of us. When we speak out both blessings and curses to others, to ourselves and even to God, James says, *"How can this be?"*

The answer is spiritual, not natural like springs and fig trees. Springs and fig trees don't deal with a sinful heart like we do. And we have to tackle spiritual problems with spiritual weapons.

There's a very important verse in Galatians 5 about this: *"Walk by the Spirit, and you won't fulfill the lust of the flesh. For the flesh lusts against the Spirit, and the Spirit against the flesh; and these are contrary to one another, that you may not do the things that you desire."* (verses 16-17)

And then a few verses later: *"But the fruit of the Spirit is love, joy, peace, patience, kindness, goodness, faith, gentleness, and self-control."*

The more the Holy Spirit grows these fruits in us—the more we yield to Him—the more our words will be like a spring of fresh water that's refreshing, thirst-quenching and life-giving.

To other people, to ourselves and to the Lord.

Dig deeper: *Psalm 19:14; Romans 6:16; 1 Corinthians 10:13*

November 8

"I dwell in the high and holy place, with him also who is of a contrite and humble spirit..." Isaiah 57:15

There's something about mountains that makes me stop and stare at them. They inspire awe, wonder and the challenge of being in such rugged terrain that can't be tamed. There's something inside of each of us that begs to go and attempt what seems impossible.

This is a part of why wild places are so amazing! They're a reminder to us of our smallness, and that we aren't the ones in control, but that God is. Mountaintop experiences are incredible! And we each seek these experiences to grow, learn and test ourselves against the power that creation and the Creator provide.

But can a person live on mountaintop experiences alone? What's there? Snow. Rock. Lichens. Pikas. Bugs. Maybe some grass. Truly, there's not a lot that thrives in this rugged terrain.

The opposite of these high mountain tops, are the valleys. Lower in elevation, they're often teeming with life. There's water and nutrient-rich soil. It's place of a wide variety of vegetation and animals to flourish. What are we missing when we rush through the valleys?

High places have always drawn people to visit, worship and sacrifice on them. People in the Old Testament worshiped God on the high places (Exodus 19; 1 Samuel 9).

There's something within us that seeks the divine on these mountaintops and high places. But there's very little to live on, and survival is incredibly hard there. Yet valleys seem dark, and hard to walk through sometimes in our lives. So why do it?

It's not in the climbing, or the sense of accomplishment we feel when we climb mountains. It's in taking the lessons and experiences and bringing them into the everyday, the mundane, the "valleys" of life.

When we return to our day-to-day, we no longer will see just with our eyes. We'll know deep down in our spirit the lessons God taught us on the mountain.

Dig deeper: *Psalm 23:4; Psalm 62:6-8; Hebrews 13:21*

Laura Watson

327

November 9

"God is light, and in Him is no darkness at all. If we say that we have fellowship with Him and walk in the darkness, we lie, and don't tell the truth. But if we walk in the light, as He is in the light, we have fellowship with one another, and the blood of Jesus Christ, His Son, cleanses us from all sin." 1 John 1:5-7

Light and darkness are the most basic realities of the world we live in. The sun is the source of our physical light. When our side of the earth faces the sun, we have light. When the sun's light is absent, then we have darkness.

Shadows are a type of darkness. They're caused when objects block some of the sun's light. It's not the deep darkness of night, when the sun's light is gone, but it interferes with the light in a limited sort of way.

There are places of darkness even when the light shines, likes caves, dense forests, deep waters—places where the light only penetrates so far.

In all these places and situations, this reality is always true: where it's dark is where the light doesn't shine. Darkness is the absence of light. If you're in a sunlit meadow at noon, you can't block the light or darken the meadow with a dark object.

But if you're in a dark cave and turn on your flashlight, that small light allows you to see everything it touches.

So it is spiritually. Spiritual darkness—sin and evil—is the absence of light—God. John is saying here that we can't both have our sin and walk with God. It doesn't work that way. Darkness is there for the very fact that light isn't.

But *"when we walk in the light, as He is in the light,"* we get fellowship with both God and other followers of Jesus—one another. Even if a little darkness gets in, when we turn to the light in repentance, Jesus cleans us up right away.

Let's walk in the light today!

Dig deeper: *Micah 6:8; Romans 13:3; Philippians 1:6*

November 10

"Give thanks to Yahweh, for He is good; for His loving kindness endures forever...to Him who by understanding made the heaven-s...who spread out the earth above the waters...who made the great lights...the sun to rule by day...the moon and stars to rule by night..."
Psalm 136:1, 5-9

The way Yahweh, Almighty God, designed the heavens, the earth, light, the moon and stars truly causes us to say, "Thank You! You are good!"

For example: "Only...where the expansion and the gravitational strength balance to within 1 part in 1,015 at 1 second after the big bang, allows life to form." (*newscientist.com*, "Gravity Mysteries: Why is Gravity Fine-Tuned?")

Electromagnetic force, strong and weak nuclear force, the expansion rate of the universe, and the mass density of the universe are other physical contributors that all have to be very precise in order for life to form.

And then we have the shape of the Milky Way galaxy, where the Milky Way is placed compared with other galaxies, where our sun is positioned within the Milky Way, what our sun is made of and its age and mass, our solar system with several planets in different orbits—all are necessary in order for us to be here.

(To read more about this, check out *God's Crime Scene* by J. Warner Wallace, a cold-case homicide detective. It's fascinating!)

"To Him who by understanding made the heavens" takes on a whole new meaning when we learn details about what the heavens are all about. The incredible complexity, vastness and yet inter-relationship between chemicals, physical forces, space and time is astonishing.

No wonder God tells us, *"For as the heavens are higher than the earth, so are My ways higher than your ways, and My thoughts than your thoughts."* (Isaiah 55:9) And yet *"His loving kindness endures forever."*

Next time you're blown away by what you see in the heavens, let it remind you of God's understanding and lovingkindness. Let it cause worship!

Dig deeper: *Psalm 86:15; Jeremiah 10:12; Romans 11:33*

November 11

"The everlasting God, Yahweh, the Creator of the ends of the earth, doesn't faint. He isn't weary..." Isaiah 40:28

Anyone who's ever hiked, backpacked, paddled or biked over long distances knows weariness! Sometimes it's a good weary. We've challenged ourselves and wanted to be able to meet that challenge. When we reach the end of the trail, or the summit, or the shore we're tired, but thrilled. We did it!

But other times we're exhausted because we got lost and had to add a few miles. Or the wind and waves came at us head-on and we had to fight for hours to make any progress. No thrill involved, just bone-weary fatigue.

I experienced that on a Boundary Waters canoe trip once with three other women. We hit a series of portages that had obviously not been well-used. We fought thick tree branches, mud, swamp and rocks for hours...then hit a dead-end. The map showed the trail angling to the northwest, but there was no trail. Just a beaver pond on one side and the dense forest on the other.

After searching for over an hour we admitted defeat. It would be dark before long. The kind of pitch black darkness when there's cloud cover in the wilderness. We couldn't stay where we were. There was barely enough clear, dry ground at the edge of the pond for four of us to stand, let alone pitch a tent. We had to turn around and face those awful portages again.

It's at those times we're most grateful for a loving Heavenly Father who doesn't faint and isn't weary. We can go after His presence and cry on His shoulder. He gives us His strength when our own has been drained:

"He gives power to the weak. He increases the strength of him who has no might. Even the youths faint and get weary, and the young men utterly fall; but those who wait for Yahweh will renew their strength. They will mount up with wings like eagles. They will run, and not be weary. They will walk, and not faint." (Isaiah 40:29-31)

Dig deeper: *Isaiah 40:9-31*

November 12

"...having gifts differing according to the grace that was given to us..." Romans 12:6

It was summer and time for the new boss to come north for the five-hour drive to visit Camp du Nord for the first time. Though I had met him in the interview process, I really didn't know him. I wondered what he'd be like, what he thought about camp, and the gifts that he'd bring to his calling as a leader.

Upon his arrival, it was clear he was very excited about being at camp. He wanted to do something to fully engage and asked if I would take him out in a canoe. We walked down to the shore and I pointed out the white caps on the lake, and the two-to-three-foot waves that were crashing pretty strongly against our shoreline.

He assured me he knew how to canoe. He looked like a pretty strong guy so I suggested he sit in the front to supply the power and I'd be best suited steering in the back. He agreed (a good start for a new boss), and we agreed to set a goal to paddle the mile across the lake and into a channel, find a place of refuge to turn the canoe around, and head back.

You might think a canoe swamping adventure was about to happen! But not so. The new boss was strong as an ox! We headed straight into the wind and waves. 30 minutes later we returned at top speed, riding the waves back to shore in about 10 minutes. We gave each other high fives and our relationship was off to a victorious start.

His gift of leadership was expressed in casting a vision to paddle across the lake, and listening to me in terms of understanding specific strategies to accomplish our goal. He was gifted to supply power in his paddling stroke, I was gifted with the ability to steer. The results? Harmony and success.

"For even as we have many members in one body, and all the members don't have the same function, so we, who are many, are one body in Christ, and individually members of one another, having gifts differing according to the grace that was given to us." Romans 12:4-6

Dig deeper: *Proverbs 18:16; 1 Corinthians 12; 1 Peter 4:10-11*

Brian Rupe

November 13

"He showed me a river of water of life, clear as crystal, proceeding out of the throne of God and of the Lamb, in the middle of its street. On this side of the river and on that was the Tree of Life, bearing twelve kinds of fruits, yielding its fruit every month. The leaves of the tree were for the healing of the nations." Revelation 22:1-2

Remember when Jesus told the woman at the well that *"He who believes in Me, as the Scripture has said, from within him will flow rivers of living water"* (John 7:38)? I wonder if He meant the same river—the river coming from the throne of God.

Just as natural rivers produce life everywhere they go, so the spiritual river of living water produces life everywhere it goes. Spiritual life. Hope. Faith. Endurance.

The river from the heart of God, the throne of God, from Jesus Himself brings life. So much life that the Tree of Life can grow on both sides of it. So much life that it bears fruit all year.

"The leaves of the tree were for the healing of the nations." That one sentence tells us several things:

First, these leaves are healing because they're watered directly from the river that comes from the throne of God. From God's throne comes healing.

Second, the healing is for the nations. The Greek word translated *nations* here is *ethnos*. *Ethnos* doesn't mean a political nation, but a culture. An ethnic group.

God's heart is for the healing of every culture, every ethnic group, every race. That healing comes through the river of water of life. I believe that's the river that Jesus said will flow out of us when we believe in Him.

Isn't that beautiful? Jesus has made us part of His family so we can be part of the healing of the nations.

Dig deeper: *Ezekiel 47:9; John 4:13-14; John 7:38-39*

November 14

"But the boat was now in the middle of the sea, distressed by the waves, for the wind was contrary." Matthew 14:24

This is the setting where Jesus walked on the water to the boat his disciples were trying to keep from sinking. Jesus wasn't walking on smooth seas, but big waves—big enough to cause distress to these professional fishermen, experienced sailors.

What must that have been like? If you've been at the ocean's coast or by one of the Great Lakes, you know the power of waves. Can you imagine walking on and among waves like that?

What do you think Jesus was thinking? Was He anxious? "Boy, I hope I can make it to the boat!!" Was He having fun with it? "This is awesome!" Was it just the quickest way for Him to get to His friends to save their lives?

Matthew simply says, *"...Jesus came to them walking on the sea."* (v. 25) His response to the disciples' fear is: *"Cheer up! It is I! Don't be afraid."* (v. 27)

I think that's partly what Jesus meant when He said, *"I came that they may have life, and may have it abundantly."* (John 10:10) Part of the abundant life Jesus came to give was the ability to meet storms head-on without fear or anxiety.

He said to His Father later, *"I have accomplished the work which You have given Me to do."* (John 17:4) One of those works was to defy the natural order by walking on top of the water during a storm. He didn't do it all the time—usually He took a boat across the sea like everyone else. But in this instance, His Father must've said, "Son, show these boys Your authority over the storm."

That same Jesus—the one who says in the middle of the storm: *"Cheer up! It's Me!"*—lives in you.

In your storms, look for Him to walk on the waves, in the middle of the wind. When He gets in the boat with you, He brings His abundant life with Him!

Dig deeper: *Psalm 107:28-31; Nahum 1:7; Matthew 14:22-36*

November 15

"The heavens declare the glory of God. The expanse shows His handiwork." Psalm 19:1

Flying in cloud is banned in paragliding competitions. When you have 150 pilots flying towards the same waypoint and they fly into a cloud, mayhem and mid-air collisions result. But when flying solo, flying in and out of cloud is glorious.

When the sun shines on the ground, it heats it up unevenly. Darker areas warm up quickly—light, moist areas more slowly. When conditions are right, a thermal will form and rise from the ground. The moisture in the air condenses and forms clouds. This is what paraglider pilots seek. This warm rising air lifts us higher and higher and enables us to fly far.

The higher we go, the more glorious the vista. We can see ridge after ridge of mountains. Lakes and rivers appear with the sun sparkling upon the waters. Forests stretch for miles, and in England the sea is never too far away to be seen. Sometimes we can see the Isle of Man or Ireland, more than 100 miles away.

It isn't safe to fly into cloud and lose sight of the ground or other pilots. If you're close to mountains you can easily lose your sense of direction and crash. Flying in cloud can also make your paraglider wet, which is dangerous. Or if you're high enough, frost can form on the glider and make it heavy.

But under clouds and along their edges is where the greatest lift is. We often play in and out of the edges or bottom of a cloud.

When you break through a cloud and come out into the brilliant sunshine with "the expanse of His handiwork" spread out before you, it isn't just *"the heavens (that) declare the glory of God"*...It's impossible not to shout for joy!

Dig Deeper: *Psalm 19*

Brian Doub

334

November 16

"Put on the whole armor of God, that you may be able to stand against the wiles of the devil." Ephesians 6:11

Do you know the difference between an *endo*skeleton and an *exo*skeleton? An endoskeleton is like ours—the skeleton is inside the body and supports the muscles, organs and tissue. An exoskeleton is like armor—it's a hard shell that protects the body from the outside.

As people, we can put on a couple different types of armor, or exoskeleton. One, the good kind...the healthy kind, is found in this verse in Ephesians: *"Put on the whole armor of God..."* It's like the exoskeleton of a crab. It's armor that protects us from something. That something is *"the wiles of the devil."*

There's another kind of armor or exoskeleton we can put on, an unhealthy kind. It's the armor we want to put on when we've been hurt by others...to keep people out. It's the armor we want to put on when we've been disappointed by God...to keep *Him* out.

Sometimes this is caused by severe trauma we've experienced, and it needs deep healing. Other times we *choose* it because we think it's easier to block others out—including the Lord—than to work it through, or to risk being hurt or disappointed again.

But Jesus' way isn't to put on an exoskeleton for self-protection. Ephesians 6 goes on to say: *"For our wrestling is not against flesh and blood (people), but against the principalities, against the powers, against the world's rulers of the darkness of this age, and against the spiritual forces of wickedness..."*

The thing about having an endoskeleton is that, yes, sometimes we get wounded. But God created our physical body with the amazing ability to heal itself. And when we walk with Jesus in this life—when we trust *His* armor to protect us—we can trust Him for healing when we get wounded. We can trust Him to redeem even hurtful situations.

Dig deeper: *Psalm 18:30; Psalm 119:14; Proverbs 18:10*

November 17

"For You formed my inmost being. You knit me together in my mother's womb. I will give thanks to You, for I am fearfully and wonderfully made." Psalm 139:13-14

It's amazing to think that all of creation was put in place by intention. God knows and sees every bird and flower. So many scientific principles work with precision to allow the earth to flourish with all its thriving ecosystems and interconnected relationships.

And as intentional as God was with the earth, we were created with even more purpose. The Bible identifies humans in Psalm 139 and Psalm 8 as having a special place in God's heart. We see that in the creation story as well.

God's word in Isaiah 41:9 shows how deliberately placed and designed we are when it says, *"You whom I have taken hold of from the ends of the earth, and called from its corners, and said to you, 'You are My servant, I have chosen you and not cast you away.'"*

God showed this to me once while sitting in an art museum. Claude Monet painted beautiful scenes of God's creation. As I sat in front of his breathtaking painting of water lilies on a pond, I considered how highly that painting is valued—priceless. Protected by a building, a security system and a team that takes care of it.

I heard God say to me, "As beautiful as this painting is, its value is nothing compared to the value of the homeless man sitting on the steps outside this museum...and nothing compared to your value. This painting and the location depicted in it will pass away, but love for the people around you will have eternal impact."

God uses all of creation to declare His goodness and majesty, and to show us that there's purpose to every moment in life.

May God show us how to recognize the value in ourselves and in the people around us today. You are chosen. You are seen. You are loved.

Dig Deeper: *Genesis 1; Psalm 8; Psalm 139*

Emilie O'Connor

November 18

"...whoever drinks of the water that I will give him will never thirst again; but the water that I will give him will become in him a well of water springing up to eternal life." John 4:14

Jesus was a master at taking the ordinary things of life and making a spiritual lesson out of them. In this case, Jesus is talking to a woman he met at a village well. She had come to draw water like she did every day.

Jesus told her that He had water to give her that would become internal—*"a well of water springing up."* The Greek word translated *well* in this verse is *pégé.* It's also translated as *spring* or *fountain* or *flow.* In other words, it keeps coming and coming!

Natural springs produce a continuous supply of pure, uncontaminated water. A clue to one of these springs is the lush vegetation around it. This water nourishes life. Another clue is animal tracks leading to it—they're coming to get that life, too.

That's what it's like to get this living water Jesus is talking about—it's His life in us that flows continuously like a spring or fountain. It produces eternal life. But that eternal life doesn't start for us in heaven after we die, it's starts now! It starts when we turn from living for ourselves, when we repent from our sin and turn our lives over to Jesus.

Paul, in his letter to the Galatian Church, says it like this: *"I have been crucified with Christ, and it is no longer I who live, but Christ lives in me."* (Galatians 2:20) Christ Jesus living in us is like a spring or fountain of water—always flowing, always nourishing.

As it flows up and through us, that life of Jesus will attract others to get some of that nourishment, too. It'll water everything around us and give life wherever it touches.

That's why it's so important to nurture our relationship with Jesus! He's where the living water comes from.

Dig deeper: John 4:1-47

November 19

"...I will give freely to him who is thirsty from the spring of the water of life." Revelation 21:6

This reminds me of Jesus' words to the woman at the well in John 4, that the water He gives is like a spring or fountain, a continuous flow of living water. This is the spring within each of us who believe in Him and follow Him.

The last two chapters of Revelation describe the future—the new heavens and the new earth, the New Jerusalem. What life will be like after the end—the new beginning.

The *water of life* here is described in the first two verses of Revelation 22:

"He showed me a river of water of life, clear as crystal, proceeding out of the throne of God and of the Lamb, in the middle of its street. On this side of the river and on that was the tree of life, bearing twelve kinds of fruits, yielding its fruit every month. The leaves of the tree were for the healing of the nations."

This is the water of life Jesus is talking about. Why is it living water? Because its source is God's throne. Look at the effect this river has—amazing fruitfulness. Trees grow on both sides of this riverbank. Their fruit is so abundant it produces all year long. And it's not just the fruit—the leaves of these trees themselves bring healing to nations.

This is what's available to us when Jesus' living water flows from inside us and outward. Not only does it satisfy our own thirst, this living water produces fruit and healing to those "along our banks"...those whose lives we touch.

And this living water within us will become more and more important as the days ahead grow darker, which the Bible says they will.

How steady is the flow of the water of life in your own heart and spirit? Does it come in spits and spurts, or is it flowing freely? Is it coming from God's throne? As my kids used to say, "Is He the boss of you?"!

Dig deeper: *Revelation 21 & 22*

November 20

"For as the body is one, and has many members, and all the members of the body, being many, are one body; so also is Christ."
1 Corinthians 12:12

Animal bodies, plant bodies and human bodies all have this in common: each is made up of many, many parts that have different functions that work together so the whole body works the way it's designed to work.

A single-celled microscopic bacterium, a tiger, a blue whale, a dandelion, a maple tree—every living thing is made this way. Many parts, each with its own function, working together to make up the whole, functioning body.

In people, that design reached its apex, its highest form. Not only do the parts of our physical body work together seamlessly, but God designed our thoughts, attitudes and emotions to also play a role in the health and well-being of our physical body.

That's also how God designed the Church to be. Many parts that work together in different functions to benefit and contribute to the whole body:

"Now there are various kinds of gifts, but the same Spirit. There are various kinds of service, and the same Lord. There are various kinds of workings, but the same God, who works all things in all. But to each one is given the manifestation of the Spirit for the profit of all." (1 Corinthians 12:4-7)

The chapter goes on to compare people in the church to parts of the human body, and asks: *"But now God has set the members, each one of them, in the body, just as He desired. If they were all one member, where would the body be?"* (verses 18-19) The body isn't made of just feet, or just eyes, or just lungs.

The point? Every member has a different function and every member is important. While some members of the Body of Christ are more visible—pastors, evangelists, teachers—*all* members are key to the healthy function of the body.

The goal? Unity. Verse 7 says, *"...to each one is given the manifestation of the Spirit for the profit of all."*

Dig deeper: *1 Corinthians 12*

November 21

"Beware of false prophets, who come to you in sheep's clothing, but inwardly are ravening wolves. By their fruits you will know them..." Matthew 7:15-16

Jesus gives us a picture here of a wolf dressing up like a sheep so it can get into the sheepfold to kill and eat the sheep.

A wolf's intent is purely instinct and survival—it eats meat to live. But here, Jesus warns us about people who twist God's word for their own gain and selfishness. They look like sheep, but they're actually wolves. Their motive isn't instinct, but evil.

In these days when anyone can build a blog and social media page there are some who spend all their time accusing other Christians of being false prophets.

The key, Jesus says, is *"By their fruits you will know them."* While we do want to be discerning, let's not assume someone's a false prophet just because he or she believes God's word differently than we do.

Yes, there are non-negotiables about what the Bible teaches as truth: Jesus is God's Son. He's the only way to the Father. Our salvation is through faith alone, by grace alone. There are truths that are foundational to historical, biblical Christianity.

But many of our disagreements are just differences. Some say God wants us to be blessed and prosperous. Some say no. Some say healing is for today, others say healing ended with the apostles. Some say infant baptism, some immersion. Paul talks about these kinds of arguments in Romans 14.

What if the Lord gives us different revelations about Himself so we have different convictions about different sides of an issue? In the end, Jesus says, *"By their fruits you will know them."* The fruit is a godly life—the person loves and obeys Jesus, lives by the fruits of the Spirit, loves and serves people.

And in the end, *"Why do you judge your brother? Or you again, why do you despise your brother? For we will all stand before the judgment seat of Christ...each one of us will give account of himself to God."* (Romans 14:10,12)

Dig deeper: *Matthew 7:1-5; Matthew 7:15-20; Romans 14*

November 22

"...looking carefully lest there be any man who falls short of the grace of God, lest any root of bitterness springing up trouble you, and many be defiled by it" Hebrews 12:15

Here in Minnesota we have a non-native species of large shrub called buckthorn. Once established it takes over the native plants quickly and crowds them out. Its fibrous root system makes it tough to remove once it's established.

I remember an uncle of mine spending an entire summer working to clear buckthorn from their wooded backyard so the native plants and flowers could flourish instead.

That's what a root of bitterness is like in our heart. The Greek word translated bitterness is *pikria*. It means a bitter or resentful spirit. This kind of spirit or heart isn't from God—it's not native to His character. It could be the result of any number of things—things that happened to us, or things we chose.

We learn a few things in this one short verse: 1) We have a responsibility here. 2) We need God's grace for it. 3) A root of bitterness affects others, too, not just us.

Like buckthorn, it's a whole lot easier to be sure a root of bitterness doesn't get a chance to grow in the first place. The sooner we deal with a hurtful situation through God's grace—probably involving forgiveness, His kind of love, patience and other fruits of the Spirit—the easier it is to get rid of.

Allowing a root of bitterness and resentment to remain in our heart will affect our relationship with both God and others. It can cause spiritual blindness and open us up to deception. It can crowd out God's purposes for us if we allow it to stay, temporarily or even permanently. It can even affect our physical health. That's pretty serious.

Do you need God's grace to help remove a bitter or resentful spirit? He'll do it! Sometimes it just takes a season of complete surrender, repentance and prayer. Sometimes it takes help from others, maybe even professional counseling.

Having that root out, though, is intensely liberating! It's so worth it.

Dig deeper: *Proverbs 14:30; Isaiah 5:20; Ephesians 4:31*

November 23

"For as the rain comes down and the snow from the sky, and doesn't return there, but waters the earth, and makes it grow and bud...so is My word that goes out of My mouth. It will not return to Me void, but it will accomplish that which I please, and it will prosper in the thing I sent it to do." Isaiah 55:10-11

The word of God is unstoppable!

He gives us this picture of a common occurrence in the natural world: rain and snow fall to the earth, water it and—in partnership with other elements of God's design—cause the earth to grow, bud and bring forth life.

Sometimes the rain and snow are abundant, sometimes they're scarce. Sometimes the life grows right away and sometimes it can take weeks or months. It's amazing to see deserts green up suddenly with the rains. The seeds and dormant plants seem lifeless, but they're just waiting for the moisture. When it comes, they respond.

With snow, most of the new life won't come until the ground has thawed and the snow and ice have melted. But the life comes eventually.

Our Creator has designed our physical world to need water for vegetation to grow and produce life that supports the rest of life here. It's a picture of how His word produces life in our soul (our mind, will and emotions) and spirit.

That's why it's so important that, as believers, we soak up God's word. It's that rain and snow that produces life in us. It's what feeds us. And that's why it's also important that when we share about Jesus' love to those who don't know Him yet, we use His word—the Bible.

I recently heard the testimony of a woman who grew up in an atheist home, attended a liberal Ivy League university, knew no Christians, and, there, became a follower of Jesus simply by reading a Bible.

His word will prosper in the things He sends it to do!

Dig deeper: Isaiah 55

November 24

"For as the body is one, and has many members, and all the members of the body, being many, are one body; so also is Christ." 1 Corinthians 12:12

One theme you'll notice as you read Paul's letters to the various churches of his time—a large portion of the New Testament—is his emphasis on *unity* among Christians.

Here in 1 Corinthians 12, he illustrates what he means by unity in the church, in the body of Christ. He compares the church to the human body. Each "member" of the human body has a different but very important function. If a member were to be cut off from the body, it would cause damage. Sometimes even trauma or death.

You know what it feels like to have even a minor cut or scrape? Our whole body and mind is affected by it. You stub your little toe and your whole body knows about it!

Paul is saying "That's how we need to look at the Body of Christ!" Each individual church or home fellowship can be seen as a body...but Jesus sees all Christians everywhere as the Body of Christ, His church.

The Greek word used in the New Testament that's translated *church* is *ekklésia*. It means "called out from and to." It's people called out from the world to His Kingdom. That's all of us.

Part of that calling is another major theme in Paul's letters—believers being willing to "give up my right to myself" (as Oswald Chambers says, in *My Utmost for His Highest*) in order to be both a witness to non-believers and a servant to other believers. *"For the profit of all,"* Paul says in verse 7.

How can we walk that out in daily life? One way is to commit ourself to a local church, which is part of the Body of Christ. Don't flit around from church to church looking for what you can get out of it. Commit yourself and give yourself. Serve with the spiritual and natural gifts the Holy Spirit has given you so that local church—that body—is strengthened.

Dig deeper: 1 Corinthians 12

November 25

"He said to his disciples, 'Therefore I tell you, don't be anxious for your life, what you will eat, nor yet for your body, what you will wear. Life is more than food, and the body is more than clothing. Consider the ravens: they don't sow, they don't reap, they have no warehouse or barn, and God feeds them. How much more valuable are you than birds!' " Luke 12:22-24

Aspects of nature are often used throughout scripture to illustrate important truths. These illustrations serve as reminders, and can help us understand scripture in a tangible way. Here, Jesus is telling His disciples not to be troubled or anxious about their needs.

Anxiety comes in many forms and severities. Like temptation, having anxious thoughts isn't wrong. What matters is what we do when we feel anxious.

Verse 29 of Luke 12 says, *"Don't seek what you will eat or what you will drink"* for these are worldly things, but instead *"seek God's kingdom"* (verse 31).

We can't wave a magic wand and will anxiety away. However, the more we know our God and seek His kingdom, the more we're transformed. And the kingdom of God is righteousness, peace and joy in the Holy Spirit (Romans 14:17).

While the birds don't worry about food, nor do they attempt to store it up for later, they do work to care for themselves and feed their young. Jesus isn't prohibiting planning, promoting laziness, instructing His disciples not to prepare, or promising a worry-free life. He's asking them to focus on what to *do* with their life, rather than what they *need* for their life.

What needs are you dwelling on that cause anxiety? What are you setting your heart on? Let the ravens of the skies be a daily reminder to set our heart on seeking His kingdom above all else.

Dig deeper: *Luke 12: 22-31; John 15:4; Romans 14:17*

Ariella Carter

November 26

"I will give thanks to You, For I am fearfully and wonderfully made. Your works are wonderful. My soul knows that very well."
Psalm 139:14

I thought I was Super Woman. After four months of literally everyone in my life falling ill, I had remained unscathed. I kept my workout regimen, drank my daily dose of apple cider vinegar (I have no idea if it actually does anything), ate healthy and slept well.

Then came the worst bout of stomach flu I can remember. Thirty hours into it I had lost seven pounds in water weight. I'm no large person to begin with. It took me 20 minutes to get a glass of water from the kitchen because I couldn't stand up longer than three seconds.

By hour 48 I had a wonderful God moment: *"I praise You because I am fearfully and wonderfully made!"* My body, which was slowly getting better, was handmade by a creator God who made it to heal itself!

This body that powers my bicycle through glorious summer rides, pumps blood into my arms to kayak the lakes, and helps me dance through white blankets of snow on my outdated military surplus snowshoes, also heals itself.

Astounding isn't it?

But here was my connection: how often do I express my gratitude and utter amazement to my Lord for giving me this body? It's a miracle. It's unexplainable. It's mine for free.

The challenge for all of us as we read this is to stop and take five minutes right now, right where you are, to do nothing but thank God for all of the good in life. Jot it down, speak it aloud or silently pray. But now and everyday should be a lifetime resolution of gratitude in the daily ups and downs.

We live in a miraculous world with miraculous bodies and we have the chance to thank the Creator who made it all. Let's do so!

Dig deeper: Psalm 139

Tracy Blesi

November 27

"...that which you yourself sow is not made alive unless it dies. That which you sow, you don't sow the body that will be, but a bare grain, maybe of wheat, or of some other kind. But God gives it a body even as it pleased Him, and to each seed a body of its own." 1 Corinthians 15:36-38

Jesus' death and resurrection makes our resurrection life in Him possible. Our earthly body and heavenly body will be as different as that of a seed to its fully-developed mature plant.

Paul's meaning in this chapter is about our literal earthly and heavenly body—encouraging followers of Jesus everywhere and for all times that physical death isn't the end for us, but rather the beginning. That gives us unshakeable hope.

We can also apply this to our spiritual walk with Jesus while we're here on this earth. In Paul's letter to the Galatian church, he talks about the difference between our natural, evil desires (the dead seed) and what the Holy Spirit produces in our lives (the living, growing, fruitful plant).

"Those who belong to Christ have nailed their natural evil desires to His cross and crucified them there." (Galatians 5:24) That's like planting the seed. I willingly crucify (execute) my natural desires... I plant the seed.

Paul describes some of those natural evil desires in verses 19-21: impure thoughts, love for lustful pleasures, idolatry (placing things as more important than God in my heart), hatred, jealousy, anger, self-centeredness, drunkenness, criticisms.

When I plant that seed of death to those natural desires, I'm saying to the Holy Spirit: "You control me! I want Your fruit in my life!" And *"when the Holy Spirit controls our lives He will produce this kind of fruit in us: love, joy, peace, patience, kindness, goodness, faithfulness, gentleness and self-control..."* (Galatians 5:22-23)

That's as night-and-day difference as the dead seed to the living plant it produces! And, again, the prerequisite for the living plant? Death of the seed.

Dig deeper: *1 Corinthians 15; Galatians 5:13-26*

November 28

"He said to them, "Come, and see." John 1:39

I am always struck by the power of simple invitations in scripture. I often find myself strategizing—trying to make the most amazing invites that are full of wonder, detail and mystery. Then I see the pattern of the Gospels, that the invitations were usually very simple, like *"Come, and see."*

I often get the privilege to lead hiking trips to beautiful places in the Canadian Rockies. On one such trip we were at an alpine lake with crystal blue water. You could even see the glacier that fed it in the beautiful sun. Having been there before, I knew that the real treat, though, was a waterfall around the corner. The campers explored extensively, then eventually came and asked me, "Is there anything else to see here?" I replied, "There's a waterfall. We might as well go see it."

Undersell, overdeliver. Business classes taught me that. And so I led them to a 200-meter cliff overlooking a wooded valley with a crystal blue vein of water spilling down. At the end of the long valley were black clouds with thunder and lightning, and we were above it all. It was one of the most spectacular sights many of us had ever seen.

Jesus does this all the time with His invitations.

He doesn't promise the spectacular. Instead He simply invites us to be with Him, and then the spectacular happens. The earliest disciples modeled it too, with Phillip saying the same words, *"Come, and see."*

Whenever you don't feel smart enough, capable enough or trained enough, remember—our part is simple. Come, and see Jesus, and invite others to do the same.

Dig Deeper: *John 1:35-50; John 4: 28-30; Acts 8:34-35*

Hogan Brimacombe

November 29

"...all of you clothe yourselves with humility, to subject yourselves to one another; for 'God resists the proud, but gives grace to the humble.' Humble yourselves therefore under the mighty hand of God..." 1 Peter 5:5-6

Every animal has a self-defense mechanism and a strong self-protection instinct. For some it's *flight*—run, fly or dig. For others it's *fight*—stink, spines, claws, horns. For still others it's camouflage—hide, stillness.

It wasn't always like this, and it won't always be like this for them. In the Garden of Eden everything lived in harmony before man chose to rebel against God (commonly known as *The Fall*). And the Bible promises that kind of harmony again one day, in the new heavens and the new earth (Isaiah 11:6-9).

Because of the fall, we humans also have a very high self-protection bent. It's not just physical, but mental and emotional, too. "Look out for #1" means it's *my* needs, *my* wants first, then I'll think about everyone else...even God.

But Jesus says, "No! That's not My way." A big part of humility is being willing to lay down that natural bent towards self-protection. To *"subject yourselves to one another"* means to place yourself under others. Not because they're better than you, but because that's what Jesus does. He showed that when He washed His disciples' feet—a job always designated to the servant.

It takes humility to place yourself under others. The way we can do that as followers of Jesus is because we trust Him. When your identity is based on you as God's daughter, God's son, then you have nothing to prove to other people. You can trust your Father, your Savior, your Counselor to take care of every situation you're in...including with other people. Even those who may hurt you or hate you.

God's promise for those who humble themselves before Him is *Grace*. He *gives grace to the humble*. He'll help you through it. You don't have to protect yourself. He's there. You can trust Him.

Dig deeper: *Proverbs 22:4; Mark 9:35; Philippians 2:3*

November 30

"Don't be conformed to this world, but be transformed by the re-newing of your mind..." Romans 12:2

In elementary school we learned this big scientific word: *metamorphosis*. Even today when I read or say that word, I think of a monarch butterfly in its chrysalis. That wonderful transformation it goes through from caterpillar to butterfly. From green striped wiggly worm-thing to graceful orange-and-black-winged beauty. From crawling to flying.

Metamorphosis means "change of physical form, structure or substance especially by supernatural means" (did that dictionary just say *supernatural?* Hmm). And "a striking alteration in appearance, character or circumstances." (*www.merriam-webster.com/dictionary*)

That's the word Paul uses in Romans 12:2, above, when he urges us: *"Don't be conformed to this world, but be transformed by the renewing of your mind, so that you may prove what is the good, well-pleasing, and perfect will of God."*

When we come to Jesus for salvation and discipleship, He transforms or metamorphosizes our mind—change by supernatural means! A striking alteration from what was our selfish, worldly, sinful way of thinking to a mind that *"may prove what is the good, well-pleasing, and perfect will of God."* A mind that may prove—*dokimazo* in Greek—test, examine, reason out God's will.

Earlier in Romans Paul says, *"the mind of the flesh is hostile toward God..."* (Romans 8:7). We can't understand or submit to God's ways and purposes without that metamorphosis of our mind.

And going back a step further we see clearly the difference from crawling worm-thing—*"For the mind of the flesh is death"*—to winged beauty—*"but the mind of the Spirit is life and peace."* (Romans 8:6)

That's true metamorphosis! And, like the monarch, it doesn't happen overnight but is a process...a supernatural process.

Is your mind *con*formed or *trans*formed?

Dig deeper: *Romans 8*

December

S. BRODIN

December 1

"Enter in by the narrow gate; for the gate is wide and the way is broad that leads to destruction, and there are many who enter in by it. How the gate is narrow and the way is restricted that leads to life! There are few who find it." Matthew 7:13-14

One of the accusations against Christianity is that it is narrow-minded. The exclusive claim of salvation only in Christ goes against the modern open-minded thinking, and in our postmodern world this claim has become a joke.

Jesus concludes His most comprehensive message on life in the Kingdom of God, the Sermon on the Mount, by reducing it all to two gates, two ways, two trees and two homes.

Our passage is annoyingly narrow. We might be tempted to find ways of showing our faith is not like that. One option would be to swallow hard and to accept that while our faith is narrow, in the end we will be proven right. In Romania we have a saying: *He who laughs at the end, laughs better*. Is this what Jesus has in mind?

Is this call to enter the narrow gate and follow the narrow path a consolation in that while we are ridiculed now, we will be proven right in the end, and that makes it all worth it?

I grew up in a context of ridicule during Communism where believers were laughed at in school for being narrow-minded. This image is coming back these days, but this understanding is too small for what Jesus is saying.

There is a striking contrast in Jesus' description between the way and the destination. The narrow gate and path lead to *Life*. The wide gate and path lead to extreme narrowness: death and destruction.

This reversal is ironic—the wide leads to narrowness and the narrow leads to wide-open life.

Dig deeper: *John 1:1-14; John 6:35; James 4:4*

Emil Toader

December 2

"Enter in by the narrow gate; for the gate is wide and the way is broad that leads to destruction, and there are many who enter in by it. How the gate is narrow and the way is restricted that leads to life! There are few who find it." Matthew 7:13-14

We all seek life, safety, identity, truth and meaning. The need and void for such are in us all and it bears a divine shape that can only be fulfilled by God.

Isn't this what Adam and Eve wanted in the Garden? Open eyes! True life and meaning! Real freedom! And the serpent whispered that God wanted them blindsided. "Don't be narrow-minded. The fruit will open your eyes so you will be like God." They chose wide.

The story is the same. Sin promises freedom and life, largeness. But it leads to death, bitterness and slavery separate from God.

Only dead fish swim with the flow! Christ is calling us to enter through Him and walk in Him.

Jesus doesn't just place two options in front of us, pointing a finger to say "I told you!" No! He is calling us to enter through the narrow gate, through Him, to choose true life.

He is not an indifferent merchant with a "take it or leave it offer." He so much wants all to enter that He personally came and made Himself the door. He alone—through His life, death, and resurrection—fulfilled the impossible golden rule, lived the perfect life and opened the door to life for all.

The narrow gate is a Person. It is Christ Himself. That is why it is narrow—because it is too good to be true! He is the way, the truth and the life.

Dig deeper: *John 14:6, Acts 4:12, 1 Timothy 2:5*

Emil Toader

December 3

"Enter in by the narrow gate; for the gate is wide and the way is broad that leads to destruction, and there are many who enter in by it. How the gate is narrow and the way is restricted that leads to life! There are few who find it." Matthew 7:13-14

Recently, walking through Timisoara, my home city in Romania, this passage has received a deeper meaning.

European cities take pride in squares and cathedrals, and Timisoara is no exception. The Union Square is our *social well* of the city—a beautiful large square surrounded by beautiful buildings.

I learned from an architect that the contrast between the narrow streets and the wide square is intentional. It is meant to impress the viewer. After walking the narrow streets fenced by tall buildings, suddenly this opening comes as a major contrast. It is beautiful!

Union Square is like that. You walk into it impressed by the beautiful Serbian Orthodox Cathedral and the Catholic Dome. By the Palace of Culture and beautiful buildings. Even more, you feel welcome and invited to one of the tens of terraces serving great food, coffee and refreshments.

You just want to be there.

In the middle of the square our city placed a statue of the Holy Trinity—a column reminding people of the end of the plague of 1780. The statue was moved in the middle of the square during Communism. What an image! God the Trinity, in the middle of the square as a symbol of healing, restoration and defeating death and plague.

At the end of the narrow street of faith, God—expressed in the beautiful perfect communion of Father, Son and Holy Spirit—is inviting and welcoming. He makes that abundant life available to us. God is in the square...and will have coffee and pizza and a great banquet with us one day!

Dig deeper: *Psalm 31:19; John 1:12; 1 Corinthians 2:9*

Emil Toader

December 4

"...you don't know what your life will be like tomorrow. For what is your life? For you are a vapor that appears for a little time, and then vanishes away." James 4:14

I was snowshoeing on the lake near our home in fresh December snow one morning. I knew people had been ice fishing on the lake already, and I could see both snowmobile tracks and ski tracks. So I felt safe on the ice.

All went as usual. I enjoy exploring the cattail marshes along the shore, walking into the nooks and crannies. Being on the lake in the winter is completely different than in a canoe or kayak in the summer. It's unique to us northerners—an advantage of being part of "the frozen chosen"!

I was following some fox tracks deeper into the cattails when I suddenly stepped through the ice and into the water!

What a shock!

I wasn't in any real danger. The water was only knee deep in that spot. The surrounding ice was firm enough, and since it was just my right leg that went through I was able to scramble out, albeit a bit awkwardly with my snowshoe on.

Several thoughts went through my mind as I walked the mile home a bit earlier than intended: I don't remember even noticing how cold the water was...My right foot is squishy inside my soaked boot, but the wool sock is keeping it plenty warm, even in 16° F...Apparently the ice isn't as firm around thick clumps of cattails this early in the winter...

But most of all: *Life can happen so fast.* One moment I was snowshoeing on top of the lake ice and the next moment I was struggling to get out of the muddy water. I know people who were in this life one moment and with Jesus the next moment.

It made me remember my life is a vapor, and I'm not guaranteed tomorrow. None of us is. Events like this remind us to keep the right perspective about what's important and what isn't!

Dig deeper: *Proverbs 27:1; Matthew 6:33-34; James 4:13-17*

December 5

"Go and make disciples of all nations..." Matthew 28:19

I will always wonder if I've been, or currently am being obedient to that call.

It helped when I heard a pastor comment on that verse: "While you are going, make disciples!"

Maybe it isn't that hard. Maybe the "disciples" come to us. I recall an afternoon over 35 years ago that makes me ponder how we may start the process and another may finish it.

My husband and I were in Bangladesh working at a Mission Hospital. On a rare day off, we took a hike and somehow got separated. Within moments, out of the dense jungle, as if I were an expected visitor, a little girl came and took my hand. She quickly realized I was unable to understand her language, so she sought to teach me. Pointing to a tree or cloud, she would tell me how to say it and wouldn't move on until I had repeated it correctly. She loved being my teacher.

Then in this deep, dense forest we landed at the feet of a golden statue of Buddha. Here, alone in the jungle, was a well-visited icon of idolatry.

My little friend bowed low and pulled me to do the same. I wouldn't. Instead I began to sing "Jesus loves me, this I know..." This quickly brought my friend to her feet and, smilingly, she turned to me. She wanted to learn my song!

She had a high, squeaky little voice but her words were clear to me and foreign to her. "Yes, Jesus loves me, Yes, Jesus loves me!"

I prayed for that child for many years. Like the eunuch from Ethiopia in Acts 8, would God bring someone to tell her of the One she was singing about? I would love to believe that, now grown, she's heard, believed and is now loving the same Jesus who loves me and her.

Dig deeper: Mark 16:15-18; Matthew 28:16-20

LeaAnn Schroeter

December 6

"For You formed my inmost being. You knit me together in my mother's womb. I will give thanks to You, for I am fearfully and wonderfully made.

"Your works are wonderful. My soul knows that very well. My frame wasn't hidden from You, when I was made in secret, woven together in the depths of the earth.

"Your eyes saw my body. In Your book they were all written, the days that were ordained for me, when as yet there were none of them." Psalm 139:13-16

This is one of the most beautiful passages in literature describing God's intimate knowledge of each one of us: *"You formed... You knit...my frame wasn't hidden from You...Your eyes saw..."*

It speaks of the value and destiny of each one of us—born and unborn: *"In Your book they were all written, the days that were ordained for me, when as yet there were none of them."*

And it recognizes what our response should be: *"I will give thanks to You, for I am fearfully and wonderfully made."*

What a revelation David (the author of this psalm) had about himself because of his close relationship with God. This youngest son, looked down on by his older brothers and even his father... this shepherd boy knew he was loved by God, formed by God, and given destiny by God. And it shaped the way he saw himself. In turn it shaped the destiny of his country and his generation.

That's what godly truth does. God Himself tells us we—you and me—are made in His image, in His likeness, with purpose. When we believe that and live like it's true, we open ourselves up to the destiny God created us for.

Identity is a powerful thing, and it's under assault both in areas of society and by our enemy, the devil. If you're a follower of Jesus, it's so important you understand your identity through His truth. Take these words of David's and speak them over yourself. Pray them to your Heavenly Father. And go live out the days that were ordained for you!

Dig deeper: Psalm 139; Ephesians 1

December 7

"For the word of God is living and active, and sharper than any two-edged sword, piercing even to the dividing of soul and spirit, of both joints and marrow, and is able to discern the thoughts and intentions of the heart." Hebrews 4:12

What is "the word of God" that it can be living and active? I was always taught that the Greek word *logos*, used here for *word*, means the written word of God, the Bible. And it *does* mean that...but it's not limited to that.

Logos also means speech, the expression of a thought. So *logos* can be written or spoken. And what makes God's *logos* living and active? It's the Holy Spirit. The Greek word we translate *spirit* is *pneuma*, meaning breath or wind. The Holy Spirit breathes on His word and causes life.

It's like Genesis 2:7 says: *"Yahweh God formed man from the dust of the ground, and breathed into his nostrils the breath of life; and man became a living soul."* So the Holy Spirit breathes on God's words to us and they become alive.

Now, His word, though alive, doesn't always produce good in us. That depends on us. Earlier in this chapter of Hebrews it says: *"For indeed we have had good news preached to us, even as they also did, but the word they heard didn't profit them, because it wasn't mixed with faith by those who heard."* (verse 2)

Remember Jesus' parable of the farmer and the seed? It's in both Matthew 4 and Luke 8. The lesson is that the same seed is scattered on different types of ground. The seed—the word—is good. It's the ground that allows or doesn't allow the seed to take root and flourish.

So it is with the living, breathing, active word of God. The Spirit has already breathed His life into it. If we mix it with faith—if we believe what God says—then all the rest of Hebrews 4 is ours.

Watch over the soil of your own heart. Invite the Holy Spirit to breathe more of His life into His word for you today!

Dig deeper: Isaiah 55:10-11; 2 Timothy 3:16; Hebrews 4:12-16

December 8

"He who loves his brother remains in the light, and there is no occasion for stumbling in him. But he who hates his brother is in the darkness, and walks in the darkness, and doesn't know where he is going, because the darkness has blinded his eyes." 1 John 2:10-11

It really couldn't be more clear—there's no room for hate in God's kingdom!

Anyone who's ever done any backcountry hiking or backpacking can relate to the difference between taking a trail in the daylight compared to nighttime. Some trails have so many hazards it's even a challenge to make it in the daylight without stumbling. Darkness hides all those hazards—mud, twists and turns, fallen trees, rocks and roots, thorn bushes, cliff edges.

When someone chooses hate over love towards a brother (the Greek word has a range of meanings including biological brother, fellow worker and a fellow Christian) it's like walking a treacherous trail at night with no moon or headlamp. And this verse implies the darkness isn't just towards that other person, or group of people. The one doing the hating walks around in life in the dark, blinded.

To clarify, this kind of love doesn't mean warm fuzzy feelings. It's a patient, kind, humble, others-focused, tenaciously good way of thinking about and treating others (see 1 Corinthians 13:4-8 for a detailed description).

Hiking a backcountry trail at night is sort of like physical blindness—we might as well be blind for all the good our eyes do us. The darkness John is talking about here is spiritual blindness.

We can't see things clearly in the Spirit or in our own spirits when we're in spiritual darkness. We can't hear clearly from the Lord when we're in spiritual darkness. That's pretty serious.

When Jesus says the greatest commandment is to love God with everything we have, and then to love our neighbor as ourself, He means it. Our faith journey depends on it.

Dig deeper: *Mark 12:28-31; 1 Corinthians 13*

December 9

"We...bring you good news, that you should turn from these vain things to the living God, who made the sky, the earth, the sea, and all that is in them..." Acts 14:15

In Acts 14, Paul and Barnabas were in a city called Lystra and had just healed a man who had been crippled from birth. The people there were so astonished by that miracle that they immediately tried to worship these two men as gods.

Like so many others, these people put their hope and trust in created things (in this case, people) rather than the Creator.

We've heard it said that people need something to worship. When they don't know the living God, their Creator, they'll find other things to worship—to set up as all-important. You'll know you "worship" something when it's the all-consuming thing in your life. The Bible calls these things *idols*.

It's easy for us to idolize our outdoor passions: hiking, backpacking, kayaking, rock climbing, biking, skiing, whatever. They can become all-consuming in our lives so much that we prioritize our money, time and energy after them.

The words of Paul and Barnabas here are calling us to turn from vain things, these idols. The Greek word translated *vain* here is *mataios*. It means useless, unreal, unproductive, fleeting.

They're saying, "Why would you set your heart and affections on these unproductive, useless and temporary things when the living God has made a way for you to Himself? He's the one who made all these things you think are so important. Turn to Him!"

Have you ever read the book of Ecclesiastes? It's all about what happens when people chase after vain things. They get vanity. The Hebrew word is *hebel*—mere breath, vapor, delusion, fraud, useless, nothing. The writer was Solomon. He was the wisest and wealthiest person on the planet in his day. And this is his conclusion, based on his own life experience.

But turn to the living *God who made the sky, the earth, the sea* and life has purpose, not vanity.

Dig deeper: *Ecclesiastes; Acts 14:8-18*

December 10

"Before the mountains were born, before You had formed the earth and the world, even from everlasting to everlasting, You are God." Psalm 90:2

Someday we'll know how old the earth and the universe are. When we're with God in eternity, we'll know the history of everything we see around us. There are theories about this, but these theories are peoples' best guesses, based partly on data and partly on presupposition (such as whether or not they believe in supernatural causes).

There are both new earth and old earth creationists—followers of Jesus who believe the Bible is God's word, but disagree over when God did His creating.

Does it matter that much? Whether God created the universe, the earth and life 6,000 years ago or 4.5 billion years ago, can He still be the author of it? After all, our main point is that God formed it, created it—at some point in history.

We believe God is eternal, and the verse above from Moses' psalm emphasizes that: Before all this appeared, *You are God.* Present tense. It was to Moses that God explained His name as: *I AM,* also present tense (Exodus 3:14).

In Revelation 1:8 the Lord explains it a bit differently: *"I am the Alpha and the Omega,"* says the Lord God, *"who is and who was and who is to come, the Almighty."* God always *has been* in existence and always *will be* in existence.

What comfort and security that gives us! Before you and I were born, He is God. Before our grandparents and great-grandparents came along, He is God. Before the mountains were born, He is God. Long after we leave this earth, He is God.

We don't need all the answers. We don't have to figure everything out to believe and know He is God. So many things aren't as important as simply having that anchor. He is God, *even from everlasting to everlasting.* Forever.

Where do you need to believe that in your life today?

Dig deeper: *Psalm 90; Psalm 93*

December 11

"Delight yourself in Yahweh, and He will give you the desires of your heart." Psalm 37:4

When times are difficult it's natural to want to escape what's going on. We try TV, movies, social media, outdoor pursuits, food or alcohol. Anything that helps us feel better, even though the circumstances haven't changed, and might feel hopeless.

There *is* hope, though—in Christ Jesus! There's a future and destiny for each person on Earth! One small way to bring that hope and joy into your life when you feel stuck or overwhelmed is to make goals.

Setting small and reachable goals is a great way to help you focus on your own personal journey and less on the trials you and others might be facing.

It can be as simple as a short prayer walk two or three times a week, memorizing a scripture verse as you brush your teeth, listening to one worship song as you commute to work or school, writing down one thing you're grateful for each day.

Celebrate the days you stayed focused on your goals and learn from the times you didn't.

In my own life, God revealed to me to start taking these small steps for myself, and it gave me the confidence to dream really big dreams with God that at the time seemed impossible. It allowed me to learn to trust God and myself, but also for God to trust me.

Your dreams might also seem impossible, but nothing is impossible with God! He wants to dream big dreams with you and see them come to pass. Start small, and set some reachable goals for yourself to escape the current trials and stress in your life, to reconnect with yourself, with your dreams and with God.

It will bring life and peace to you in the midst of hard times and circumstances. It sure worked well for me and brought me greater measures of peace, hope and confidence in overcoming the trials of today.

Dig deeper: *Psalm 138:8; Matthew 7:7-8; Philippians 1:6*

Laura Watson

December 12

*"He said, "My presence will go with you, and I will give you rest."
Exodus 33:14*

Our spiritual walk is often reflected by the world around us. An example is the seasons. Different life seasons hold certain purposes and activities. The same is true for how the earth responds to changing seasons. One characteristic that's part of the season of winter is rest. The earth rests.

The Bible teaches us to include seasons of rest in our life, both for the earth and for the people who live in it. Science has shown that this isn't just an outdated practice—rest promotes health and fullness of life. The word God uses to teach this is *sabbath*.

In farming, allowing the soil a rest period gives it time to replenish nutrients. And as the earth rests in the winter, the rocks beneath the soil are pushed to the surface.

Just like the earth needs to rest, so do we. And just like the earth pushes up the rocks while it's resting through winter, I've found God uses seasons of rest in my life to reveal places where growth and healing are needed. This allows God to redeem and restore us, and help prepare us for the work He wants to do in us and in the world around us.

One day during a season of rest and healing I journaled this: "My healing was waiting for me—I didn't have to force any of it or try to make it happen."

Farmers don't dig around to find rocks in their fields. At the right time they come to the surface and can be removed. In that same way God allowed the right things to come to the surface in my life at the right time, and then brought healing and restoration.

Is God bringing rocks to the surface in the soil of your life? How is He asking you to implement sabbath rest in your life? How are these two questions connected for you?

Dig deeper: *Ecclesiastes 3:1-8; Matthew 13:3-9, 18-23; Mark 2:27*

Emilie O'Connor

December 13

"He said, 'My presence will go with you, and I will give you rest.' "
Exodus 33:14

In its physical sense, wilderness brings up connotations of a desert, forest or arctic wasteland away from civilization.

In a spiritual sense, it's a distancing from the Lord, a lifelessness in our Christian walk. What we call a *wilderness experience* can happen through things like disobedience, a tragic life event or significant change in circumstances.

Experiencing *physical* wilderness can be the antidote to *spiritual* wilderness when it also means *social* wilderness—leaving our surroundings to be alone in the outdoors. We place ourselves out of reach to purposefully meet with the Lord. We're laid bare and vulnerable to the elements. It also makes us vulnerable to the Lord and to His Spirit working in us. It's important for our restoration and learning.

In the wilderness environment our senses are sharpened. Our awareness of God's presence is heightened as we're free from busyness and messages, advertising and expectations. Our hearts are softened and our heads decluttered. We make space for Him.

One of the ways I've felt vulnerable to the Lord was in the physical demands of summer work at a northern Minnesota wilderness ministry. It was a place for me to be alone, to reflect, to meditate on His word. To be present with Christ and be laid bare. But part of the deal was to work on the property: stack hay, feed horses, clean stalls, mow lawns, repair bunk houses, disinfect latrines, mend fences and fill holes in the hayride tracks.

It was in this muscle-aching tiredness I'd go in the late afternoons and walk the back trails, find a quiet spot in the woods and *be*. Physically and spiritually vulnerable, alone in the wilderness, God showed up.

Does the thought of being alone and vulnerable scare you or enliven you? Do you have wilderness within reach to venture away and experience His presence in a deep, transformative way?

Dig Deeper: *Isaiah 40:3-5; Hosea 2:14-15; Luke 4:1*

Paul Scoringe

December 14

"Now the fruit of righteousness is sown in peace by those who make peace." James 3:18

What kind of fruit do you want your life to produce?

Fruit is one of God's great gifts to us! So many varieties, full of natural goodness and delightful flavor. Even the array of colors in fruit—bright reds, vivid greens, yellows and oranges, blues and purples—makes it fun to eat!

Each of the fruits we love to eat are designed for specific conditions. They thrive best when those conditions are met: the right amount of rain, the right amount of sunlight, the right nutrients in the soil, the right climate. When those conditions are met, the fruit is vibrant and healthy.

If we want the healthy, vibrant fruit of righteousness in our life we need to pay close attention to the conditions we're providing. The Greek word translated *righteousness* in this verse is *dikaiosuné*. It also means justice or a judge's decision.

In the New Testament, that judge is God. It's *His* righteousness that matters, not what's right in the eyes of people. The New Testament writers use this word often, and it always refers to what God says as righteous and just.

The proper conditions in order for this fruit of righteousness to grow in us is *peace*, or in the Greek, *eiréné*. This word, like the Hebrew word *shalom*, carries all kinds of rich meaning: wholeness, favor, harmony, tranquility, peace of mind, rest, healing.

And James makes it clear in this verse that the seeds of peace that produce the fruit of righteousness aren't separate from the one who sows or plants these seeds. No, these seeds are *"sown in peace by those who make peace."* By peacemakers.

Jesus had something to say about peacemakers, too. He said: *"Blessed are the peacemakers, for they shall be called children of God."* Children of God produce good fruit because they carry God's peace on the inside of them.

How can you carry more of God's peace inside you today? Tomorrow? In your life?

Dig deeper: *Psalm 34:14; Philippians 4:4-9; Colossians 3:15*

December 15

"He heals the broken in heart, and binds up their wounds. He counts the number of the stars. He calls them all by their names. Great is our Lord, and mighty in power. His understanding is infinite." Psalm 147:3-5

Isn't it interesting that healing the broken hearted and counting the stars are listed together in this song of David's?

I wonder if he wrote this one while sitting out with his father's sheep as a teenager. Looking up into the night sky and seeing stars upon stars (there was no such thing as light pollution in those days!). Knowing how God had healed his own broken heart—something he'd come to know well in the future.

One of the truths we can take from this is that God sees both our broken hearts and the stars in the universe. He knows the intimate and He knows the expanse. He not only knows and heals my own broken heart, and yours—but those of people we've never met, in times we've only read about.

If this Creator God has named the stars—billions of them— He also knows *your* name. There's a verse in Revelation that says: *"To him who overcomes, to him I will give of the hidden manna, and I will give him a white stone, and on the stone a new name written, which no one knows but he who receives it."* (Revelation 2:17)

He'll do that for each of us. He knows our name. He knows our stuff. He knows our secret sorrows. He knows our hopes and dreams. Go to Him for healing and binding up. If He counts and names the stars, of how much more value are you to Him? So much more.

And, as David always does in his psalms, take that and go to the Lord in praise and worship. *"Great is our Lord, and mighty in power. His understanding is infinite."*

Dig deeper: *Psalm 23; Matthew 6:27-34*

December 16

"Yet He didn't leave Himself without witness, in that He did good and gave you rains from the sky and fruitful seasons, filling our hearts with food and gladness." Acts 14:17

This verse comes right after Paul said that God *"allowed all the nations to walk in their own ways"* apart from Him. Even though He created them (the nations, people) He never forces them to follow Him. He's always given people free will to choose their own way, their eternal destiny.

And yet in His mercy He doesn't leave us without a witness. Paul goes on to describe some of what this witness looks like: His goodness through rains, fruitful seasons, created things that give us fulfillment and gladness.

This parallels closely to Paul's words to the church in Rome: *"...that which is known of God is revealed in them, for God revealed it to them. For the invisible things of Him since the creation of the world are clearly seen, being perceived through the things that are made..."* (Romans 1:19-20)

The natural world tells us about the Creator of that world. Even though nature is under the curse of sin like we are, it still holds some of its original goodness, wonder, beauty and power put into it by God.

And just like the creative works of artists tell us (or witness) about the artist, so these created things in nature witness to their Maker. According to the Bible, it's not just God's people who recognize this, but God has caused these things to be a witness of Himself to everyone, everywhere.

Everyone—whether they love God, hate Him or say He doesn't exist—gets to experience the blessings and goodness of His created world. The rains for their crops. The fruitful seasons.

The serenity or thrill or wonder that the natural world offers all point to Him. Will we recognize that? Will we give Him glory for it?

Dig deeper: *Job 12:7-10; Acts 14:8-20; Romans 1:16-22*

December 17

"Yahweh, how many are your works! In wisdom, you have made them all. The earth is full of your riches." Psalm 104:24

In the last couple of months I was on the road and out in nature a lot. In some moments I was so amazed, like the psalmist. For me, nature is one big miracle. I would like to tell you about a few moments of wonder.

In Slovenia we were in a huge stalactite cave. This cave by itself was absolutely wonderful and its beauty touched me. There we saw *grotto olms*. They are amphibians. They live in complete darkness and only eat something every twelve years! That way they become 70-100 years old. Wow!

In an animal park in Austria we saw some goats. Looking closely we discovered a little goat that stumbled through the area. It was really cute to look at. We figured out the little baby was just born. Immediately after birth the little one gets on its feet and can not only stand but walk straight away. Wow!

At a small beautiful mountain lake we unpacked our outdoor stove and ate our breakfast. Two ducks swam by—a male with a female. When another male duck approached, he was chased away. Ducks live monogamously and stay together until the chicks have hatched. Also many other animals like rainbow parrots, wolves and penguins live in a monogamous relationship. Wow!

We cannot see God. But creation tells us so much about Him:

God is *beautiful*. He has invented colors and shapes and the most different plants and animals.

God is *thinking through*. Everything goes together and has a wonderful system.

God is *love*. We live in this beauty and diversity. I believe that nature is a wonderful gift to us humans and a sign of His love for us. A gift that gives us joy and makes us marvel!

Take time to go into the creation. Go out into nature. I'm sure you will experience moments of wonder, too. Take time to watch and to praise our marvellous Creator.

Dig deeper: *Psalm 104*

Steff Weber

December 18

"The Spirit and the bride say, 'Come!' He who hears, let him say, 'Come!' He who is thirsty, let him come. He who desires, let him take the water of life freely." Revelation 22:17

The water of life described here is the same water Jesus talked about early in His ministry to the woman at the well. Do you remember that story? (John 4). He told her He could give her living water and she wouldn't thirst anymore.

At the time she didn't know He was talking about spiritual thirst, not physical thirst. But when He proceeded to "read her mail" and tell her several details about her life He couldn't possibly have known other than by the Spirit of God, she believed He was the promised Messiah. She received the living water and her spiritual thirst was, indeed, quenched, along with a bunch of others from her village.

It's this same living water here in Revelation: *"He who is thirsty, let him come...let him take the water of life freely."* Why does this water have life in it? The Greek word translated *life* is *zóé*—it refers to both physical and spiritual life, the life that comes from God Himself.

Earlier in Revelation 22 we learn where the river comes from: *"Then he showed me the river of living water, sparkling like crystal, flowing from the throne of God and of the Lamb..."* (verse 1)

The living water comes from the place of God's authority (His throne) and His sacrifice (the Lamb). It's freely available to us because the Lamb of God became the sacrifice for the sin of the world, including you and me.

Jesus paid the price so we can drink of that water of life freely. And just like all life relies on water in the natural world, our spiritual life relies on water, too—this living water from Jesus.

Dig deeper: *Isaiah 12:3; Ezekiel 47:9; John 7:38*

December 19

" 'I Myself will be the Shepherd of My sheep, and I will cause them to lie down,' says the Lord Yahweh. 'I will seek that which was lost, and will bring back that which was driven away, and will bind up that which was broken, and will strengthen that which was sick...' "
Ezekiel 34:15-16

This chapter in Ezekiel is a pretty harsh word against the leaders in Israel whom God had entrusted to care for His people. They were messing it up pretty bad. They weren't taking the care of their people seriously.

God compared these not-so-good leaders to a shepherd neglecting his sheep. Because the shepherds weren't doing their job, the sheep *"were scattered, because there was no shepherd. They became food to all the animals of the field, and were scattered. My sheep wandered through all the mountains, and on every high hill. Yes, my sheep were scattered on all the surface of the earth. There was no one who searched or sought."* (verses 5-6)

In that culture, sheep were a common livestock animal, valued for many reasons. The shepherds who cared for them had an important job to do—protect them from predators, provide First Aid for sickness and wounds, bring them to good pasture and water, find a safe place for them to bed down at night.

That's what God expected the leaders in Israel to do with the people under their authority and care, too. And that's what Jesus expects of His leaders—pastors, church elders, mentors.

Of course, Jesus calls Himself the Good Shepherd, and goes even further than simply caring for the sheep. He says, *"The Good Shepherd lays down His life for the sheep."* (John 10:11)

Are you a "sheep"? Then respond willingly to the shepherds in your life, as well as to the Good Shepherd. Keep yourself under their care.

Are you a "shepherd"? Then protect, lead, strengthen, guide and heal the sheep Jesus has placed in your care. Use Jesus as your model of what that looks like.

Dig deeper: *Psalm 23; Acts 20:28; 1 Peter 5:2*

December 20

"Don't be wise in your own eyes. Fear Yahweh, and depart from evil. It will be health to your body, and nourishment to your bones."
Proverbs 3:7-8

I recently read that the Book of Proverbs is full of spiritual *principles*, not *promises*. This is a great example.

If you look at the state of our world today we see a world that is *wise in its own eyes*. That doesn't fear the Lord at all. Most people either don't believe He exists or don't know anything about Him and His ways, and, frankly, don't care. Instead of departing from what the Lord calls evil, our world is running towards it.

We also live in a world with skyrocketing anxiety, depression and suicide. Doctors have known for decades now that 85-90% of physical illness stems from lifestyle-related causes, with stress a major factor.

While Solomon likely didn't know the scientific connection between our choices, mental health and physical health almost 3,000 years ago, his wisdom came from God. And God definitely knows—He's the one who created us!

The Lord designed us to be interrelated—our mind, thoughts, emotions and body. And He designed us so that our body would be healthiest when our choices reflect God's ways.

"Don't be wise in your own eyes." Humble yourself before God and others. Recognize you don't have all the answers. *"Fear Yahweh, and depart from evil."* Come under God's authority and agree with what He calls *sin*. Walk in His ways, obey what He says to do and not do.

"It will be health to your body, and nourishment to your bones." When you follow Jesus and His ways, when you live by the Spirit and not the flesh (Galatians 5:16), the fruits of the Spirit will grow in you. These include joy and peace, kindness and self-control. These are the opposite of depression, anxiety, fear and self-protection.

This doesn't necessarily mean you'll never get sick. But as a principle: what a person, a family or a culture plants, that's what will be harvested.

Dig deeper: *Galatians 5:16-25; Ephesians 5:1-21*

December 21

"In the beginning was the Word, and the Word was with God, and the Word was God...All things were made through Him. Without Him, nothing was made that has been made." (John 1:1-3)

The Hebrew word used for *Word* in this scripture is *logos*. The definition given by the Interlinear Bible (which goes back to the original Hebrew and Greek used in the Bible) is "a word, speech, divine utterance; expressing the thoughts; reasoning expressed by words."

John is talking here about Jesus being the *Logos*, the *Word*— the divine utterance or spoken thoughts of God. *"The Word became flesh, and lived among us. We saw His glory, such glory as of the one and only Son of the Father, full of grace and truth."* (John 1:14)

Now take a look at Genesis 1, the creation story:

"God said, 'Let there be light...' God said, 'Let there be an expanse...' God said, 'Let the earth yield grass, herbs, seeds, fruit trees...' God said, 'Let the waters abound with living creatures...' God said, 'Let the earth produce living creatures after their kind...'"

The Hebrew word used in those verses for the verb *said* is: *amar*. It means to say, utter, command or declare.

That's why John describes Jesus as the One through whom everything was made—everything in the heavens, on earth, under the earth, in the seas. All things were made through Him. God spoke, Jesus was the Word He spoke, and all these things came into being.

And this Jesus was the same one who humbled Himself to become a helpless baby. To grow up in an average Hebrew family in an out-of-the-way place. To spend just three years of ministry healing, delivering, teaching and training. And then to offer Himself as the sacrificial Lamb for you and me so we could be reconciled to our Heavenly Father.

If you're a child of God, Jesus lives in you. He's still the Word, the *Logos* of God. He can and will speak His divine words through you. That's pretty cool!

Dig deeper: *John 1:1-18*

December 22

"He doesn't delight in the strength of the horse. He takes no pleasure in the legs of a man. Yahweh takes pleasure in those who fear Him, in those who hope in His loving kindness." Psalm 147:10-11

I've loved horses since I was a little girl. I think they're one of God's most perfect creatures. When I ride I feel at home somehow. I love the feeling of their strength and movement beneath me. I love their eyes and the way their coats glisten in the sun. The way the wind blows their long mane and tail.

God made the horse strong and beautiful. The verses in Job 39:19-25 depict God talking to Job, telling him of the horse: *"Have you given the horse might? Have you clothed his neck with a quivering mane?..."*

So when the verse above tells us *"He doesn't delight in the strength of the horse"* it's not that God doesn't like horses! *"He takes no pleasure in the legs of a man"* doesn't mean God despises His own creation.

This is a comparison. *"Yahweh takes pleasure in those who fear Him, in those who hope in His lovingkindness."* In other words—don't put your trust and hope in created things, even the best created things. Put your trust and hope in the Creator of those things. He's the one who has the strength you'll need all through your life.

He's the one with wisdom that's so far above ours that He says: *"For as the heavens are higher than the earth, so are my ways higher than your ways, and my thoughts than your thoughts"* (Isaiah 55:9).

The Lord takes pleasure in His people who fear Him, reverence Him, obey Him, love the things He loves, hate the things He hates. He takes pleasure in those who hope in His love, strength, grace, forgiveness, kindness, mercy and justice.

Where is your hope today? What are you trusting in to give you strength?

Dig deeper: Psalm 30; Hebrews 10:19-23

December 23

"He has made the earth by His power; He has established the world by His wisdom. And by His understanding has He stretched out the heavens." Jeremiah 10:12

Have you ever stood in awe before a mountain range and just thought, "Wow, God, You're so amazing! Thank You for this!"

If you're like me, you've experienced this dozens of times. On a mountain. By a lake with its mirror reflection. Along a coast with huge waves crashing on the rocks. Next to a thundering waterfall. Looking up into a dark night sky at billions of stars.

As His children, this should pull deep gratefulness out of us. That's what worship is—"God, You're incredible! I'm so grateful for Your goodness. Thank you so much for Your power, wisdom and understanding."

Everything we see in nature is a reminder of who God is. Have you ever thought of making a habit of thanking Him each time you stop to appreciate it?

I think that's part of what Paul meant when he wrote to the church in Thessalonica to *"Always rejoice. Pray without ceasing. In everything give thanks..."* (1 Thessalonians 5:16-18)

We have constant reminders of Him every time we step outside, really. That makes it easy for us to find things to be thankful for, and to turn that thankfulness into praise!

"Shout for joy to Yahweh, all you lands!
Serve Yahweh with gladness.
Come before His presence with singing.
Know that Yahweh, He is God.
It is He who has made us, and we are His.
We are His people, and the sheep of His pasture.
Enter into His gates with thanksgiving,
And into His courts with praise.
Give thanks to Him, and bless His name.
For Yahweh is good.
His loving kindness endures forever,
His faithfulness to all generations." (Psalm 100)

Dig deeper: *Psalm 95:1-6; Colossians 3:17; Revelation 5*

December 24

"For the creation was subjected to vanity [futility], not of its own will, but because of Him who subjected it, in hope that the creation itself also will be delivered from the bondage of decay into the liberty of the glory of the children of God." Romans 8:20-21

When sin entered the world through peoples' rebellion, God's curse over that sin affected all of creation. Genesis 3:17 says: *"To Adam He said... 'the ground is cursed for your sake. You will eat from it with much labor all the days of your life.'"*

Verse 3 of our beloved Christmas song, *Joy to the World*, says:

No more let sins and sorrows grow
Nor thorns infest the ground...

Those things represent the curse: sin, sorrow, thorns...also bee stings, mosquito bites, sunburn, allergies, aggressive wild animals, destructive weather, death and decay.

That's a world subjected to futility—without purpose. It often seems meaningless, even hopeless. But we have a living hope that creation won't stay that way! *"...the creation itself also will be delivered from the bondage of decay into...liberty..."*

The song goes on:

He comes to make His blessings flow
Far as the curse is found, far as the curse is found.

What wonderful news! While we're waiting for and working towards that day when we and all creation will be set free from this bondage of sin, we can help "make His blessings flow far as the curse is found."

We do that when we pray, "Your kingdom come and Your will be done on earth as it is in heaven." We do that when we bring the presence of Jesus into our everyday lives. And we do that by taking care of this wonderful creation He made and will one day redeem.

How can you "make His blessings flow far as the curse is found" today?

Dig deeper: Revelation 21:1-5; Revelation 22:1-3

December 25

"...there is born to you today, in David's city, a Savior, who is Christ the Lord. This is the sign to you: you will find a baby wrapped in strips of cloth, lying in a feeding trough." Luke 2:11-12

This was no ordinary baby. This was God made flesh—God Himself in the form of a human infant...Jesus. In Hebrew, His name is *Yeshua*, which means *to rescue, save* or *deliver*.

In John 1, Jesus is called the Word: *"In the beginning was the Word, and the Word was with God, and the Word was God. The same was in the beginning with God. All things were made through Him. Without Him, nothing was made that has been made."* (verses 1-3)

Did you get that? This baby—Jesus...Yeshua—was responsible for Creation. *"All things were made through Him."* In verse 10, John says again: *"the world was made through Him"* and then *"The Word became flesh, and lived among us."*

I love how Chris Tomlin and Matt Maher wrote it in their Christmas song, *He Shall Reign Forevermore*:

"Here within a manger lies the One who made the starry skies..."

Before He became the Word made flesh, Jesus spoke the stars into existence. He created the galaxies, our sun and solar system, the earth we live on. And then, in order to rescue the human race from our sin and bring us back into fellowship with the Father, He humbled Himself to become a helpless infant.

As C.S. Lewis said: "The Son of God became a man to enable men to become sons of God."

And as Linus says, "And that's what Christmas is all about, Charlie Brown."

"You will find a baby wrapped in strips of cloth, lying in a feeding trough..." This Creator of the starry skies became *"the Lamb of God, who takes away the sin of the world."* (John 1:29)

Dig deeper: *John 1:1-18; John 3*

December 26

"But, according to His promise, we look for new heavens and a new earth, in which righteousness dwells." 2 Peter 3:13

What's behind all the efforts in our culture to make things just? Fair? Right? Where do we get those ideas, that there's such a thing as justice? Rightness? Goodness? Why do we long for things like acceptance? Loving relationships? Fulfillment?

C.S. Lewis, in his book *Mere Christianity*, says, "If we find ourselves with a desire that nothing in this world can satisfy, the most probably explanation is that we were made for another world."

The Bible gives us both a history and a look into the future. It describes God's original creation—the one we're living in now. The one that started as paradise, and has been crumbling apart ever since sin entered the world (as told in Genesis 3). There's a reason we think things should be just and right—because that's the world we were made for.

Ever since sin came in, people have rebelled against God and His authority. We've wanted to have our own way. To tell *Him* what to do, instead of Him telling *us* what to do. So God initiated a rescue operation. It's described in all four Gospels in the Bible—Matthew, Mark, Luke and John.

And the Bible describes the future *"new heavens and a new earth"*—that's what's coming someday for those who follow Him. The world we were made for. It's not going to come easily, though. In fact, what the Bible describes is terrible. The books of Daniel, Isaiah, Jeremiah, Ezekiel, Hosea, Joel, Matthew, Thessalonians (both of them) and Revelation are just some of those that deal with what the Bible calls the Last Days. It's not pretty.

But...the end result will be *"according to His promise, we look for new heavens and a new earth, in which righteousness dwells."*

If our current world, despite the corruption and ugliness, is so beautiful...imagine what the new heavens and new earth will be like without that ugliness. With righteousness all the time, everywhere, for everyone. Sounds heavenly, doesn't it?

Dig deeper: 2 Peter 3; Revelation 21:1-4

December 27

"For the creation was subjected to vanity, not of its own will, but because of Him who subjected it, in hope that the creation itself also will be delivered from the bondage of decay into the liberty of the glory of the children of God." Romans 8:20-21

I love the way the New Living Translation says this:

"Against its will, creation was subjected to God's curse. But with eager hope, the creation looks forward to the day when it will join God's children in glorious freedom from death and decay..."

When Eve and Adam chose to rebel against God by eating the fruit, their action didn't just bring the curse of sin and death on them—but on all of the created world: *"The ground is cursed for your sake,"* the Father said to Adam. (Genesis 3:17)

The final fulfillment of God's promise of redemption isn't just for us as His children—it's for all of creation! Revelation 21:1 says, *"I saw a new heaven and a new earth: for the first heaven and the first earth have passed away..."*

If you think nature is full of beauty and wonder now, just wait! There are a handful of prophecies, both Old and New Testaments, that describe life in this new age, including this one:

"For, behold, I create new heavens and a new earth; and the former things will not be remembered, nor come into mind...The wolf and the lamb will feed together. The lion will eat straw like the ox." (Isaiah 65: 17, 25)

And this one:

"He showed me a river of water of life, clear as crystal, proceeding out of the throne of God and of the Lamb, in the middle of its street. On this side of the river and on that was the Tree of Life, bearing twelve kinds of fruits, yielding its fruit every month. The leaves of the tree were for the healing of the nations." Revelation 22:1-2

How we look forward with hope for that day!

Dig deeper: *Revelation 21-22*

December 28

"We proclaim him, admonishing every man and teaching every man in all wisdom, that we may present every man perfect in Christ Jesus; for which I also labor, striving according to his working, which works in me mightily." Colossians 1:28-29

The bugs were everywhere—in the sand, in the grass, flying in the air, crawling in his ears, biting his feet and flying into his mouth. He literally could not get away from them. Even when hunkering down inside the tent, they came in with him.

Besides the bugs were the constant and chilling rains that just seemed like they'd never abate. Finding a place to set up the tent was next to impossible due to the thoroughly saturated ground.

It was miserable...and yet glorious! The breath-taking views of snow-capped mountains, glistening ocean waves and grizzlies meandering along the shoreline were all worth it.

We sat in awe as my nephew gave us a slideshow of his month-long kayaking journey from Vancouver Island up to Alaska. The journey was long, difficult, mentally straining and physically demanding.

But we were all astounded by the experiences he had and the views he was able to see only because of his will and stamina to pursue his goal of getting to Alaska by kayak.

There is a goal we should all have in life as believers as well. It also can be quite the challenge but in a very different way. It's the goal, as Paul said, to *"present every man perfect in Christ."*

Paul described it as labor that every one of us should strive for. The end results are astounding when we see those we touch with the message of Christ: hope, love, peace, grace.

God promises to powerfully work in us to attain this goal. It's not done in our own strength.

Add that goal to your bucket list!

Dig deeper: *Matthew 28:16-20; Romans 12:1-2; 2 Timothy 2:20-21*

Tracy Blesi

December 29

"The God who made the world and all things in it, He, being Lord of heaven and earth, doesn't dwell in temples made with hands. He isn't served by men's hands, as though He needed anything, seeing He Himself gives to all life and breath, and all things." Acts 17:24-25

It's tempting to think we're doing God a favor by giving Him a few minutes of our day. Or a couple hours of our Sunday. Or even a year of our life for Bible school, or ten years for missions or church work.

"Isn't He lucky to have me on His team? In fact, what would He do without me?" It's tempting to pat ourselves on the back for all we're doing "for God."

And in His love and grace, the God who made the world and all things in it, the One who gives us breath and life, has His ways of reminding us of our place, and *His* place.

John Bunyon's classic novel, *The Pilgrim's Progress*, written from his prison cell between 1678 and 1684, describes some of these ways God uses to refine us: the Hill Difficulty, the Valley of Humiliation, the Valley of the Shadow of Death, the town of Vanity, By-path Meadow and Doubting Castle.

(If you've never read *The Pilgrim's Progress*, I highly recommend it!)

Our faithful, loving God has no need of our service, our churches, our religious works. But He gives us each breath, each day of our life. He gives us the wonders of nature that surround us. And He gives us relationships with other people, whom He loves just as He loves us.

Instead of seeing our service and sacrifice, our time and money as a favor we're doing for Him, let's see it as our partnership with Him. This God who created everything we see, He so wants us to be part of His family, His household of faith.

Accept each day, each breath with profound gratitude. Recognize the One who gives it, and step into real, living relationship with Him!

Dig deeper: *Acts 17*

December 30

"Behold, I send you out as sheep among wolves. Therefore be wise as serpents and harmless [innocent] as doves." Matthew 10:16

Jesus' plan for His followers wasn't to save them and then keep them safely tucked away from the wolves in some hidden place. His plan wasn't "keep it secret, keep it safe."

Jesus' plan for His followers then and for His followers ever since has been to *"Go and make disciples of all nations..."* (Matthew 28:19). It started here in Matthew 10 when He sent them out for the first time, just to their fellow Israelites. Kind of a practice run.

Both sheep and wolves were commonplace in that time. Jesus' disciples would've been very familiar with the danger sheep experience among wolves. So when He used that metaphor, they understood the risk. He told them to be *"wise as serpents."* Thoughtful, prudent, discreet—wise. The opposite of thoughtless and foolish.

He also told them to be *"harmless as doves."* Innocent, blameless, simple—harmless. Can you imagine a dove hurting anything?

That doesn't make much sense to us because we're used to thinking like the world thinks. We have to protect ourselves. Be a survivor. Be ready to fight back or run like heck when the wolves attack. It's easier just to stay in our own flock away from the wolves.

That's why before Jesus sent His disciples out, He did two things: *"He called them to Himself"* and He *"gave them authority"* (Matthew 10:1). Being sent out by Jesus involves, first, coming to Jesus. It's complete trust in Him and His love.

And then it's going out in His authority, in His presence, with His Spirit filling us. That's how we can go among the wolves with both wisdom and innocence.

Our society is obsessed with safety. But safety isn't Jesus' first concern for us. It wasn't His first concern for Himself. His first concern was obeying His Father. Actually, that was His *only* concern. That's what He lived for. That's what He calls His followers to live for. But not alone—you always go with Jesus, and usually with other believers, too.

Dig deeper: *Matthew 10*

December 31

"It is the glory of God to conceal a thing, but the glory of kings is to search out a matter." Proverbs 25:2

Whenever I read this verse in Proverbs I think of the natural world. When God created the heavens and earth, He included everything on the planet humans would need to live and thrive.

Food sources...medicines...fuel for heat and cooking...materials to make tools and build structures...minerals, metals, gemstones. When God created people, He didn't give them a hammer and nails. He gave them the intelligence, curiosity and determination to develop them out of the natural materials around them.

God filled the world with animals and plants of all kinds in every kind of habitat, and even today, we're still discovering new species! According to *Smithsonian Magazine* (an article published in 2010), 300 species of mammals had been discovered in the previous decade. That doesn't include all the other animal and plant species discovered since then.

It's like a divine treasure hunt! Imagine how, when God put the DNA strand in each cell, He must've looked forward to the time when people would discover it. It took thousands of years for scientists to get to that point—and once they realized such a thing exists, it opened up an entire new field of study. Imagine God's delight in that!

I remember how fun it was for my husband to hide our kids' Easter baskets. How fun it was for us to watch them look all over the house...then the joy on their faces when they discovered the hiding place.

I feel like that every time I hike in the mountains in the late spring. There are tiny and intricate alpine flowers that we only find at those high altitudes. How amazing that God put them where so few people would see them. And when we discover and take joy in what He's hidden, what joy it must give Him as our Father.

To search out mysteries, to look for "hidden treasure" is a gift. It keeps wonder and curiosity alive. It's a doorway to humility, gratitude and praise!

Dig deeper: 1 Chronicles 16:31; Romans 11:33-36; Colossians 1:16-17

Authors & Artists

It's been a joy to work with these brothers and sisters in Christ from across the United States and around the world. Some make their living through the outdoors in one way or another. Others simply love nature and love God.

For photos, a more thorough bio of each one, and links to their organizations, please go to: *brodinpress.com/devotional.*

Sharon Brodin is the principle author and editor of *Heaven and Nature Sing.* She lives near Minneapolis, Minnesota. Sharon owns *Brodin Press LLC* as well as two outdoor blogs, *Twin Cities Outdoors* and *Active Outdoor Women.* She wrote 260 devotionals for this project.

Tracy Blesi studied Christian ministry and has an extreme passion for anything active and outdoors. She lives near Minneapolis, Minnesota, and travels frequently. Tracy wrote four devotionals: pages 32, 104, 345, 379.

Hogan Brimacombe has been working as a campus minister for *InterVarsity Christian Fellowship Canada* for many years. His outdoor experiences come from leading youth into the wilderness hiking and canoeing. Hogan wrote three devotionals: pages 99, 174, 347.

Stephen Brodin has been a career artist his whole life and is a long-time lover of the outdoors, especially fishing. He happens to be Sharon Brodin's father-in-law, too. Steve drew eight of the illustrations: pages 1, 63, 95, 159, 191, 255, 287, 351.

Mark Bullington is currently the owner of *Amelia Island Kayak Excursions* in Amelia Island, Florida, along with his family. He loves sharing his passion with thousands of guests each year. Mark wrote one devotional: pages 288.

Brian Doub served God overseas for 32 years and now lives in the beautiful Rocky Mountains of Colorado where he can paraglide and worship God 10-20 thousand feet in the air. Brian wrote six devotionals and drew four of the illustrations: pages 17, 18, 33, 127, 133, 214, 223, 269, 319, 334.

Jung Ho Park is an assistant pastor in Los Angeles, California. He actively spreads Jesus' love and message through his award-winning photography. His photo "Little Corona Beach" is the cover photo for *Heaven and Nature Sing*.

William Hayes is Associate Chaplain and Director of Wilderness Ministry at *Ohio Wesleyan University*. His campus work includes taking students on wilderness treks all over the US and to South America. William wrote three devotionals: pages 146, 183, 294.

Emilie O'Connor grew up enjoying the outdoor adventure opportunities of northwest Pennsylvania, and does the same in her new home state of Minnesota. She currently works as a registered nurse. Emilie wrote 20 devotionals: pages 12, 13, 41, 68, 83, 100, 114, 128, 145, 168, 193, 205, 224-226, 266, 281, 312, 336, 363.

Nancy Patten worked alongside her husband, Mark, for 40 years as he directed *Okontoe*, a ministry in the wilderness of northeast Minnesota. Since his passing in 2019, she continues to live and serve at Okontoe. Nancy wrote one devotional: page 229.

Beth Poliquin has lived in many different parts of the US including Virginia, Hawaii, Arizona, Minnesota and now Maine. She's a paddling instructor and guide, and enjoys outdoor activities of all kinds with her family. Beth wrote five devotionals: pages 8, 71, 140, 211, 256.

Brian Rupe is a retired camp director, having served in leadership positions in five different YMCA camps over 34 years. He now resides near Minneapolis, Minnesota. Brian wrote 26 devotionals: pages 7, 20, 37, 54, 64, 76, 77, 110, 123, 137, 150, 163, 180, 196-204, 246, 263, 292, 331.

Nathan Russell and his wife, Betsy, have pioneered multiple outdoor ministries at *YWAM Montana - Lakeside*, where they continue to serve. He is an avid outdoor adventurer and also teaches backcountry medicine. Nathan wrote one devotional: page 322.

Drs. Neal & LeaAnn Schroeter are ER physicians in Ashland, Wisconsin. They own and help manage *Whitecap Kayak*, a business that operates to mentor youth in leadership through kayak guide training. They wrote seven devotionals: pages 158, 251, 306-309, 356.

Paul Scoringe works as a freelance sports marketing consultant is his native New Zealand. He's lived, studied and worked in Canada, Minnesota and Germany over the years as well. Paul wrote two devotionals: pages 270, 364.

Tasse Swanson is a marriage and family therapist, having worked for 25 years in a local hospital, and currently in her Minnesota church. She's traveled extensively and loves many kinds of outdoor activities. Tasse wrote two devotionals: pages 165, 220.

Summit Adventure is a wilderness ministry based in California that focuses on experiential education, adventure programming and cross-cultural immersion. Three of its team members contributed devotionals: pages 284, 316, 344.

Emil Toader serves as President of *Missio Link International Foundation*, based in his native Romania. One of their missions is *Alpinis Leadership Center*, which works with youth through camps and the outdoors, and through training and conferences for adults. Emil wrote six devotionals: pages 172, 302, 303, 352, 353, 354.

Kirsten Voorhees currently works in Human Resources for one of the world's leading paddle companies, not far from her Minnesota home. She floats down a local river in her kayak every chance she gets. Kirsten wrote one devotional: page 317.

Laura Watson is an environmental educator and wilderness guide with *Solid Rock Outdoor Ministries* in Laramie, Wyoming. She loves using the wilderness to teach identity and grow disciples. Laura wrote ten devotionals: pages 11, 50, 70, 118, 154, 237, 274, 298, 327, 362.

Timon & Steff Weber lead a ministry in the paragliding community of Europe's Alps called *PARA|DISE*. Their vision is to see disciple grow in the paragliding scene. They wrote three devotionals: pages 186, 241, 368.

Matt White loves to train, support and be in community with people in natural spaces while they discover their next steps with Jesus. He does this at Adventurous Christians in Grand Marais, Minnesota. Matt wrote four devotionals: pages 28, 61, 94, 297.

www.ingramcontent.com/pod-product-compliance
Lightning Source LLC
Chambersburg PA
CBHW070900030426
42336CB00014BA/2270